Citizens of an Empty Nation

THE ETHNOGRAPHY OF POLITICAL VIOLENCE

Tobias Kelly, Series Editor

A complete list of books in the series is available from the publisher.

Citizens of an Empty Nation

Youth and State-Making in Postwar Bosnia-Herzegovina

Azra Hromadžić

PENN

UNIVERSITY OF PENNSYLVANIA PRESS

PHILADELPHIA

Copyright © 2015 University of Pennsylvania Press

All rights reserved. Except for brief quotations used for purposes of review or scholarly citation, none of this book may be reproduced in any form by any means without written permission from the publisher.

Published by
University of Pennsylvania Press
Philadelphia, Pennsylvania 19104-4112
www.upenn.edu/pennpress

Printed in the United States of America
on acid-free paper
10 9 8 7 6 5 4 3 2 1
Library of Congress Cataloging-in-Publication Data
ISBN 978-0-8122-4700-8

Contents

Introduction   1

Part I. Integrating the School

1. Right to Difference   29

2. Cartography of Peace-Building   63

3. Bathroom Mixing   86

Part II. Disintegrating the Nation

4. Poetics of Nationhood   105

5. Invisible Citizens   139

6. Anti-Citizens   156

Conclusion   181

Epilogue. Empty Nation, Empty Bellies   188

Notes 193

Bibliography 211

Index 225

Acknowledgments 237

Introduction

On July 23, 2004, eleven years after the destruction of the famed Old Bridge in Mostar, Bosnia-Herzegovina,[1] and after a decade of painstaking international diplomatic efforts and more than thirteen million U.S. dollars invested in the reconstruction,[2] the new "Old" Bridge was reopened to the public. Together with thousands of "internationals" and "locals," I witnessed the opening ceremony. Numerous speeches were given by key international and local leaders who spoke about the significance of the event for the city's divided people and the country's future. Popular singers and actors gave inspiring speeches and sang patriotic songs. Boats passed under the bridge, and celebrated divers leaped into their river from the rebuilt bridge. After several hours of emotionally charged entertainment, children from the two divided sides of the city, the Bosniak/east side and Croat/west side, met in the middle of the bridge. This moving "bridging" act officially opened the bridge to the public.

While absorbing the excitement, I followed the crowds and carefully crossed the new bridge packed with people. Then I returned to the streets. They were crammed with people celebrating, drinking, eating, or simply walking around, wanting to take part in the event. Without thinking, I found myself crossing the main boulevard, the onetime front line of battle, and walking over to the Croat west side of the divided city. I was stunned by the contrast between the two sides: there were no crowds on these streets; there was no celebration; it was business as usual. Some youth were sitting in bars, ignoring the lights and noise coming from the other side. I felt confused—how is the rebuilding of the bridge a symbol of national reconciliation if the majority of Croats in Mostar do not even acknowledge its rebirth?

In the weeks following the opening ceremony, I scrupulously investigated those tensions. As I was grappling with the competing meanings and emotions surrounding the reconstruction of the Old Bridge, I realized that its restoration could not fulfill the international and local expectations of national reconciliation since the bridge's former symbolism did not match the postwar social and political context. What is more, another postwar initiative and different type of "bridge-building" was simultaneously taking place, powerfully reflecting and encapsulating the concerns of ordinary Mostarians. Challenging negotiations about the reintegration of the famous high school in town, the Mostar Gymnasium, were occurring in the shadows of the new bridge; they included multiple local and international actors and groups. My curiosity was immediately stimulated: what was giving substance to these contested processes and events of intervention and reintegration? How were they perceived and experienced, fabricated and contested by the actors involved and the general public? This initial curiosity would mark the beginning of my long-term research at the school, where I ethnographically captured the complex processes that are at the heart of this book: the effects of postwar international state-making interventions on "ordinary people,"[3] especially youth.

My fascination with the Mostar Gymnasium was amplified by my own experiences of war-interrupted schooling. During the war (1992–95), together with my family and people of Bihać—a northwestern Bosnian town on the border with Croatia—I spent three and a half years under siege, with no electricity or regular food supplies. Prior to the war, my classmates were youth of all ethnoreligious backgrounds; Bosnia's Serbs, Croats, Bosniaks (Bosnian Muslims), and others coexisted peacefully in my town and in my classroom. After several months of increasing rumors and reports about violence elsewhere in the country, in early May 1992, I came to school to find many students' desks empty—almost all Serb students were gone from their desks as well as from our town, including Nataša, one of my best friends. Some of my classmates and teachers left Bosnia-Herzegovina altogether, while others moved to the Serb-dominated part of the country, including the surrounding hills. Literally overnight, they became the "enemies" who would bomb our hometown for the next three years. Their empty desks provoked rumors, sadness, confusion, anger, and anxiety among those of us who remained. This palpable classroom *emptiness*—a reflection of my town becoming rapidly "overcome by nationhood and nationalism" (see Brubaker 1994; Drakulić 1993)—and the related, hasty transformation of a classmate into "an enemy" profoundly shaped my life, including the course of my academic career. This ethnography is thus deeply informed by my experiences of going to school in the Balkans during the 1990s, the times of war and peace.

My experience of the half-empty classroom is an illustrative example of how schools in (post)war regions become places where intimate relationships, friendships, and connections powerfully converge with some of the major instruments used by local and international political actors to manage, impose, compose, solidify, fragment, legitimize, and promote certain goals (Mosse 2005; Latour 2000), including the implementation of postconflict reconstruction projects.[4] Therefore, it should not come as a surprise that for the international political actors and local political elites in postwar Bosnia-Herzegovina, schools and youth became a prolific site for imagining (ethno)national identities and were prioritized as means to unify or dispute the postwar state. At the same time, schools emerged as a powerful terrain for demonstrating war-produced political and social divergences and collisions.

As a result of these larger and uninformed processes, and the unique symbolic and geographical place of the Mostar Gymnasium, the school instantaneously felt like a perfect academic and personal fit, allowing for an intense ethnographic and anthropological engagement as well as a profound personal reflection, challenge, and growth. The school, popularly known as Stara Gimnazija (the Old Gymnasium), has a unique place in Bosnia-Herzegovina, past and present. Built in 1898 in the Austro-Hungarian orientalist, Moorish revival style, it is a historical institution and national monument. It was one of the most famous and academically prestigious educational institutions in the former Yugoslavia, and among the best in Bosnia-Herzegovina. Due to its academic rigor and popularity, the school attracted more privileged and high-achieving youth. Many of the school's students later became famous young revolutionaries, freedom fighters, world-famous artists, academics, and scientists. Given its illustrious history—and the fact that someone from almost every family in Mostar has attended this school—a lot of emotion surfaces in conversations about the school and its future.

The school's importance and symbolism are enhanced by its location in the very center of Mostar, on the Croat west side of the main boulevard, which currently divides the city. In prewar Mostar, the boulevard was the center of economic and social life. At the time of my research, however, it was an eerie, empty strip of land, drained of much of its former life and content, "a twilight border zone of hostile and uneasy separation between

Figure 1. Stara Gimnazija, summer 2005. Photo by the author.

the two halves of the divided city" (Wimmen 2004:3). This "no-man's-land," with its ghostly remains of brutal violence, was in complete opposition to its former central place in the life of Mostar.

Given this illustrious history and geography, and the school's importance in the contemporary politics and projects of peace-building and state-making in Bosnia-Herzegovina, the Mostar Gymnasium replaced the Old Bridge as the most potent icon of the postwar peace-building and state-making project, and of the social (re)organization in the segregated city. While the new "Old" Bridge physically replaced the destroyed Old Bridge, it could not retain its former symbolism. The political project of "socialist humanism" (see, among others, Cohen and Marković 1975; Horvat 1982), which invested the Old Bridge with a unique idea of Yugoslav coexistence and Bosnian multiculturalism, was shattered with the destruction of the state and its Old Bridge. As a result, the new "Old" Bridge stretches today above the Neretva river as a residue of the history of coexistence and the recent bloodshed. Instead of pride and resistance, it provokes the mixed feelings of betrayal, rejection, international governance, and ethnic membership. On the other hand, the processes of reunification of ethnically segregated students at the highly symbolic Mostar Gymnasium disclose the praxis of cooperation and resistance involved in the reconstruction of the postwar state, which the new "Old" Bridge fails to capture. More specifically, it is via discourses and practices of the school's reconstruction that the international diplomatic (di)visions, local ethnopolitical projects, and ethnicization of everyday life reveal themselves most vividly, congealing to produce what I call an *empty nation* in Bosnia-Herzegovina.

This book is an ethnography of an empty nation that emerges as an effect of the ill-fitted (di)vision of the Bosnian-Herzegovinian state. This vision originated in powerful and destructive forces of "local" ethnonationalisms, but it was also adopted by the majority of the international peace-building and state-making actors in Bosnia-Herzegovina (see Gagnon n.d.; Campbell 1998). In order to ethnographically capture the complex "agency of actors" (Mosse 2005:6), and the convoluted processes, visions, and ideologies that brought this unique, neither united nor divided school into being, I approach Stara Gimnazija in a way numerous anthropologists would approach "their person" and tell their story. My intent is to give the *sense* to emptiness that is experienced by Bosnian youth targeted for reconciliation by the international humanitarian intervention. By doing this, I illuminate, localize, and bring to life the main dilemma of the contemporary international interventions in postwar societies: whether and how to knit back together war-divided ethnic groups. Furthermore, I show how these international interventions, as fields of interconnected visions, people, and activities, are experienced by those who are most affected by them—in this case, the Bosnian youth.

The main concern of this book is thus to show *how* peace-building and state-making projects "work in practice" (Ferguson 1994:xiv; Moore 2013), what kind of effects and structural changes they produce, and how they fragment, subjugate, silence, reorganize, create, empower, and erase the "local" (Mosse 2005:4). I invite the reader to join me on this journey as I descend into the school's most intimate spaces, capture its inhabitants' dynamic and seemingly contrasting practices, reveal the school's "hidden transcripts" (Scott 1990), and place these processes into the global political context of postwar peace-building and state-making in the era of global governance, permanent emergency (Pandolfi 2010), and "new development" (Duffield 2001).

Encountering Emptiness

It is a mid-September day in 2005, the first month of my fieldwork at the Mostar Gymnasium. The school is only partially reconstructed with some rooms more equipped and ready to receive students than others. The most impressive room is the new computer lab, a donation to the school by the Japanese government. Since the first day of my fieldwork, I have tried to visit the lab, but the door is always locked. Today, I press the door handle and for the first time in the last few weeks, I find it open. I push the door, which is large, heavy, and made of fine wood. It has been recently painted—the strong scent of paint invades my nostrils as I enter the room.

A young man is standing there, his shaved head and orthodontic braces shining in the Mostar sun pouring through an open window. His name is Damir,[5] and he is the employee in charge of the lab, he explains. Sure I can look around, he tells me. The interior is filled with numerous computer screens, sitting on clean desks arranged in neat rows. The screens' blackness is in sharp contrast with the Mostar daylight. The buzzing sound of equipment underscores the silence created by human absence. I stroll down, occasionally patting the empty chairs in front of computer screens. Why is this perfectly equipped computer lab always empty? What is its purpose? Who, if anyone, is supposed to use it and how? I ask Damir these questions.

He explains to me that there was a gap between the donor's request for the lab's use and the "spirit" of the reunified school. He tells me that the Mostar office of the Organization for Security and Cooperation in Europe (OSCE)—the main international organization overseeing education in Bosnia-Herzegovina and the integration of this famous school—used integrationist rhetoric when asking for the money from the Japanese government.[6] The donor responded in the spirit of the call; it donated the money under the condition that the lab should be used exclusively for joint student activities. This meant that activities would include students from both curricula.[7] Since the school was never fully integrated but rather administratively reunified (see Chapter 1), and the curricula are still completely ethnically separated, there are no mandatory joint activities that could meet the donor's request. In order not to lose the privilege of using an extraordinarily well-equipped computer lab, the informatics (*informatika*) instructor, Igor, the only teacher who teaches in both curricula, developed two joint extracurricular activities, "animation" and "the Internet." In "the spirit of integration," the OSCE named these joined extracurricular activities "open to all." Damir was very excited about this progress, which he called "modernization."

Since the two ethnically divided curricula were already overloaded, many students could not afford the time to join extracurricular activities, so they were never able to use the fancy lab. Meanwhile, the regular information technology classes in both curricula were held in the old-fashioned computer facility, with outdated equipment that was falling apart. One student told me that most keyboards missed at least several keys. In practice, very few students visited the new lab. While open to all, during the school year 2005–6, the lab remained *empty* of its intended beneficiaries.

The story of the empty lab captures the effects of the tension at the heart of internationally designed state-making in Bosnia-Herzegovina: institutionalization of a school/state that rhetorically supports and even imposes reunification, while institutionally recognizing ethnic segregation at the expense of common schooling, and by extension, common citizenship, peoplehood, and nationhood. Materialization of the empty lab thus captures the main paradox that this book examines: that the efforts to rehabilitate and rebuild a postwar nation and its citizens, and to promote reintegration, democracy, and stability, inadvertently reinforce the perpetual emptying of the state of its citizens.

The school's computer lab is only one visible effect of this paradox; there are numerous other highly symbolic empty spaces, dotting the postwar landscape, encapsulating and reflecting the tension between integration and segregation, and between state-making and nation-breaking. Consider, for example, a young man's encounter with an empty space, nicely captured in Markowitz's (2010) ethnography of Sarajevo. The author explains how her informant, Ernest, took the anthropologist to the place in the city that, in his opinion, represented the most important Sarajevan and Bosnian-Herzegovinian monument—the eternal flame. The flame and the stone niche that surrounds it were erected in the very heart of the Bosnian-Herzegovina capital after World War II to celebrate the Tito Partisans' victory over Nazism. Engraved on the stone niche is the dedication to Partisan groups representing different ethnic backgrounds in Bosnia-Herzegovina and the former Yugoslavia.

For Markowitz's informant, this diversity and multiplicity, its Brotherhood and Unity,[8] is precisely what Bosnia-Herzegovina stands for, despite the war and destruction. On a warm day in August 2002 when they visited the niche, however, the flame was out, and "Ernest was mortified that independent Bosnia-Herzegovina, his native country, could not support its most important monument. We were standing in the middle of the city in an *empty space*, devoid of its brightly burning flame" (Markowitz 2010:40; emphasis added).

Even though the explanation for the flame's absence was not, to Ernest's relief, straightforwardly political—this part of the city experienced a shortage of gas that day—in the eyes of the informant and some other passersby the lack of the flame was immobilizing.[9] Ernest's reaction, a mixture of paralysis, anger, and sense of betrayal, resembles numerous other experiences and articulations of postwar emptiness I witnessed in Mostar and beyond: the empty space where the bridge in Mostar used to stretch for centuries, the empty boulevard by Stara Gimnazija, the neglected World War II Partisan graveyards and abandoned monuments to this era[10] all over Bosnia-Herzegovina and the former Yugoslavia, the eradication of the word "Bosnia" from the names of towns and streets (Sorabji 1995:92), the parking lot on the site where the famous sixteenth-century Ferhat Paša or Ferhadija mosque proudly stood in the formerly ethnically mixed city of Banja Luka,[11] and empty desks and empty homes of my classmates at the beginning of the war are all ghostly remains of shared history and the power of war-produced "ethnic cleansing" and postwar institutionalization of ethnic nationalisms over interconnected life.

Ordinary people confront this war-produced destruction and related political, spatial, and existential emptiness daily, as they perpetually negotiate their empty state. These empty spaces are intimately connected, in everyday life, with political, national, and ethical forms of vanished political agency and personhood. For example, Bosnia-longing, Tito-loving, Yugo-nostalgic Sanja describes her experience with the state-level, national emptiness vividly, using the spatial metaphor of a house to talk about the former Yugoslavia and Bosnia-Herzegovina, which she referred to by a popular description of Bosnia as *Jugoslavija u malom* (miniature Yugoslavia):

Let me tell you how it is . . . it is like you had one big house, where you moved around freely. In that house you had your own room, but you spent much time in the living room, visiting with other people. Or you [would] go and see them in their own rooms, which always stayed unlocked. You loved that house . . . now, there is no living room . . . the space where it used to be is destroyed and neglected, covered in shit and dirt. No one goes there anymore. And people . . . they do not leave their rooms, which are locked at all times. . . . But we all remember how we once had a house.

With the arrival of "peace" in 1995, the war-produced emptiness only grew deeper and stronger, as Sanja's example shows so powerfully. The sense of emptiness, ironically, was given new legitimacy through the postwar reconstruction projects since the "organizing principle of vision and division" (Bourdieu 1990:134), its epistemes, and its ethos highly resemble local ethnonational projects that perpetually (attempt to) drain away the connective tissue from the citizenry and the nation.

In the chapters that follow, I address this unfinished consolidation of emptiness conjured up by the scenes above. I also ethnographically explore how this emptiness comes into being: which contradicting forces and epistemes converge to generate the powerful spaces of absence, including the empty lab, and, by extension, the Bosnian state? Furthermore, I look at how the school's inhabitants live, make sense, negotiate, inhabit, or resist this emptiness, thus producing unique if unexpected sites of "cultural intimacy" (Herzfeld 2005). Investigating these processes ethnographically will reveal the main argument of this book: that youth in Bosnia-Herzegovina come of age structurally constrained by three deeply interwoven processes that generate the empty nation in Bosnia-Herzegovina: the rigid visions and practices of international peace-building; ethnic nationalisms and the mistrust they generate; and war-initiated, rapid ethnicization of everyday life. In individual chapters of the book, I treat different dimensions of this emptiness in their depth and their complexity, to show how emptiness manifests in and refracts into the lives of youth. Furthermore, the chapters ahead show how this emptiness is deferred and ignored rather than resolved into a new, deeply optimistic international ideological formation—a postwar democratic state.

Empty State, Empty Nation

After more than three years of failed negotiations, bloody conflict, over 100,000 deaths, and the displacement of 1.5 million people as refugees, on

December 14, 1995, the Dayton Peace Agreement,[12] brokered by the United States, brought an end to the Bosnian war. By constituting the state as a consociation democracy, it also solidified and legitimized a shallow state model in Bosnia-Herzegovina. The consociational power-sharing model presumes cooperation of political elites across ethnic divides in order to manage conflicts. This model of power-sharing (Lijphart 1977) rests on the recognition, institutionalization, and proportional allocation of resources to ethnically, religiously, or linguistically defined collectivities (Van den Berghe 2002). Fears of ethnic domination are therefore reduced by extending self-rule and segmental autonomy as far as possible to each community (Palmer 2005). This leads to absolute political institutionalization of ethnicity on the substate entity level,[13] protected by the autonomy of self-government, veto rights for each of the ethnic groups, and systems of proportionality and administrative power-sharing.

The Dayton Agreement was envisioned to accommodate sociopolitical diversity, while safeguarding the sovereignty and integrity of the state. Additionally, it promised to limit opportunities for ethnonationalism to take over the state's political and social space. In order to achieve these goals, the Agreement divided Bosnia-Herzegovina into two entities: the Federation of Bosnia-Herzegovina (FBiH), with a 51 percent share of the territory and inhabited mostly by Bosniaks[14] and Bosnian Croats, and the Republika Srpska (RS), with 49 percent of the territory and populated almost exclusively by Bosnian Serbs. The entities were given all the characteristics of states within a more complex state.[15] Furthermore, the agreement separated the FBiH into ten largely autonomous cantons, with little intermixing between the ethnic groups.[16] While claiming to have reconciliation, democracy, and ethnic pluralism as its objectives, the agreement inscribed in law the ethnic partitioning of Bosnian (Eastern Orthodox) Serbs, Bosnian (Catholic) Croats, and Bosniaks (Chandler 1999). Therefore, the Dayton Peace Agreement created a state that was "an empty shell with the Serb Republic governing itself autonomously and the Croat cantons in the Federation having a comparable degree of self-governance" (Bieber 2005:40).[17]

This division of the state is the product of ideologies of "cultural fundamentalism" (Stolcke 1995) and ethnopolitics projected by the majority of local and foreign policy actors in Bosnia-Herzegovina. In order to implement a nationalist vision of creating ethnically homogeneous political and territorial units out of heterogeneous spaces and identities, local ethnic elites used an ideology of cultural fundamentalism, which emphasizes the importance of distinctive cultural identities. This ideology of cultural purity presumes the encirclement of culture by territory and incommensurability of mutually hostile, spatially segregated ethnicities, which are treated as rooted, bounded, and homogeneous (Verdery 1994). This approach to the region is also the basis of the internationally designed Dayton Peace Agreement, thus revealing the uncanny resemblance between the international state-making design and the ethnonationalist political project. For example, from the very beginning of the Bosnian war, every peace plan put forward by the international actors echoed the ideology of "incommensurable cultural identities" rooted in local nationalisms (Sarajlić 2011:63; see also Gagnon n.d.; Stolcke 1995).

In order to better grasp this (di)vision of Bosnia-Herzegovina, I, following Sally Engle Merry (2001), call the nexus between people and territory "spatial governmentality"—the ideological, political, and social mechanism of spatial segregation and disciplining of ethnically conceived peoples.[18] These internally generated and externally regulated policies reinforce the social divisions at the heart of the conflict. Although this logic was designed to provide clear dividing lines between the warring populations, the demographic circumstance of Bosnia-Herzegovina, such as intermixed territories, undermined this intent (Campbell 1999:407). This particular "reading" (and writing) of Bosnian future, sociality, and territory annihilates the shared public spaces that are crucial to the history of public sociality; and it ignores the fact that "until the war the three communities in Bosnia-Herzegovina did not have compact geographical strongholds, but lived in ethnically mixed territories" (Kasapović 2005:8) or sometimes in smaller homogeneous enclaves. During the war, however, the country was transformed from "being highly intermixed in 1991 to nearly full segregation of the three nations" (Bieber 2005:29; Hayden 1996). As a result, the marriage between consociational democracy, cultural incommensurability, and spatial governmentality led to the perpetual diminishing of lived interconnectedness and to the destruction, marginalization, and trivialization of memories of a shared past (Sorabji 1995) and the possibilities of a joined future, including supraethnic political alternatives.

Consociational Troubles

There are two closely related tensions at the heart of the consociational model in postwar Bosnia-Herzegovina. The first is the incongruity and disjuncture between the nation and the state in Bosnia-Herzegovina. This historically informed disjuncture is cemented through the political project of international military and humanitarian intervention, where state-making (understood as the creation of institutions and capabilities that dispense and legitimize power and rights) and nation-building (i.e., building of a sense of a common pannational identity across and above ethnic groups), while deeply intertwined, are not identical processes, and they derive from two opposing traditions and diverging understandings. The first is the "myth of ancient hatreds" particular to the Balkan people, where in order to preserve peace in the Balkans, one has to keep the Bosnia-Herzegovina people—Serbs, Croats, and Bosniaks—at a safe distance from one another. Furthermore, this tradition has also shaped the international policies of postwar state-building, which reinforced and inscribed in law ethnic division of peoples. This "myth" also generated a diplomatic mood that painted Balkan politics as "too complicated to understand." The emphasis was put on the local "cycles of violence," which repeat themselves, and where foreign powers cannot do very much to help. Outsiders were thus unwilling to intervene, "innocently or willfully imagining that ethnicity was the primary sorting mechanism of society" (Hunt 2011:xxvi). This picture of the Balkans was used by numerous national leaders, including U.S. president Bill Clinton to justify their inaction and slow response to the mass killings in the region.

This "myth" of ancient animosities is often contrasted with another "myth" embraced by a number of international actors: the notion of multicultural heaven in Bosnia-Herzegovina where Orthodox, Catholics, Muslims, Jews, and others have coexisted peacefully for centuries, and where a "true" synergy of different cultures could emerge and flourish. The description of Sarajevo's unique urban core where "mosques, synagogues, Catholic and Orthodox churches stand side by side" (Sells 1996:48) best illustrates this position. It assumes that the resilient, hybrid, and unique "Bosnian spirit," which developed over long centuries of interconnected life, cultural exchanges, and historical interrelations, will possibly reemerge, organically, from the shared history and proximity of life projects. This notion of a "truly" multicultural Bosnia-Herzegovina was incorporated into the calls for the international humanitarian intervention, providing it with a considerable moral dimension. In this way, Bosnia was framed as "the key test of the newly proclaimed international order based upon moral and ethical foreign policy" (Chandler 1999:31; see also Mertus 2004).

The second tension that grows out of consociational democracy is that it enshrines in law spatial governmentality, and thus the ethnic tensions that generated the conflict. This approach assumes that ethnic tensions and animosities are the primary cause of the recent bloodshed (Bardoš 2010; Bougarel 1996; Burg and Shoup 1999; Hayden 2005, 2007) and takes the existence of separate ethnonational groups in Bosnia-Herzegovina at face value. These arguments are often opposed by numerous claims of scholars who argue that the international diplomatic, humanitarian, and military efforts that legitimized political division of ethnic nations in Bosnia-Herzegovina are truly problematic (Chandler 2006; Campbell 1999; Gagnon 2004; Hunt 2011; Jansen 2005; Maček 2009).

Without minimizing the historical importance of ethnoreligious identity for ordinary citizens or arguing against the history of lived interconnectedness in Bosnia-Herzegovina, there are problems with both these positions; while different peoples have been coexisting in the Balkans for centuries, their coexistence was neither romantic nor ethnically hostile and blood-spattered. Rather, people in Bosnia-Herzegovina had to continually negotiate tensions and conflicts that are integral parts of everyday life in any community, especially in culturally diverse regions that have been under foreign occupation for much of their history (Bringa 1993, 1995; Bougarel, Helms, and Duijzings 2007; Jansen 2005; Mujkić 2008). These messy everyday negotiations and identifications—the product of unique historical encounters—are absent from the crude multicultural logic underlying the Dayton Peace Agreement.

Ethnicity (Dis)embodied

Focusing on the interconnected histories of different groups within what is today Bosnia-Herzegovina does not eliminate the fact that ethnic nationalism is important to ordinary Bosnian-Herzegovinians. On the contrary, the (post)war-amplified ethnic nationalism saturates the political imagination and informs much of public opinion on the future of the state and its people. Whether they are in idioms of humor or complaint, politics or religion, capitalism or corruption, discourses of ethnic nationalism saturate the popular imagination in contemporary Bosnia-Herzegovina. The effects of this massive mobilization and transformation of multidimensional Balkan people, history, and memory into "flat" ethnonationalisms will become clearer as I describe the remarkably demarcated and narrow nature of ethnic identification at the Mostar Gymnasium and beyond. This inflexible differentiation sometimes obscures the fact that all ethnic identities are constructed, contingent, and fluctuating. Ethnic nationalism and ethnopolitics are thus more complicated than they first appear, regardless of their deceptively smooth surface; they do not reveal underlying fissures easily (Herzfeld 2005:2; Kurtović 2011; Maček 2009).

My own experience with ethnicization of everyday life in postwar Bosnia-Herzegovina captures this dynamic. Since the day of my arrival in the city of Mostar, I tried to fight the "ethnic box" to which I was assigned during and after the war.[19] Because of my identity and war experience, I continue to carry and live the wounds caused by the war between the Serbs and the Bosniaks in my region. The most important consequence of this war experience is a deep feeling of betrayal and mistrust between Bosniaks and the Serbs who left our town.

In my hometown I had not experienced a conflict between Bosniaks and Croats. Regardless of the tensions between the two groups, the two populations were united against "the Serb aggressor" that kept both groups besieged.[20] Given this history of the conflict in Bihać, I was not prepared for the extent of the Bosniak-Croat violence and distrust when I arrived in Mostar. Although my name and my speech indexed, however unreliably, my Bosniak identity to all people in Mostar, "since in Bosnia your name tells people who you are" (Bringa 1995:19), I did not feel, at least not initially, that this was really "my conflict." As a result, I crossed the city divide, impatiently, without much thought or fear, as if protesting its existence.

Once I started to socialize with the Croats in Mostar, I learned that "simply" because I was a Bosniak I could not rise above the situation on the ground. My experience in the United States provided some room for social maneuvering; but I never felt "on my own territory" in the Croat-dominated part of Mostar, regardless of the fact that the most genuine friendships I built during my fieldwork were with several Croat individuals. One of the reasons for this feeling was an excess of symbols of Croat nationhood, which excluded me. The new architecture on the west side (including a huge cross erected on top of the hill overlooking Mostar, which glows at night, causing frustration to many Bosniaks) embodied and amplified symbols of Catholicism and the state of Croatia. For example, the west side's public institutions, such as schools and ministries, displayed not the flags of Bosnia-Herzegovina, but the icons of Croatia or Herceg-Bosna.[21]

Due to this massive and speedy ethnicization of the city spaces and Mostarians' interpretative frames and ways of being, it took some time, personal frustration, and effort to confront these barriers, even though the majority of students and teachers from the "other" ethnic group continuously expressed their support and approval of my presence. The "revelatory incident" (Fernandez 1986:xi) of "acceptance" came unannounced, despite the tensions, during a foreign language class, a few months into my fieldwork. The students were especially unruly that day, and the teacher had difficulty keeping order in the classroom. Finally she said, "Please behave, kids. Do not embarrass me in front of a foreign woman." Hearing the comments, Dejan got up from his seat and said, unhesitantly, "You mean Azra? She is ours" [*Ona je naša*], where *naša* indexed both commonalities and tensions between us.

For different reasons, such as the increasing importance of religion in shaping human conduct, I never felt fully at home on the Bosniak-dominated side of town either. For example, the growing influence of Islam on everyday practices overwhelmed me. One time, I was criticized by a Bosniak professor at the Mostar Gymnasium for not observing Ramadan, as a "good Muslim should." In addition, I found the label Bosniak too confining and I did not feel at ease with the increasingly Islamized content of that term. As I was sinking deeper into the raw life of the city, I felt these issues to be increasingly challenging and the city's divide became a huge load to carry around, causing frustration and sadness.

It has taken me a long time to reflect, analytically and emotionally, on my own initial experience of Mostar and its frustrating ethnic divisions. I realized that with my oppositionality and anxiety, I supported and solidified the war and postwar ethnic scripts. I was myself a product of war and postwar habitus. My own understanding of Mostar and my place in it revealed that war was still in me, making it possible for these divisions to happen, creating categories out of people, and black and white "truths." At the same time, lacking proper grammar, boundary, and space, I and others around me daily fought against it.[22]

My frustration with different but related forms of ethnic homogenization of everyday life in places such as Mostar and Bihać points at the ubiquitous supremacy of ethnoreligious identity as the organizing principle of social, cultural, and political life in contemporary Bosnia-Herzegovina. While I theoretically understand the fluctuating nature of ethnicity, living ethnicity in Bosnia continuously reminds me of its persistent and resilient nature, especially when it is politically institutionalized. As a consequence of the critical transformation of ethnoreligious background into ethnonationalist political ideology, Bosnia-Herzegovina became "overcome by nationhood," to use the powerful phrase by the Croatian writer Slavenka Drakulić. Drakulić (1993:50–52) writes:

> Being Croat has become my destiny. . . . I am defined by my nationality, and by it alone. Along with millions of other Croats, I was pinned to the wall of nationhood—not only by outside pressure from Serbia and the Federal Army but by national homogenization within Croatia itself. That is what the war is doing to us, reducing us to one dimension: the Nation. The trouble with this nationhood, however, is that whereas before, I was defined by my education, my job, my ideas, my character—and, yes, my nationality too, now I feel stripped of all that. I am nobody, because I am not a person anymore, I am one of 4.5 million Croats. . . . I am not in a position to choose any longer. Nor, I think, is anyone else . . . something people cherished as part of their cultural identity—an alternative to the all-embracing communism . . . has become their political identity and turned into something like an ill-fitting shirt. You may feel the sleeves are too short, the collar too tight. You might not like the color, and the cloth might itch. But there is no escape; there is nothing else to wear.

What Drakulić skillfully explains is the ethnicization of ordinary life, of "narrative and interpretive frames, of perception and devaluation, of thinking and feeling" (Brubaker 1996:21; see also Mujkić 2007). Furthermore, this powerful transformation leads to the calcification of ethnicity and to the perpetual silencing and marginalization of alternative, still-lingering and potentially agentive transethnic identities, politics, and language. In addition, the overwhelmingly ethnonationalist context of everyday life flattens complex identities by creating "terrible categorical simplicity of ascribed nationality" (Brubaker 1996:20).

Even though I struggle daily to resist the ethnic box in which I was placed in the aftermath of the war, in this book I still employ, however reluctantly, the homogenizing terms Bosniaks, Croats, and Serbs. I criticize the international actors and organizations for their rigid understanding and institutionalization of these categories, but I am responsible for relying on the same concepts. There are several interrelated reasons for this "double standard." First, during the period of my research, there was very little visible official *political* opposition to the ethnic order of things in Bosnia-Herzegovina; ethnic nationalism was the main principle under which political actions, economic and everyday life unfolded. Furthermore, under the internationally designed framework of consociational democracy, ethnic nationalism continues to be the key political and social factor in the divided and fragmented postwar state, so that there is no incentive for politicians or lay people to create cross-ethnic coalitions. In other words, the ethnic ideologies of identity constitute "a ready-made model of sociality, a persuasive heuristic for international actors to understand, govern, and perhaps most importantly, legitimize their state-building interventions in Bosnia" (Gilbert 2008:193). This narrow understanding of Bosnian history, culture, and politics provides an ideal ground for the transformation of contingent ethnic identities into seemingly primordial ethnic nationalisms.

Therefore, even when in my writing I utilize, however hesitantly and cautiously, "Bosniaks," "Croats," or "Serbs," I do not mean to say that all the people who identify with these groups or who are identified by others as members of these groups agree with the politics that are done in the name of these groups. In addition, I do not think that these individuals give the same or permanent meanings to the identity constructs, nor do they inhibit them in the same way. The contrary examples are plenty. Instead, I understand the idioms "Bosniak," "Croat," or "Serb" as powerful cultural and political ideas, as modes of conflict, and not as fixed and permanent entities. Furthermore, by using these labels throughout the book, I stress that what makes the use of these categories effective is not only the recent war, but also the postwar consociational model of state-making, which legitimized and institutionalized ethnonational differences.

In reality, a significant number of people in postwar Bosnia-Herzegovina I spoke with during my fieldwork, some of whom populate the ensuing pages, disagreed with the limitations and predatory nature of ethnonationalist politics and they waited for better times to arrive, without organizing into a significant opposition (but see the Epilogue). At times, regardless of their "resistance" to the ethnic order of things, these individuals perpetuated the very existence of this order through their actions and discourses. Others, frustrated and weary of ethnic divisions and politics, left (or hoped to leave) the country in pursuit of more politically diverse and economically prosperous societies. In the meantime, the ideologies of ethnic nationalism continue to energize, supply, and shape the fragmented body of the state. And that is why I chose to use, however carefully, the terms "Bosniaks," "Croats," and "Serbs" in this work, even though I critique their hegemonic status in Bosnian politics.

What is more, the internationally installed democratic order makes the isolationist programs both logical and justifiable. Under the existing hegemony of corrupt local ethnonationalisms and internationally directed state-making, any genuine attempt by international and local actors to demand integration of people, territories, or institutions of Bosnia-Herzegovina is interpreted by the local ethnopolitics and the large section of Bosnian-Herzegovinian ethnicized, politically detached citizenry, as an attack on their cultural/ethnic autonomy, on the Dayton Agreement, and, by extension, on democracy itself. Thus ironically, even those international actors who full-heartedly try to implement reconciliation and reunification of the Bosnian-Herzegovinian people, territories, and society found themselves caught in the bad scripts that the military and "humanitarian development aid apparatuses" (James 2010:8) assisting Bosnia-Herzegovina have spun.

"International Community"

Like civilization in the nineteenth century and development in the twentieth, "new development" (Duffield 2001) became a dominant interpretative grid in the late twentieth and early twenty-first centuries, through which many of the wartorn and conflict-ridden regions are known to us, including Bosnia-Herzegovina. What makes the military and humanitarian intervention in Bosnia-Herzegovina unique is that it was the first extensive international project since the U.S.-directed occupations of Germany and Japan in the aftermath of World War II (Chandler 2006:1). For these reasons, Bosnia-Herzegovina emerged as a "template for new experiments in international administration and external assistance in state reconstruction and post-conflict reconciliation" (1; see also Bose 2002) in the post-Cold War context, creating an example of a "maximal nation-building" (Marina Ottaway, cited in Brown 2006:8). As a consequence, the international humanitarian and military intervention in Bosnia-Herzegovina has brought troop presence and foreign investment that have, by the time of my research, exceeded those in other parts of the world (see Brown 2006:8).[23]

The principal international actors coordinating the Bosnian transition and recovery are the Office of the High Representative (OHR), Office of Security and Cooperation in Europe (OSCE), and UN Mission in Bosnia and Herzegovina (UNMBiH), and International Crisis Group (ICG 2001:2).[24] OHR was established formally by the Peace Implementation Council (PIC), as the instrument through which the "international community" would monitor the implementation of the peace settlement and oversee the civilian aspects of the Dayton Peace Agreement.[25] The high representative, the highest civilian authority in the country, who is also the European Union special envoy, was invested with ultimate power of decision-making.[26] In addition to OHR, the OSCE mission to Bosnia-Herzegovina has been very important for the implementation of the Dayton Agreement.[27] Accompanying these larger organizations were hundreds of large and small transnational governmental and nongovernmental agencies, including USAID, Save the Children, Red Cross, and CARE International, which took part in the reconstruction and rebuilding efforts. Finally, numerous ambassadors and embassies have played a crucial role in the civilian affairs of the postwar country (ICG 2001:3).

Regardless of the tendency in most academic and policy accounts to unify and reify the international community and refer to it as an abstract, unformed, and static "it" (Coles 2007:54), this entity is a dynamic, complicated, overlapping, uncoordinated, and conflicting bundle of simultaneously converging and diverging people, projects, interests, agendas, and practices (see Moore 2013). As a result of these complexities, in this work I avoid using the unifying, objectifying notion "international community"; or if I do use it, I put it in quotation marks to acknowledge that this social and political construct is "too neat to capture the unwieldy myriad of forces and practices that are subsumed within this conceptually diffuse term" (Coles 2007:39). Rather, I use international actors, entrepreneurs, and diplomats, or where appropriate, I use the real persons whom I encountered and befriended during my fieldwork to demonstrate their agentive capacities, differences, and struggles.

All the larger organizations have their Bosnian headquarters in Sarajevo, but they all also have (or had until recently) regional offices in several larger

Bosnia-Herzegovina cities, including Mostar. Due to the complex nature of the conflict in the city, as well as the political circumstances caused by the fighting, Mostar has had a special status vis-à-vis the "international community." As a result, the presence of international actors has been extremely visible in Mostar, where, in the early postwar years, a number of main posts in the civilian domain were headed and handled by foreigners. For example, in 1994, the European Union Administration of Mostar (EUAM) was established and headed by a German, Mr. Hans Koschnick (to be later replaced by Mr. Perez Casado), Mostar's first postwar mayor. In addition, EUAM efforts and civic activities were supported by the Western European Police.[28]

In the case of Mostar Gymnasium, where the presence of the aid community was extremely visible, the most prominent international organization was the OSCE. Even though the OSCE usually does not focus on education in other contexts, but rather addresses the issues of free elections and institution-building, its mission in Bosnia-Herzegovina established a Department of Education in 2002, mostly to focus on the education reform process. Due to OSCE's education-related mandate, most of my interactions with the "internationals" in Mostar and elsewhere happened through this organization, and especially its Mostar-based regional office, and its education officer in charge of the school's reunification, Martin.

The OSCE's presence at the school was made possible by donations coming from numerous Western states. Soon after I arrived at the school, I heard the teachers, students, and administration workers mention "German heating," "Japanese computer lab," "Spanish façade," "Spanish Square," and "French language lab." Quickly I learned that people were referring to different aspects of the school that were reconstructed with donations coming from different European and non-European governments. In this way, the widely circulating and vague umbrella term "international community" dissolved into the much more colorful and recognizable names of eleven different states.

The international presence at the school was further enforced by constant visits from foreign ambassadors, diplomats, journalists, researchers, NGO workers, and film crews, whom the local people commonly referred to as *stranci* (foreigners) (see Jansen 2007). Some *stranci* would stay for fifteen minutes, take a few pictures, or shake a few hands. Others stayed for weeks, even months. A few came almost daily, especially Martin and some

NGO representatives who hoped to include the school in their reconciliation, democratization, reconstruction, and other projects.

This foreign "invasion" created much resentment among the school's leaders, teachers, and students toward the international presence, regardless of how grateful they felt for the financial assistance they were receiving from these international organizations. While the "local" people used the homogenizing category *stranci* to talk about international actors at the school, they would often single out a certain organization, or more frequently one or more individuals they found especially (un)helpful. The following quote from one of the school employees illustrates the struggle between being grateful to certain international organizations and individuals for their support and feeling subordinate and constrained by their governmentality.

> Anyone who invested any amount of euro in this project feels like they own the place [the Mostar Gymnasium], that they can come at any time, take pictures of the school with them in it . . . I do not know, I mean . . . that they show themselves in this light, . . . like *dobročinitelji* [Croatian, the ones who do good deeds] . . . and I cannot say it is not really like that . . . that is the fact . . . and, I mean, you have the Spanish, who really, more than any others, invested so much money, and they plan to invest more in the future . . . and in general, the Spanish ambassador did so much good for Bosnia-Herzegovina, and I would think it was not just his personal interest . . . But what I want to say is that everyone wants to build something into this project so that they can secure their own personal . . . I mean . . . promotion at work, to move up on the ladder. And we, we are forced to accept that kind of aid. And it is normal, I think, when we look at that [we see] that this "high politics" came with a clear aim to Bosnia-Herzegovina, to Mostar, and to this school.

This quote captures the double nature of peace-building and school/state-making in Bosnia-Herzegovina—its simultaneously emancipatory and regulative character. The ownership of the school that foreign diplomats, workers, and journalists claimed made teachers feel that Bosnian-Herzegovinian education was a playground for experimentation, "a large laboratory" (Coles 2007:27) in state-making, because, one teacher explained, "we are just marionettes in the hands of people with power. The Balkans have always been a good place for experimentation, and one day you will understand that your research will not change anything about it."

In addition to feeling powerless to control or even impact the scope and nature of international intervention and interpretations of events at the school, the school leadership, teachers, and students often complained about these constant visits and obstructions, as I learned at the teachers' meeting in August 2005:

> We cannot bear any more those hundreds of *stranci* who come to our school, to our classroom, without letting the teachers know in advance. That is why I appreciate that Azra came and introduced herself to us. Both the students and we feel like we are in a zoo. I cannot have a regular class under these conditions.

The "zoo" comment was especially popular among the "locals." Saying that they felt like they are at the zoo indexed their dissatisfaction with the "right" of foreign diplomats and aid workers to enter *their* school at any time, and to examine, observe, and rearrange the school's space and its population, "as if we are some unique animal species" (teacher's comment).

Rather than contributing to the important and growing scholarship on the "international community" and its relationship to the "locals," and instead of documenting the internal conflicts and differences within the international field of intervention (Moore 2013), in this book I focus on the everyday effects of the "logic of recognition" (Povinelli 2002) shared and (re)produced by the majority of these actors. More specifically, this logic approaches Bosnia-Herzegovina "ethnically" (Coles 2007:53)—as a place of *ethnic people* rooted in *ethnic territories* (Campbell 1998; Ćurak 2004; Gagnon n.d.). This vision is only seemingly in stark opposition to the "local," ethnonational view of the Bosnian-Herzegovinian state and society; rather, the two discourses are tangentially intertwined and mutually constitutive. While international and local political elites have had different end goals—democratic reunification (internationals) versus ethnic segregation and manipulation (local ethnonationalist leaders)—their understanding of Bosnian-Herzegovinian people and territories has been uncannily similar, caught in narrow scripts of ethnicity and nationalism.

When put in this context, the materialization of the school's empty lab becomes clearer: it emerged from the tension within the peace-building and state-making project itself; the international political actors in Bosnia-Herzegovina faced the task of forming an ethnically plural, integrated, and peaceful school/state in which power is shared equally, while accepting the permanent existence, segregation, and institutionalization of the main ethno-national groups within the state/school. This required reconciliation of two different sociopolitical impulses—the call for integration into one school/state through the shared notions about Bosnian-Herzegovinian history and citizenship, and simultaneous establishment of a model of democracy that favored ethnic citizenship, territorial segregation, and autonomy. The Mostar Gymnasium became the public site where these two visions of Bosnia-Herzegovina converged and clashed, creating vacant heterogeneous public spaces, well captured in the materialization of the school's empty lab.

Chapter Outline

This book is divided into two parts and six chapters. Part I, Integrating the School, includes Chapters 1, 2, and 3. It further introduces the reader to the Mostar Gymnasium, outlining its reunification, spatial organization, and everyday life. While this part zooms into the school, it also addresses the wider sociopolitical context that shaped the "rebirth" of the school. Part II, Disintegrating the Nation, includes Chapters 4, 5, and 6. It retains the focus on the school but widens the analytic and ethnographic lenses; here we zoom out of the Mostar Gymnasium to examine the meaning of Bosnian statehood, nationhood, and citizenship for the country's youth. The two parts differ in how they construct "the field," but both address the issues of language and identity, spatial segregation, possibilities and consequences of mixing, and "illicit" activities in Mostar and beyond.

Chapter 1 explores the tensions surrounding language instruction at the unified school. Unpacking the passion and politics surrounding the contested issue of language instruction, the chapter demonstrates how a particular, neither united nor segregated school came into being. Here I illustrate how the ethnonational leadership successfully mobilized the wider community to resist the demands for integration of the school by removing the struggle from the sphere of elitist politics into the realm of society and culture, especially language. Thus, the school becomes a powerful metaphor for the country as a whole, where simultaneous segregation and integration of people, through the mechanisms of language, culture, and history, take place in politics and everyday life.

In Chapter 2 the focus shifts to spatial governmentality at the school. The chapter makes visible how the international power brokers in Bosnia-Herzegovina adopt the main postulates of ethnonationalist politics that see Bosnia-Herzegovina as an ethnic problem that requires a particular spatial solution. This facilitates development of a meticulous and rigid spatial cartography of ethnic difference at the school where certain features of belonging and practices of ethnic intermixing became unmappable.

Expanding on the previous chapter's analysis of the school cartography and geography, Chapter 3 follows the everyday life of students at the school. More specifically, it introduces the reader to the illicit bathroom smoking. The secluded school bathroom emerges as the most dynamic place for cross-ethnic citizenship. The youth's willingness to engage in these practices makes visible the paradox of postwar spatial governmentality—the absence of shared geography in the city where youth could mix and continue to learn about each other by confronting the past and engaging in a dialogue about a shared future.

Chapter 4 examines the interpretations, articulations, and practices youth in Bosnia-Herzegovina assign to the notion of *narod* (nationhood, peoplehood). The chapter explains how for youth in Bosnia-Herzegovina there are two predominant understandings of the term narod: the accentuated notion of narod at the level of an ethnic group and narod as a transethnic, politically uncultivated category. The chapter concludes that transethnic narod, as a space of interconnectedness, morality, economic suffering, and living proximity still lingers and powerfully informs discourses and practices of ordinary Bosnians-Herzegovinians.

Chapter 5 combines the themes of mixing and narod and focuses on the transformation of Yugoslav mixed citizens into "invisible" citizens. Here I investigate the everyday experiences and struggles of those Bosnian citizens, labeled as "Others," who do not fall into the Serb-Croat-Bosnian ethnonational grid. The struggles of invisible citizens in postwar Mostar make especially visible the difficulties with which these people maneuver their hybrid and embodied histories in the context where these practices and identities become disputed, marginalized, and undesirable.

Chapter 6 broadens the discussion of citizen-identity, and it examines the nature of the relationship between the state, citizenship, and morality as it is experienced by youth in the country. The chapter argues that when coupled with the war-generated ethnic fragmentation described in previous chapters, the massive corruption and "decline in morality" that youth associate with the recent history of peace-building and state-making generate a mixture of cynicism, lament, resignation, frustration, and detachment of youth from their Dayton state.

PART I

Integrating the School

Chapter 1

Right to Difference

After the declarations of independence by Slovenia and Croatia from Yugoslavia in the early 1990s, Bosnia-Herzegovina found itself faced with a choice between independence (supported by the majority of Bosniaks and Croats) and remaining in the Yugoslav federation (supported by the majority of Serbs). In February 1992, a referendum for independence from Yugoslavia took place, which was boycotted by the Serb leaders. Regardless of the boycott, Bosnia-Herzegovina became an independent state on April 6. On the same day Bosnia-Herzegovina was officially recognized, Serbian paramilitary units and the Yugoslav People's Army (Jugoslovenska Narodna Armija; JNA) attacked Bosnia-Herzegovina's capital, Sarajevo, and started the war in Bosnia-Herzegovina.[1] The army of the self-proclaimed Republika Srpska (RS) within Bosnia-Herzegovina, with the help of troops and weapons from Serbia, succeeded in conquering close to 70 percent of the country's territory by the end of 1993. It also perpetrated some of the most brutal acts of violence exercised against the non-Serb populations, which involved mass killings, rape, and torture.

The collapse of Yugoslavia and Bosnia-Herzegovina was particularly destructive in Mostar. First, the Serb-dominated JNA attacked Mostar from the eastern hills of the city, driving the inhabitants to the western part of town in search of protection and encouraging most Serbs to leave the town (Vetters 2007). After the Croats and Bosniaks initially defended the city against JNA forces jointly, fighting then broke out between the two groups, leading to the complete division of the town into a Croat-dominated western and a Bosniak-dominated eastern side (Vetters 2007). In addition, a "quasi-state of Croats [Herceg-Bosna] was created during the war in the

Croat dominated regions" (Malcolm 1996:252). When Croatian nationalists destroyed the sixteenth-century Old Bridge in November 1993, this punctuated the physical and symbolic segregation of the two communities. Faced by a brutal destruction of this ancient city, its famous bridge, and its population, the "international community," and especially the United States, brokered the Washington Peace Agreement in March 1994. The Agreement stopped the violence in Mostar and the wider region of Herzegovina. In addition, it created the Bosniak-Croat Federation, which is still in place. The war in the rest of the country continued, however, causing further slaughter and expulsions.

Mostar is a very appealing place when visited for a few days, but everyday life is full of hardships. The difference between the two sides of the city is still palpable. The east side, populated almost exclusively by Bosniaks, was almost totally demolished during the war. As a consequence, it is still poorer than the west side, which suffered less destruction. Several of my informants mentioned that the Bosniak side was neglected and had more social problems; they called it the "Gypsy side" because of the high number of Roma who roam its streets.[2] The Croat side appears richer and more polished, with wide, clean streets and three well-stocked shopping malls. Moreover, the population on the Croat side is generally wealthier, but both sides experience an increasing gap between the political and economic elites and the poor and less powerful. The key reason for Croats being more prosperous has to do with the part of the city they inherited from "old" Mostar. While the Bosniak side includes densely populated residential areas and the major tourist destinations, such as the Old City and the rebuilt bridge, it lacks any important administrative facilities, institutions, or factories. The Croats inherited public spaces and facilities, such as the aluminum company Aluminij d.d., which was, at the time of my fieldwork, among the most successful companies in Bosnia-Herzegovina and employed almost exclusively Croats. In addition, "west Mostar attracts Croat capital from all over Bosnia-Herzegovina, while Bosniak money mostly gravitates to Bosniak-dominated centers, most of all to booming Sarajevo" (ICG 2009:9). As a result, Croats are perceived by numerous Serbs and Bosniaks in Bosnia-Herzegovina as wealthier, "Western," and entrepreneurial. For example, some of the cities with the highest standard of living in Bosnia-Herzegovina are predominately Croat towns in western Herzegovina.

Bosniaks in Mostar generally shop on the Croat side of the city because there is not a good shopping mall on the east side.[3] These excursions are limited, however, as one of the teachers at the Mostar Gymnasium explained: "I go, purchase what I need and I leave. . . . Only if I really feel like it, I would have a cup of coffee at the Rondo [the shopping mall]. Then I leave. I never go out there in the evening." More than a few Bosniak families returned to their original prewar apartments on the west side, from which they were forced out during the war. Still, they mostly socialize on the east side. They refer to the west side as *njihova strana*, "their [Croat] side," signaling that they do not feel they really belong there.

There are also those Bosniaks who never left the west side during the war. The children in these Bosniak families frequently went to Croat schools during and after the war. There were three students in "my" Croat curriculum class who fell into this category. All three students said that they were not sure why their families decided to stay, but they hinted at several possible reasons, such as, "we did not know where to go," "we were not directly attacked," or "people at my parents' work were good to them." All students mentioned, however, that they knew of Bosniak families who were forced out of their apartments and tortured. Therefore, these students shared memories of anxiety and fear related to their place of residence. They often balanced these testimonies with examples of "good Croat neighbors" (see Kolind 2007) hiding them from the Bosnian Croat army, and thus saving their lives.[4]

The few Croat families who lived on the east side before the war generally preferred to sell their apartments or exchange them for ones on the west side rather than return. There were no Croat students in "my" Federal (mostly Bosniak) curriculum classes. All this points to the fact that Bosniaks in general, and Bosniak youth especially (because of shopping and entertainment facilities), cross the inner-city divide more frequently than Croat youth. Most of the Croat students told me that there is almost nothing for them to do on the east side.[5]

Regardless of the reconstruction of the new "Old" Bridge in 2004 and the increasing crossing from one side to another, people in postwar Mostar remain sharply divided, and "Mostar is today Bosnia and Herzegovina's only truly divided city" (ICG 2009:1). The city's ethnic structure and "political landscape are similar to Bosnia's, but with the players reversed [Croats are the numerical majority in the city, but the numerical minority in the FBiH and Bosnia-Herzegovina]. Alone among Bosnia's cities, it runs on laws and institutions built on the same, internationally designed framework used to build the Bosnian state" (1). As a result of this high resemblance between the internationally designed and governed Bosnian-Herzegovinian state and internationally designed and (initially) governed Mostar, I approach Mostar as an ideal context to ethnographically grasp the dynamic nature and effects of international humanitarian intervention in Bosnia-Herzegovina.

As a result of this war-generated and internationally legitimized ethnicization of Mostar's institutions, governance, and everyday sociality, a fluid and relational notion of group difference, which sees groups as "overlapping and criss-crossing" (Young 1990), ceased to be an option in the postwar city. Instead, the spatialization of the "problem of cultural difference" (Povinelli 2002:4) in Bosnia-Herzegovina, which most visibly manifested itself in the absence of heterogeneous public spaces, reduced the chances for youth to get to know each other, and it located Bosnia-Herzegovina citizens in one of the three possible "ethnic boxes." This created the "thickening of space" (Moore 2013:2) and the context of "ethnic apartheid" (Campbell 1999) in the place where, not that long ago, the Old Bridge proudly stretched over the fast currents of the Neretva River.

The Mostar Gymnasium

The international actors have made the integration of schools, and especially the Mostar Gymnasium, a crucial element of their peace-building and state-making efforts. They saw the Mostar Gymnasium as a powerful symbol—the integration of this socially momentous school, in a fiercely divided city, would signal to the local population and to the world that ethnically divided people in Bosnia-Herzegovina could live together. Therefore the OSCE—the international agency in charge of implementing reunification—channeled much of its power, energy, and symbolic and economic capital to the project of the school's integration. For example, based on the OSCE January 2005 report, eleven "Western" countries together donated 1.219 million euros for the reconstruction of the school (OSCE 2005:13).

The idea of an integrated Mostar Gymnasium had a strong institutional backing in the OSCE and the rest of the international humanitarian field. In addition, Martin—the OSCE's educational officer in charge of integration—exercised incredible persistence and effort while negotiating integration of the school with the local politicians in Mostar and with individuals at the school. Many international diplomats and numerous foreign ambassadors, presidents, and prime ministers visited the school and openly supported its reunification. Numerous international organizations and individual governments reinforced calls for integration by offering significant donations in support of the project.

On the local side, the main representatives in negotiations were the leaders of the two main ethnonationalist political parties in Mostar, the Croat Hrvatska Demokratska Zajednica (HDZ) and the Bosniak Stranka Demokratske Akcije (SDA). The talks also included education experts and ministers from both sides, as well as the mayor of Mostar. Due to this heavy involvement and the conflicting agendas of multiple actors, the first principal of the school told me that he felt like a marionette in the hands of local and international political elites.

After two years of heated negotiations, demonstrations, petitions, and the investment of large sums of money in reconstruction, the school was finally administratively and legally reunited in February 2004. Administrative and legal unification included the following: "appointment of one School Director; appointment of one, multi-ethnic School Board; registration of school as one legal body with a single school name; establishment of joint administrative personnel; development of a joint budget; and participation of School Directors and teachers in joint planning activities for the new school year" (OSCE 2003:2). In addition, reunification created a symmetrical, horizontal, and spatialized world of separate "ethnic equals."[6] These multifaceted processes of integration make the Mostar Gymnasium a powerful metaphor for the postwar state, where simultaneous integration and segregation of people and territories take place in everyday life.

Discourses of Integration

Of the nine secondary schools in Mostar before the war, all but two schools were located on the present-day Croat side of the city (OSCE 2005). Since the beginning of the Croat-Bosniak conflict in Mostar, the Bosniaks were not able to use any of the seven schools located on the west side. Faced with homelessness, Bosniak students and teachers established temporary secondary schools using the primary schools on the east side of town. This lack of space introduced some logistical problems: the number of school shifts was increased from two to three in most of the schools. The number of shifts on the Croat side remained two, however, since they did not face the shortage of space.

For years, numerous international actors, especially OSCE, have tried to convince the Bosniak leadership in Mostar that they will be able to return to the original buildings, but by the end of my fieldwork in 2006, the return had yet to take place. Given the fierce division of the city, and the Croat leaders' monopoly over the west side's educational institutions, the idea of return proved to be too ambitious. As a result, more than 2,400 Bosniak high school students had been studying in overcrowded and poorly equipped temporary schools for the past two decades. Croat teachers and students, on the other hand, used all but two high schools in the city (OSCE 2005:3)

In 1999, when the city was still officially divided into Croat and Bosniak municipalities,[7] the Croat-dominated city council transferred authority over the Mostar Gymnasium to the Croat-controlled Cantonal Ministry, which in turn transferred authority to the Croat Municipality South West (OSCE 2005:4). The Croat leadership in Mostar almost immediately set about some small-scale repair work on five different classrooms, renamed the building "Fra Dominik Mandić,"[8] and began teaching 257 students using the Croat curriculum and Croat language (4). The school became a "Croat school" and stayed Croat-dominated until its reunification in 2004. The rhetoric that supported the Croatization of the school is nicely summarized in the following quote: "This school is located in Croat territory. In this area, the war started because nobody knew what belonged to whom. I want this to be a representative Croat school that will train and produce Croat intellectuals" (Croat teacher at Mostar Gymnasium cited in Wimmen 2004). Meanwhile, the Bosniak leaders established a temporary high school, the "First Gymnasium," in the Seventh Primary School in an old neighborhood on the east side known as Mahala (OSCE 2005:4).

The first concrete stimulus for the reintegration of the Mostar Gymnasium came from the United States government, when it offered $1 million in assistance to the school under the condition that 392 students in the temporary Bosniak Gymnasium be reintegrated (into the Mostar Gymnasium) (OSCE 2005:3).[9] The Bosniak leadership accepted this proposal immediately, since they wanted to return to the school and end their forced exile in the primary school in Mahala. Similarly, earlier research on the processes of educational reform in Mostar shows that the Bosniak leaders generally have favored integration (Freedman et al. 2004:231). However, the Bosniaks' position in this process is more complicated than earlier research on the topic and popular rhetoric have suggested. While it is true that the Bosniak leadership supported the prointegrationist policies in the Federation of Bosnia-Herzegovina (FBiH), where they represent the clear majority (roughly 70 percent), their politics shifted when their numeric dominance was undercut by integration (Wimmen 2004:5–6). Due to their dominance in FBiH as a whole, however, they did not feel threatened by the processes of integration as the Croat community and leadership did. In addition, Bosniaks' support for integration was not always motivated by a desire to better their relationship with the Croat community in Mostar (see also Freedman et al. 2004 and Wimmen 2004). Instead, Bosniak leadership had more self-interested goals; while using the rhetoric of reconciliation and peace, they mostly wanted to return Bosniak students to the Mostar Gymnasium (also see Weinstein et al. 2007). Some teachers did not hide these motivations from their students, as Melita explains: "Our teacher Senija told us: 'We do not want to make peace; we just want our building back.' Imagine when a teacher says that in front of 40 children. . . . How can I believe that they want us to reconcile, when we and they [Croat students] get together in the hallways in front of the classrooms and they [teachers] force us back into the classrooms?"

In addition to the Croat community's fear of Bosniak dominance in the FBiH as a whole, many Bosniaks in Mostar felt that Croats in Mostar discriminated against them. Croats, who are a numerical minority in the FBiH, are slightly more numerous and visibly more prosperous than Bosniaks in Mostar. Additionally, the Bosniak leadership believed that Croats were also more privileged by the OSCE, which treated them "too softly," and let them be in charge. As one of the school's employees explains: "Azra, remember . . . there is one rule here . . . what is Croat is Croat; what is shared it is also Croat. . . . You will see this in four years when the rotation of the principal and vice-principal should take place. . . . Croats will protest that a Croat is not the principal."[10]

In addition to their criticism of those in charge as "too soft" with Croats, this person voiced other uncertainties related to the future reunification, such as identity loss, decrease of quality in education, and the asymmetries in the "international community's" approaches:

I fear that with this unification we will lose our Bosniak identity. . . . Only if we had another high school . . . the Bosniak one and this united one[11] ... and ... you know, Azra, I can tell you this because you understand ... we [Bosniaks] are so soft, we let go, everything is okay to us ... but Croats ... they are constantly complaining.... The OSCE should tolerate them less ... but imagine, *šehidska djeca* (Muslim martyrs' children) will go to that Croatian school ... and, I do expect that the grades will drop, it will be hard to keep the kids focused on the school material, when so much other stuff is going on.

These comments illustrate multiple doubts that the project of integration presented for Bosniaks. First, it points at the Bosniak fear of "identity loss" on integration. This fear has to be understood in the context of a "politics of difference" in the former Yugoslavia, where Muslims became officially a separate nation only in 1971, almost three decades after Serbs or Croats were recognized as separate nations within the socialist Yugoslavia. This memory of perceived former inequalities and discrimination against Bosnian Muslims in the former Yugoslavia is furthered by three additional factors: the present-day claims by the Serb and Croat nationalists that Bosnian Muslims are converted Serbs or Croats respectively (see Malcolm 1996); the late development of the Bosniak national consciousness in comparison to Serb and Croat nationalisms; and the fact that Bosniaks were the most numerous victims of the recent war.[12] These combined experiences make Bosniaks anxious about the preservation of their war-strengthened and war-nationalized ethnoreligious group identity.

Second, the fact that this person called Stara Gimnazija a Croat school is significant, due to the emotional and historic identification that most Bosniaks in Mostar feel toward the school. What he intended by naming the school "Croat" is to underscore the process of Croatization of the school immediately after the war, and to point at what he perceived to be the present-day power asymmetries between the two sides—"while the school will unify, Croats will stay in charge." This situation, he feared, could lead to the weakening of Bosniak ethnonational identity upon the unification. Importantly, on a different occasion, the same person addressed another dread of integration, the economic one. He said that he feared that the joined curriculum would lead to the laying off of numerous teachers in both curricula, since a joined curriculum would require fewer teachers than two separate curricula.

These comments encapsulate the multidimensional nature of fear of unification; they are in agreement with the research findings of Freedman et al. (2004), who discovered that "many objections to school integration were grounded in two basic, but related, fears: fear of conflict and of loss of identity" (231). Another reason for worry among the Bosniaks was the fact that Martin and the new school management agreed that during the year 2004–5, only grades two and three (U.S. ten and eleven) in the federal curriculum were to attend the lessons at the reunified school building, while grades one and four (U.S. nine and twelve) were to continue using the "rented" space at the primary school in Mahala. With a heavy dose of irony, a teacher remarked, "Instead of two schools under one roof, we got one school under two roofs."

The official reason for the decision to keep half of the Bosniak students in the elementary school building in Mahala was the lack of reconstructed classroom space at the reunited Mostar Gymnasium. Most Bosniak students, parents, and teachers, however, believed that the real reason for splitting their school between two locations was the script of an absolute ethnic equilibrium at the Mostar Gymnasium, a "seamless, ethnically ordered world of Croats, Muslims and Serbs, in which no other conceptions of identity have political imports, and where group relations cannot be other than mutually exclusive and conflictual" (Campbell 1999:418). Since the Bosniak student population was more numerous than the Croat one,[13] if all the Bosniaks would return to the Mostar Gymnasium at once, "the Croats would freak out" (Bosniak parent's comment), in other words, feel threatened by the numerical dominance of Bosniaks. Many Bosniaks dismissed the "fear of small numbers" (Appadurai 2006) by saying that Croats, even if numerically smaller, have more economic capital and support of the "internationals."

Regardless of the continuous expressions of feelings of inferiority, fear of identity loss, and the self-interested motivations for reunification, Bosniak leaders readily accepted all calls for integration that came from the OSCE. The official rhetoric that supported integration closely resembled and often embodied the Bosniaks' official rhetorical support for the multiethnic and unitary Bosnian state. The Bosnian Croat representatives, however, initially refused the offer, explaining their rejection as an acknowledgment of the will of the wider Croat public. The reactions of the wider Croat community bordered on the "hysterical" (Wimmen 2004:7) in claiming that "cultural genocide had been carried out against the Croat people," calling the Croat leadership who agreed to integration "traitors of the nation, if they support the project," and "evoking images of 'new janissaries'[14] being created from Croatian youth" (7). In the context of the increasingly ethnonationalized Croat community, the political elites were seen as compromised traitors of nationhood, incapable of properly representing and protecting the rights of the Croat "minority."[15] The Croat community was thus much more openly resistant to the idea of an integrated school than were the Bosniaks (also see Freedman et al. 2004; Wimmen 2004) and much more eager to argue and defend their position. The Croat leadership in Mostar passionately argued that its calls for self-determination were in service of protecting the group's "cultural/linguistic rights," in the spirit of Charles Taylor's (1994) description of a "politics of difference,"[16] where ethnic distinctiveness and authenticity form the main postulates of social and political life. The state/ethnonational disjunctures thus become embedded in the discourses of "rights," which "inform the practice of everyday life in any given plural society where different ethnonational groups compete for state power" (Neofotistos 2010:285).

Integration Contested

The Croat leaders' and wider community's passionate resistance to integration of the school becomes clearer if it is examined in the context of majority/minority politics in the emerging state. Seen through the lens of what Wimmen terms a "trapped minority," the prospect of the school's integration unleashed what is perceived as an unnatural and dangerous fragmentation of the Croat nation (Wimmen 2004:7).[17] Politically speaking, the school's integration was understood as a forced incorporation and assimilation of the Bosnian Croat population into what they saw only as a seemingly equal, power-sharing, pluralist Bosnian-Herzegovinian state, which, for most Croats, is experienced as one of Bosniak hegemony.

In Bosnia-Herzegovina the Croats are not officially a minority because they are one of the three constituent peoples.[18] Numerically, however, Croats represent roughly 15 percent of the total population of the country, less than the two larger constituent groups, Serbs (roughly 37 percent) and Bosniaks (roughly 47 percent).[19] In addition, Croats represent about 25–30 percent of the population of FBiH, significantly less than the Bosniaks, who represent roughly 55–70 percent of the FBiH population. Even more important, Bosnian Croats perceive themselves as a disadvantaged minority. Mostar, the only large Bosnia-Herzegovina city that is numerically dominated by Croats, is the site where the anxieties surrounding the "Croat status" are most visible and where the tensions between inclusion and exclusion are most passionately articulated.

The anti-integrationist stance articulated by the Croat minority arose within the field of various intersecting and often conflicting positions. On the one hand, there were the international diplomats and humanitarians with a clear mandate, agreed in Dayton, to challenge the ethnic segregation and segmental autonomy itself given to the ethnic groups by Dayton. On the other hand, the local and regional separatist discourses, largely infiltrating from the nationalist leadership in neighboring Croatia and Serbia, and adopted and furthered by the local nationalist party leaders, challenged the integrationist approaches. The overarching position of the Croat leadership stressed that Bosnia-Herzegovina and FBiH were political arenas for the ethnic dominance of the majority group in Bosnia-Herzegovina, the Bosniaks. This "ethnocracy," or disproportionate dominance of one ethnic group over other groups in a shared state, had been hidden, they claimed, behind the language of consociational politics, peace-building, and ethnic pluralism. As a result, the Croat leadership appropriated and revived the language of cultural rights in order to resist integration into a shared nation based on principles of ethnic pluralism, which they did not trust. Therefore, the Croat ethnic "minority" became increasingly suspicious of consociational forms of integration, which they saw as "ideological masks for substantively nationalizing and ethnocratic forms of rule, as assuring the cultural predominance and political autonomy of the dominant [Bosniak] nation" (Brubaker 1996:50). The fact that at the same time, due to the war-strengthened fear of the loss of identity, the Bosniak political leadership and parts of the wider community underwent Islamization further distanced Croats from the FBiH and Bosnia-Herzegovina as a whole.

The resistance to integration by the Croat group should be understood in the context of regional Croat nationhood, citizenship, territorial belonging, and political aspirations. The Croat position is not unique in Europe and beyond—most minority groups in Eastern Europe find themselves mismatched by being attached by formal citizenship to one state, yet by ethnonational affinity to another (Brubaker 1996:7). Unlike most of these groups, however, Croats in Bosnia-Herzegovina hold dual citizenship, in both Bosnia-Herzegovina and Croatia (see Štiks 2006, 2010).[20] The fact that they hold dual citizenship further diminishes their connection to Bosnia-Herzegovina, since they have better privileges as citizens of a more prosperous Croat state (for example, a more desirable passport and the EU membership). In addition, Croats in Bosnia-Herzegovina have a very strong territorial attachment, not to Bosnia-Herzegovina as a whole, but to its geographically defined southern region, Herzegovina. They conceive of Herzegovina as geographically, historically, socially, and politically distinct from Bosnia in the north (see Chapter 4).[21]

Like citizenship regimes, the sense of nationhood in Bosnia-Herzegovina has to be examined in the regional context. In the case of the Croat population in FBiH, a national sentiment is not confined to the Croat population in Bosnia-Herzegovina but is shaped by the triad of relations between the emerging Bosnia-Herzegovina state, the Croat national minority, and its external homeland, Croatia.[22] More specifically, for the Croats in Mostar, the Croat national community stretches from the Croatian border with Slovenia on the west to the boulevard in Mostar on the east, unifying the Croatian homeland with its national minority in Bosnia-Herzegovina. While this spatial understanding of Croat nationhood is not as ambitious as that claimed by the proponents of the Greater Croatia, the current national imaginary still captures a large portion of what is officially today an independent and sovereign Bosnia-Herzegovina.[23]

While most Herzegovina Croats did share some *territorial* identification with the Yugoslav Republic of Bosnia-Herzegovina, historically they have conceived of themselves as members of a distinct nation, which corresponds not to the (republic) state boundaries but to the less territorially restricted notion of *domovina* (homeland). This transborder national sentiment has been especially pronounced after the fall of Yugoslavia, when the "homeland" has been powerfully rearticulated as Croatia, so that Croats from Bosnia-Herzegovina and those in Croatia are seen as conationals, fellow members of a single, transborder nation (Brubaker 1996:5). In other words, Croatia is experienced as domovina or a true homeland by the majority of Croats in the region and beyond, regardless of which state they were born in, live in, and officially belong to. Regardless of their emotional detachment from Bosnia-Herzegovina and the vague idea of the multiethnic Bosnian nation, the political engagement of Croats in Bosnia-Herzegovina is understood as crucial for the protection of the Croat nation and domovina as a whole. The conviction that the Croatian nationhood is defended and guarded within the political structures and territory of

Bosnia-Herzegovina makes much more comprehensible the "hysteric" (Wimmen 2004) response of the Croat minority and their resistance to the integration of the school. Placed in the field of regional politics of belonging and identification, the Mostar Gymnasium was removed from the center of the formerly united city to the frontline of Croat national space at its southeastern frontier. This rendered the school both marginal, in terms of its physical location, and central, in terms of its role in marking and preserving the ethnonational boundaries of belonging. As a result, for the majority of Mostar Croats, the school was seen as one of the "building-blocks, and possibly a linchpin, of a bulwark designed to seal off 'nationalized territory'" (5).

As the Croat community's fury about the integration of the school continued to grow, it became obvious that the international actors in charge of reunification initially had not realized the significance of the Mostar Gymnasium for the Croat ethnonational community. The messages sent by the OSCE—such as "integration does not mean assimilation"[24]—did not convince the Croat leaders; just the opposite, the Croat leadership interpreted integration as an ideological mask for substantively nationalizing and ethnocratic forms of rule, assuring cultural predominance and political hegemony of the Bosniaks. In addition, the vague definition of "school integration" enabled the manipulation of the term and its meanings.

Integrated School

An "integrated school" is an educational concept with a long history in conflict-ridden societies; it is most frequently associated with Northern Ireland, and more recently, Israel.[25] It is one of a range of attempts made to bridge the divide between Protestant and Catholic children in Northern Ireland, and Palestinian and Israeli children in Israel. Although Northern Ireland has been nurturing sixty-two integrated schools since 1981, the meaning of integration has remained ambiguous for a long time (see Dunn 1986) and still means different things in different schools (Gallagher, personal communication).[26]

The meanings of integration in education in Bosnia-Herzegovina are also multiple. The local notion of integration is best captured by the phrase *biti zajedno*, "to be together" which essentially means joint classrooms and curricula. This is seen in contrast to *biti razdvojen*, "to be separated." For many people in Bosnia-Herzegovina, integration is understood either as the return to the prewar Yugoslav ethnic relations, potentially leading to a return to the territorially and socially intermixed nation (this would automatically call for the demolition of the RS and many of the Croat- or Bosniak-dominated cantons in FBiH) or as an assimilation into a larger, dominant group and a related loss of ethnocultural identity. Both are perceived by the ethnonational leaders and ethnicized citizenry as unnatural and dangerous to the survival of ethnonationally defined communities.

In Bosnia-Herzegovina the process of integration of schools emerged as a response to war-generated segregation in education. There is a whole range of ways in which integration of schools, students, and teachers has been attempted by the OSCE across schools in Bosnia-Herzegovina. The first step in this direction was the creation of so-called two-schools-under-one-roof, a peculiarity of Bosnian elementary and high school education (Hemon 2012). These schools were designed as a temporary measure to encourage the return of refugees to their homes. In this way, the returning refugees were reassured that their children would not have to follow the curriculum of the dominant, nonrefugee group. Instead, returnee students would attend school in their own language, while they would share the same school building with the students of the other ethnic group, who would attend their own school.

In these fifty-seven currently "integrated" educational institutions in FBiH (the RS has one centralized, "Serb-centered" curriculum), Bosniak and Croat children and teachers often have no mutual contact. In the most extreme cases, such as the schools in the towns of Prozor-Rama and Travnik, students enter the schools through separate entrances, have separate breaks, and the teachers do not use the same teachers' room (OSCE 2005:1). The extreme example of this type of integration is the gymnasium in the segregated town of Stolac, near Mostar, where Croat and Bosniak students attend school in different shifts, Croats in the morning and Bosniaks in the afternoon. The students share the building, but the schools are not administratively unified, unlike the Mostar Gymnasium. Furthermore, during the long and cold winter months, the heat at the school is turned off at the end of the class instruction for Croat students, which leaves the classroom unheated for the Bosniak students (teacher's comment). This is possible because the school, as well as the town politics in general, is controlled by the Croats.[27]

These examples show how the "two-schools-under-one-roof," safeguarded by the consociational democratic model that gives meaning, legitimacy, and potency to ethnically defined and segregated (educational) spaces, has not been a temporary measure toward full integration, since most of these schools remain segregated today. In some cases, such as the deeply divided Herzegovinian towns, Stolac, Prozor-Rama, and Čapljina, segregation among students has been deepened, where "two-schools-under-one roof" are fully separated into two schools, one for Bosniaks and one for Croat students. In this failed story of integration, the Mostar Gymnasium, which has been administratively unified and where the students of the two ethnic groups go to school at the same time of day and share the same extracurricular activities, emerges as a ground-breaking example. In this way, the Mostar Gymnasium most closely approximates, in practice, the vaguely articulated (inter)national ideal—national unification that recognizes rights for self-autonomy of ethnic groups.

The main international actors in Bosnia-Herzegovina considered integrated education as a norm that would speed up state-making and peace-building and bring about political and educational improvement, something that is clear from numerous declarations, such as "without integration [of schools] you will never become part of Europe" (Claude Kieffer, former director of education at OSCE Mission to Bosnia and Herzegovina quoted in Farrell 2001:17). In addition, discourses of integration produced by the OSCE in Mostar were initially unclear. Martin explains:

> We had an idea—we wanted Bosniaks back in schools, and we wanted to see them [Croat and Bosniak students] in the same classes. Initially, the OSCE was pushing for integration. And frankly, there is absolutely no reason why they should not be together. [However,] We did not succeed in fully integrating the Mostar Gymnasium. Despite our constant repetitions to the locals that it is much more complicated and expensive to work separately and stay segregated, it did not work. . . . We made a mistake because at the beginning of our "campaign" for the integration of the Mostar Gymnasium, we talked so much about the common curricula for non-national subjects. Integration was understood as a conflict of Croat national interests.

Martin's ethics, morality, and reasoning displayed in this comment were out of joint, showing contrasting obligations to public reason, morality, and political and cultural sensibility. For example, Martin's observation that there is "absolutely no reason why they should not be together" carries moral and ethical claims about what Bosnia-Herzegovina ought to be—a truly multicultural, unified nation, where communities define themselves in relation to others, thus establishing the layers of heterogeneous public and common peoplehood. In addition, practices of segregation were interpreted by Martin not only as immoral but also irrational, since they were economically more costly than integration. On the other hand, Martin continuously expressed genuine if privileged understanding of why people in these circumstances "behaved in that way." After several years of living and working in Mostar, Martin developed local sensibility that understood, made sense of, and respected the local fears and anxieties. This deep "local" knowledge is clearly observable in his other statement: "It is a broader social issue with the Croats feeling so insecure regarding their status in Bosnia-Herzegovina. . . . Maybe, if there is a constitutional reform that would get them more representation at the state level, and if there are structures that would make them feel more secure about their place in Bosnia-Herzegovina, maybe then, only then can we make further progress." This demonstrated complexity and sincere desire to understand the "locals" often coexisted with the strong belief that internationals, described as nonpartial, nonpolitical, more knowledgeable and objective (Chandler 1999; Coles 2007; Gilbert 2008; Pickering 2009), should remain in charge.

Martin's statement also illustrates the flexibility and compromise that OSCE had to exercise in order to confront the diverging and colliding discourse of integration stemming from the local resistance to the external vision. The original idea of integration, produced by the OSCE at the beginning of negotiations in the early 2000s, had two main components: the return of Bosniaks to the building and the integration of classrooms and curricula. It is the latter that spread panic among the Croat community. Understood from their standpoint, the "integrated classroom" agenda contained many of the aforementioned dangers for the Croat people, such as blurring the boundaries of the Croat-imagined community or, worse still, assimilation into the Bosniak-dominated federation and state. This political agenda of boundary maintenance and self-preservation through segregation, however, was framed and performed in the public sphere as a fear of "cultural loss," and more specifically a fear of compromising the purity of the Croatian language—the essence of Croat nationhood—which, they claimed, would be obliterated in the process of integration.

Martin and others at OSCE openly admitted that they underestimated how much their vision for the integration of classes would clash with the Croat political and sociocultural sentiments. The original vision required that students of both ethnic groups would attend classes together in the "shared subjects" deemed less controversial. These included psychology, philosophy, sociology, biology, chemistry, mathematics, physics, art, and sports education. The instruction of "national group" subjects, including language, geography, literature, religious education, and history, however, were to remain separate. While this idea seemed in accord with the existing education bills that promoted inclusive, democratic, nondiscriminatory education that was "open to all," the OSCE leadership initially failed to understand what integrated classes meant for the Croat community. While the Croat leaders accepted that Bosniak students would most probably return to the school, the boundary between *us* and *them* in the school had to be maintained in order to protect political boundaries and the essence of the transborder Croat nation. In other words, the OSCE incorrectly assumed that the controversy would concern only the subjects that were seen as "national" in nature. Soon they realized that for the Croat leadership, any mixing among students in classrooms and especially the idea of Croat students attending classes in the Bosnian language (even if it is a math or science class) was interpreted as dangerous due to the potential blurring of ethnic boundaries and related loss of cultural purity and autonomy. While some of the earlier quotes also point at the Bosniaks' fear of "identity loss," these worries, unlike the Croat leaders' opposition, stayed mostly unexpressed during the official negotiation process. Instead, Bosniaks publically supported integration of the two curricula, which made the Croat political leadership look, in this instance, like "the bad guys" in the eyes of "internationals."

The Croat minority refused the incorporation into Bosnian peoplehood for pragmatic and emotional reasons. For example, many of my Croat informants, aware of the increasing link and overlap between nationalism, racism, xenophobia, and "language purity" in Croatia (see Kordić 2010), feared that losing the language purity would threaten their children's opportunities to study in Croatia (see below), and that it would limit their group's sovereignty and membership in the transborder Croat nation. In order to achieve self-exclusion from the state- and people-making project in Bosnia-Herzegovina, the Croat leaders relied on the parts of the Bosnia-Herzegovina constitution that legitimized the ideas of politics of difference, which defined political belonging according to ethnic membership. In this way, the Croat leadership skillfully used the tension at the heart of the Dayton Peace Agreement to subvert the Agreement itself and at least temporarily immobilize the OSCE actors who found themselves caught in the equivocal Dayton script. These Croat leaders stressed the fact that the Agreement grants rights to the constitutional peoples to protect their community's rights, including the education of ethnic youth using ethnic curricula, in ethnic classrooms, and especially in the ethnonational language. It is the language of instruction that became the fiercest battleground between the sociopolitical forces and ideologies of integration, and the everyday practices and politics of segregation. This tension around language "functions as a diagnostic of the state" (Gupta 1995:389), especially since this allowed for Croat leaders to articulate their position as the one of "second-class" citizenry (Neofotistos 2010:286) in the Bosnian-Herzegovinian state.

Serbo-Croatian Language and Its Registers

Former Yugoslavia was one of the most linguistically diverse states in Europe. The official languages were Serbo-Croatian (or Croato-Serbian), Slovenian, and Macedonian. Serbo-Croatian was the primary language in Croatia, Serbia, Montenegro, and Bosnia-Herzegovina, and it served as a *lingua communis* in Yugoslavia (Bugarski 1995; Radovanović 1989). Slovenian and Macedonian were spoken in the republics of Slovenia and Macedonia, respectively. There were multiple minority languages such as Hungarian, Albanian, Romanian, Slovak, Czech, Ruthenian, Bulgarian, Ukrainian, Turkish, and so on (Radovanović 1989; also see Bugarski 1995; Škiljan 1988). Each of these official languages had many dialectical and regional variations, which further complicated any attempts to map the linguistic variations onto ethnically imagined and claimed territories.

The origins of the Serbo-Croatian language go back to the nineteenth-century Slavic Enlightener linguist and Serb peasant Vuk Stefanović Karadžić. Together with Croatian linguist and politician Ljudevit Gaj, Karadžić saw the emphasis on the united Serbo-Croatian language, based on a common *štokavski* dialect, as a "platform for the political unification of Serbs-under-Turks and Croats-under-Hungarians" (Longinović 2011:285), thus envisioning a "unified philological territory that was to serve as a cultural weapon in their struggle against the imperial rule of the Ottomans and Hapsburgs" (285). Importantly, this anti-imperial coalition between "Serbian" and "Croatian" was based on the idea of a common Slavic ethnicity that would use their shared language to develop a nation (286). As a result of this vision and its appeal to the popular masses in Serbia and Croatia, which were undergoing nationalist renaissance, both Croats and Serbs adopted Karadžić's dialect, dictionary, grammar, and orthography. This union of two "non-identical twins" (285)—Serbian and Croatian—marked the birth of a new language, Serbo-Croatian. Some regional variations and dialects between and within each language were preserved, however, and they were used as markers of different linguistic and cultural regions within and across Serbia, Croatia, and Bosnia-Herzegovina. For example, Croatian variants were based on *ijekavski* dialect and the Serb on *ekavski* speech (e.g., *mlijeko* vs. *mleko* for "milk"). In addition, Serbian variants mostly used the Cyrillic alphabet while Croatian variants employed almost exclusively the Latin alphabet. In Bosnia-Herzegovina, both alphabets were used and taught in schools. Tito's egalitarian policies tried to manage and deemphasize these differences between dialects and alphabets, especially through education and the military.[28]

When Yugoslavia started to disintegrate at the beginning of the 1990s, the differences between language variants were strengthened, amplified, and further politicized by nationalist regimes in Serbia, Croatia, and Bosnia-Herzegovina. These aggressive language policies led to the removal of the hyphen between the words "Serbo-" and "Croatian," thus signaling and symbolizing "balkanization" of their sociolinguistic and political interconnectedness. In this way, linguistic methods were used to both establish and "prove" the necessity of cultural fundamentalism, right to difference, and social exclusion, in the name of (ethno)national protection.

These now officially confirmed and institutionalized linguistic differences have been included in post-Yugoslav constitutional and legal systems devised to ensure the dominance of the majority ethnonational group within each new (sub)state (see Hayden 1992). They are also perpetually invoked and accentuated in everyday encounters to index ethnic differences (boundaries) between groups and persons they purportedly embrace. In other words, the idea that ethnic registers of language index ("essentialize") what kind of (ethnic) person you are, has been used to create linguistic, cultural, and political distancing in order to reorganize social and political relations between groups in the Balkans.

New Registers and Their Users

Since the start of the Yugoslav wars, nationalist political leaders and a significant number of lay people on all sides insisted they spoke three different languages, a claim constitutionally acknowledged in Dayton, when the partition of Serbo-Croatian into Serbian, Croatian, and Bosnian was legitimized and institutionalized (Farrell 2001:5; see also Magner 1996). As a result of this political and linguistic separation, in education and in current linguistic practice there are three official languages in use in Bosnia-Herzegovina: Croat, Serbian, and Bosnian. Thus, Bosniak and Croat students stopped being educated in the Cyrillic alphabet and Bosnian Serbs started to use the Cyrillic alphabet almost exclusively for schooling, business, and administration.[29] Specific and forceful linguistic changes were introduced to claim purity of ethnicity and to solidify distance between now official languages. For example, the "lexeme production machinery" was employed in the now independent country of Croatia, and, as a result, the new vocabulary, sometimes welcomed and sometimes ridiculed by its intended audiences, "flooded" the Croatian territory. The famous and often repeated examples include the new word for helicopter, now *zrakomlat* ("machine that beats the air," formerly *helikopter*), *časnik* ("officer," formerly *oficir*), *jezikoslovlje* ("linguistics," formerly *lingvistika*), and *putovnica* ("passport," formerly *pasoš*).

In the case of Bosnia-Herzegovina, there were two main trends that Bosniak linguists and politicians adopted. The first one was to argue that Bosnian is the language of all people living in Bosnia-Herzegovina (see, for example, Halilović 1996[30]), a claim rejected by the majority of non-Bosniak ethnonationalist leaders and linguists. The second and related strategy of the Bosniak linguists was to start privileging the vocabulary that originated in or was borrowed from Turkish. One of the most visible changes was an overemployment of the letter "h" at the beginning of many words that allegedly had "lost" their "h" in the course of history. For example, there is a belief among Bosniaks that Serbs (both in Bosnia and Serbia) tend to (purposely?) drop "h" when pronouncing Muslim names (e.g., saying Asan instead of Hasan). The first Bosnian language dictionary published during the war reflected this sentiment, introducing the letter "h" in numerous words that never had an "h" or dropped it a long time ago. Some examples include *hudovica* ("widow," formerly *udovica*), *kahva* ("coffee," formerly *kafa*), and *historija* ("history," formerly *istorija*). In the Serbian part of

Bosnia-Herzegovina, efforts were made by linguistic and political elites to impose the *ekavski* speech, spoken in Serbia but not in Bosnia-Herzegovina,[31] in media and educational contexts, resulting in constant slips by news reporters, teachers, and other governmental employees, who would accidentally switch registers in one sentence, often causing ironic comments by their audiences.

Regardless of these initial "failures," language-distancing achieved some of its main goals—it produced local linguistic populations who were ready, in the name of cultural purity, right to difference, and national-language preservation, to exclude themselves from the common Bosnian-Herzegovinan citizenship and nationhood, by constantly policing, exaggerating, embodying, living, and performing linguistic differences. The Croat language, in this framework, was elevated to the throne of Croat nationhood and its very existence as *narod* (nationhood, people). The former employee at the Mostar Gymnasium explains:

> The international community forced, I don't want to say violently, but still pushed for full integration . . . and the local political parties that were in power—they also pushed for this, because of their own interests. But the international community did not understand the complexity of the situation for the Croats. The problem [of integration] becomes most obvious when we talk about language. Our local languages are similar in some ways, but they are mostly different. And *narod* [nation, peoplehood] without language is not narod at all. Which language would students listen to at school? Parents fear that the Croat language will be destroyed. . . . This is bigger than politics; it's about society and about culture.

This statement echoes what Kordić (2010) calls the nationalist ideology of "linguistic purism," which has dominated language education in Croatia since the 1990s. The workings of this ideology are especially visible in the circulation of stereotypical statements, such as "the language is a nation's soul and its mirror" (Kordić 2010:9, my translation), and in emphasizing its affective and aesthetic states, such as Marijan's (student at the Mostar Gymnasium) comment: "I do not want to study together, since I love to speak Croatian. It is so much prettier and nicer [than Bosnian]." As a result of these larger changes in linguistic practices and tastes, ethnically, territorially, and now linguistically divided youth in postwar Bosnia-Herzegovina grow up speaking (or believing to speak) and endorsing only one language variant, that of their ethnonational group.

Performing Linguistic Difference

As a result of the marriage between the ideology of ethnic nationalism, language education, and social aesthetics, the call for the protection of language purity from "foreign" and "mixed" linguistic elements appeared natural, and socially and aesthetically necessary (Kordić 2010:10). The effects of this ideology on everyday cross-ethnic interactions became especially apparent to me in February 2006, when I met with Stipe, one of the local leaders in charge of education in Mostar at the time. Before we began the interview, Stipe asked me not to tape his answers. The reason for this became clear when we started talking about language as a barrier in the development of the "common curricula" and integrated classrooms. Stipe explained to me that he and I were speaking *mješanac* (mixed language) so that we could understand each other, but that *mješanac* was an artificial language of an artificial country (former Yugoslavia) that was meant to collapse. We could talk in *mješanac* because the two of us were educated under the old system, in the old language, Croato-Serbian. Stipe thought, however, that this language was an imposed language, neither Serb nor Croat. In addition, he claimed that if one were to use this language today, he or she would be considered illiterate. Stipe also added that teaching students in two languages at the same time would make these students confused, because they would not speak any language, but a mixture of languages. I was puzzled by our conversation because the way I spoke in that meeting and in general was the way that many Bosniaks in Bosnia-Herzegovina speak today. In a way, the education leader suggested to me that the "Bosniak" language (during our conversation, Stipe proposed that the language name change from the official Bosnian to Bosniak, since, he stressed, only Bosniaks in Bosnia-Herzegovina speak it) is most similar to *mješanac* of the past. By extension, the Bosniaks and Bosnia-Herzegovina closely resemble, in Stipe's mind, the artificial language and the artificial state in the former Yugoslavia.

My encounter with Stipe demonstrates what is at stake: for the Croat leaders and wider community, which they successfully mobilized, integrated classrooms meant the exposure of Croat students to the Bosnian language, which, in their view, was very similar to the Serbo-Croat language of the past—where the language of the past represented Serb hegemony in Yugoslavia, today it indexes Bosniak domination in the new state. The purity of the Croat language was to be protected from mixing by any means, since it is at the border between the Croat, Serb, and Bosnian languages that the political, social, and cultural boundaries between *us* and *them* are designed, disputed, sealed, and guarded.

The Croatian leadership used the discourse of ethnocultural rights to difference to claim their right to preserve the Croatian language as the only language of instruction in the Croat curricula. Possible assimilation into Bosnia(n) would be deadly to the ideal and deeply felt desire for an endangered Croat authenticity. This fear automatically led to protectionism and the politics of spatial segregation for the Croat language and people from Bosnian language speakers, even though the two languages were mutually easily understandable. The Mostar Gymnasium school board president at the time, a Bosniak, captured this linguistic tension well when she said:

> Language is a medium of communication, not of isolation. We all have a right to speak our own language—that is only democratic. But if I have a right to use my language, does it mean that only Bosnian words can enter my ear? That is what the other side is asking for. . . . If the other side uses democratic rhetoric to ask to hear only the Croat language, then I lose my democratic right to speak my language, you see? So, you cannot ask that . . . that only one language can enter your students' ears because other languages will contaminate your language—you have to be more inclusive . . . because in that case Martin, when he comes to visit the school, would have to speak in the Croatian language. . . . See what I mean? . . . You see, one of our most famous authors said that we, the people in Bosnia-Herzegovina, are unique in Europe since by being born in this country we have passive knowledge of three languages—which one I speak is my choice.

This quote demonstrates the pursuit of language/national preservation at the expense of "true" democracy (in Iris Young's sense),[32] but it also hints at the shrinking space for interethnic interaction. Instead, this space for interaction was replaced by a more rigid notion of a "right to difference," which, once politicized, led to the suffocation and marginalization of heterogeneous public spaces in which to have a "multilingual" dialogue. This reduced the chances for youth to get to know and *speak* to each other.

The political stance that framed exposure to local languages other than Croatian as a threat to ethnonational identity became embedded in many youths' vision of schooling and life in general. The following example demonstrates the shrinking space for "bilingual" interaction caused by the fear that language contamination would lead to personal failure. In this short excerpt from my field notes of September 10, 2005, I captured and documented a discussion demonstrating the anxiety surrounding the possibility of creation of a heterogeneous educational and social space. During that weekend, I spent many hours recording the interactions between student council representatives from the largely segregated small town of Strana in central Bosnia-Herzegovina. It became a common practice for the OSCE in Mostar to bring students from other segregated high schools in FBiH to the Mostar Gymnasium. By bringing ethnically segregated Strana students together at the Mostar Gymnasium, the OSCE was hoping to achieve two goals. The first goal was to introduce students to each other so that they could recognize how much they have in common. The second goal was to expose the students to the unusually prosperous (thanks to foreign donations) and newly renovated, well-furnished, reunited Mostar Gymnasium, which achieved this prosperity upon its reunification. As a consequence, in early September the selected students from Strana were attending a workshop at the Mostar Gymnasium on how to create a joint student council in their school. In their own school building in Strana there were two schools that shared the same building but nothing else. Here is an excerpt from my workshop field notes:

> I walk into the student lounge. It is quiet, colorful, spacious, and nicely lit. Danijel, the OSCE employee in charge of the workshop, is not there yet. While we wait for him to come back from lunch, the students lean back in their chairs, arranged in a semicircle, and start talking. I am paraphrasing their dialogue:
> Edin: You see how they [Mostar Gymnasium] can cooperate and have one roof, one school. Look at this fancy student lounge they got!
> Aida: That is what I have been saying all this time, we need one joint student council, not two . . . we need to unite.
> Tanja: That will never happen with us.

Edin: Yes it will, why not?
Aida: Not if it continues like this.
Andrea: How would we do it, with two different languages?
Dino: Is it really important which language it will be? I speak now and you understand me, we all understand each other! That is all that matters.
Andrea: Well, it is important to me. I do understand you and it is okay for this kind of thing ... but if I spend time with you and I hear your words, and if I use those words in my exam at the University of Zagreb, I will fail!

This example nicely captures the effects of language purism (Kordić 2010:10), which has been institutionalized, desired, and protected by ethnonationalist regimes in post-Yugoslav spaces. In this context, purism is included in all curricula, so every student, from a very early age, must be exposed and naturalized into it. At the same time, no one knows what purism *is*, which makes language an especially anxious social and ideological field in need of constant protection and policing. Youth are constantly called to accept, appreciate, welcome, and act out this "authentic" difference—the essence of cultural hermeneutics—in exchange for acceptance into the larger transborder nation and domovina's recognition. As a result, language performance acts as a social ethics and cultural technology for successes and failures of national and individual dreams.

Furthermore, the idea of integration is interpreted not only in terms of emotional attachments to the Croat narod (transborder nation), but it is also explained pragmatically—as a road to personal failure in the demonstration of fluency in Croatian. A student who wants to attend university in Zagreb, the capital of the Croat imagined national community and the external domovina of Bosnian Croats, then, the argument goes, has to speak perfect Croatian (see Hayden 1992). The majority of the young Bosnian Croats I befriended during my fieldwork wanted to continue their university studies in Croatia, for three main reasons. First, they hold dual citizenship (Croatian and Bosnian) and feel rights, duties, and obligations to Croatia first. Second, most of them told me that they felt they belonged to Croatia, which is their true domovina, and considered Zagreb their capital city. Third, Croatian universities have a better reputation for academic excellence than Bosnian ones. For these reasons, Croat students prefer to speak perfect Croatian, and, by extension, demonstrate their rightful place in the transborder Croat national community, the state of Croatia, and its universities.

Integrated classrooms threatened this project since they represented incorporation into the vague Bosnian nation and disputed state. Learning/speaking/embodying/performing Bosnian would, in addition to confusing the political field in which the way you speak supposedly indexes your ethnicity, also prepare these students to continue their university-level education in Bosnia-Herzegovina, most probably in its capital, Sarajevo. This was not seen as a desired option for the Croat youth I befriended, however. If they were not able to continue their education in Croatia, most of the Croat students opted to attend the university in west Mostar, in Croatian. This points to the fact that even though most Bosnian Croats acknowledged that they live in the territory of Bosnia-Herzegovina, their territorial loyalty to Herzegovina, their identification with the Croat nation and domovina, and their membership in the state of Croatia had to stay uncompromised.

The goal of preserving the Croat language meant that it had to be protected from local language variations. This could only be ensured if the teachers spoke Croatian and if all books were in Croatian. On several occasions I witnessed students mercilessly correcting their teachers where Bosnian or Serb words slipped into their speech. The only Bosniak teacher teaching (German language) in the Croat curriculum at the Mostar Gymnasium at the time of my fieldwork was a frequent target of such corrections:

> A student came up to my desk and said, "Why did you underline this word, professor?" pointing to a part of the homework I had just returned to him. I said, "because it is not *tačno* [Bosnian/Serbian version of 'correct'], son." Then I heard someone in the last row say *točno* [Croat version]. And I said, "You know what, if you write this *tačno*, it will be *točno!*"
>
> Another time, I think it was '93, I was in class and I said *sedmica* [Bosnian for "week"] and someone immediately shouted *tjedan* [Croat version]. I got up and wrote on the blackboard: *tjedan* = *sedmica* = *nedjelja* [Serb version] = *hefta* [Bosnian, colloquial]. As I wrote *hefta*, they cried, "Oooooo!" I said, "Yes, yes, *hefta* means seven in Persian. The more languages we know, the more we are worth, right?" They responded, "Right."

She looked at me, sighed, and said: "You have to make it funny, so that you don't get overwhelmed with sadness and start crying right there, among them." This Bosniak teacher, in order to avoid humiliation at the hands of the students or punishment by the Croat educational authorities, had to "sit down and learn those 20 main Croat words, such as *tisuća* [thousand], *kolodvor* [station], and *tjedan* [week]."

Teachers who taught the Croatian language were also under considerable pressure. Dragica described the challenges she faced teaching the Croat language in an ethnically segregated society:

> I had to study it [Croatian] myself, even though I knew the two variants of the language from before, there were always alternatives offered to us at the University. We studied both Serbo-Croatian, and Croato-Serbian. Maybe I used more Serb variants in the past, but luckily, after the changes, I was able to learn the new vocabulary quickly, maybe because I have a talent for language. But I have to prepare more now, and I have to learn as I go. Now, I always double-check everything to make sure I know all the new grammatical rules and terms. I spend more time on language now, and less on literature. In the past I did much more literature. . . . Once I was in a very uncomfortable situation: I had just begun teaching Croatian Language in Mostar, and we were reading Meša Selimović [a world-famous Bosnian author with "Muslim origins" who later declared himself a Serb], and one student walked out of class and said he didn't want to read this author. I felt terrible. I didn't know how to react. I stayed calm, and after class I went to the teachers' room and told my colleagues what had happened. They didn't react at all. And that surprised me the most.

In postwar Bosnia-Herzegovina, teachers have been required to develop unique ways to cope with the situation in new classroom environments. Teachers like Dragica, who showed disagreement with the rigid nationalization of education, generally did not receive support from other teachers and administration. Rather, the policies of language purity continued to inform their teaching, and by extension, the cultural landscapes of Bosnian and Herzegovinan youth coming of age in a postwar country.

Regardless of these war-generated, politically driven linguistic divergences, the closeness of the three languages in Bosnia-Herzegovina makes language a fragile and contested space of ethnonational politics and the implementation of the consociational democratic arrangement. Therefore, even in the contexts of the workshop, where one document could be read and understood by all workshop participants, the same document had to be made available in all three official national languages and in both alphabets. What is more, for the majority of people in postwar Bosnia-Herzegovina, the continuous display of the three mutually understandable, grammatically almost identical but politically divided languages, became not only acceptable, but a necessary and natural performance of cultural and political preservation. For example, in the summer of 2006, a Dartmouth College professor of education an a veteran director of more than forty high school and community theater productions, prepared a multiethnic, multilingual production of Shakespeare's Romeo and Juliet in Mostar. The play brought together students from the Mostar Gymnasium and other, still fully segregated Mostar high schools. The students worked hard the whole summer preparing the play. The performance was staged among the ruins of the University of Mostar library, located behind the Mostar Gymnasium. At the night of the performance that I attended, the atmosphere was dreamlike, with candlelight illuminating the ruins of the old building, which also served as a reminder of the wartime violence. Romeo and Juliet emerged from the ruins, and began to speak of their love. Something about this exchange was humorous, and I instinctively giggled, together with several other members of the audience in the row behind me: Romeo was talking to Juliet in Bosnian and she was responding in Croatian. Since most of the audience understood both languages, this performance of difference felt excessive to some people in the audience, but to many of the youth who were participating in the event, this was a necessary and "natural" public demonstration of ethnic belonging. After the play ended, feeling confused by the multilayered nature of language performance and language politics, I looked for Melita, the production manager of the play and my main informant. She shared my questioning of the language act, but then her face got serious when she said, "On the first day of rehearsal, the actors got into a fight about whether to call the local language Bosnian or Croatian."

The youth's performance of language differences at the school and beyond was constant, anxious, and often inflated. These "performances" should not be seen as necessarily bogus or calculated, however: the youth naturalized and embodied performances of language difference. In other words, performance here does not presuppose artificiality; "it is not 'put on' or antithetical to 'reality'" (D. Taylor 1997:185). Rather, following

Diana Taylor (1997) and Schechner (1985), I approach performance as a "restored" or "twice-behaved behavior" (D. Taylor 1997:185). The "restored" nature of teachers', students', and management's linguistic behavior offered to people at the school a way to cope with, negotiate, resist, and critique their own and others' actions.

Even though many scholars point at the constructed and almost tragicomical policies of linguistic nationalism in the former Yugoslavia and its consecutive states (see, among others, Kordić 2010; Longinović 2011), young people come of age in the context where many of these ideologies became legitimate world views and embodied ways of being, as I witnessed in the fall of 2005, when I attended a three-day workshop for Herzegovina students in the war-depressed town of Neum on the Adriatic coast. The workshop was organized by OSCE in order to bring students from multiple schools together to discuss the possibility of creating student councils in all Herzegovinian high schools. On a sunny Saturday morning, the first day of the workshop, I watched Danijel, the OSCE local staff member, enter the room, walk to its center, and put down three piles of paper—the typed agenda for the day. He explained to the participants that the left pile had copies in Croatian, the middle one in Serbian, and the right one in Bosnian. Without any hesitation, the students walked to the "proper" stack, signaling who "they were," before the workshop even started. I stood in the middle, confused, and finally took one copy in Bosnian. I felt constrained and somehow betrayed by my own performance. Halfway to my seat, I turned around and took a copy of the agenda in Croatian and Serbian as well. This and all the other examples demonstrate how language emerged as a powerful ethnonational symbol—a tool of political and social boundary-making between ethnically conceived communities. Given the overwhelming similarity between the languages—which enabled youth of ethnic communities to come together, laugh together, and perform together in the cracks between ethnic territories and ideologies—language continuously provoked simultaneous anxiety, desire, and fear of mixing.

Many local and foreign linguists still argue that the three new languages are variants of one now officially dead language, Serbo-Croatian, since they share a common set of grammar rules. This means that regardless of the forceful nationalist policies to distance the new languages and thus the people who speak them, the language communities in the region still understand each other's spoken languages without much difficulty (Longinović 2011). Yet the minor differences between languages became socially and politically salient, requiring constant performance of difference by members of ethnonational groups who experienced language distinctions as crucial for their existence and survival as separate, historically and culturally legitimate nations.

People at the Mostar Gymnasium—students, teachers, and the management—had to perform and thus constantly negotiate these calls for integration and pressures for segregation that were circulating in the political space. Their linguistic performance and their brilliant maneuvering of cultural similarities and differences—as in the case of the semantic/political negotiation between *tačno* and *točno*—reveal the ironic and contested nature of identification, authority, and knowledge- and subject-production. Under these new regimes of citizen-becoming, the exhibition of ethnic belonging and a dismissal of cross-ethnic similarities become a necessary way to claim autonomy, legitimacy, and citizenship in a postwar country. The performances of converging and diverging language identifications at the Mostar Gymnasium and beyond thus illustrate the contradictions inherent in the processes of peace-building and state-making in Bosnia-Herzegovina: the war-produced and internationally solidified tension between integration and segregation, and democracy caught between state-making and nation-breaking. At the same time, the naturalness with which the students performed ethnic identifications and differences via language usage made it clear that acting out this difference became a necessary routine, a personified and habitual behavior for youth coming of age in the postwar country.

From Integration to Administrative Unification

OSCE and the rest of the international actors involved in the reunification project have approached Mostar Gymnasium as a showcase for postwar state-making that favors integration as a form of social reconstruction. This approach has stressed the need not only to protect communities in order to manage conflict, but also to reconcile them in order to ensure that conflict does not recur. This stance seems to be historically sound, since the people of Bosnia-Herzegovina have a long history of interconnectedness and engagement in an ethnically mixed public, including joint schooling, under different political regimes. After all, different ethnic groups in Bosnia-Herzegovina have not been historically understood as entirely "other," but as overlapping and constituted in relation to one another (see I. Lovrenović 2001). The present-day state-making project in Bosnia-Herzegovina could be interpreted as an attempt to rejuvenate this past territorial integration and build a common multiconfessional nation based on shared territory and citizenship in Bosnia-Herzegovina.

This vision of a shared school was understood as too politically risky and threatening by the ethnonational leaders, however. Nonetheless, the OSCE initially underestimated the risk of integration for the Croat leaders: Martin's first approach to the problem of Croat resistance was to see it as a political issue that could be resolved by pressuring the nationalist parties in power, especially the party Croatian Democratic Union (HDZ). Faced with an unexpected level of resistance from the wider Croat community, which was mobilized by the political leaders, OSCE had to quickly refocus its efforts and adjust its vision and language of integration in order to continue to negotiate with the local communities and their diverging agendas.

This new understanding seems to have facilitated a shift in the discourse of integration. After almost a full year of advocating integration, Martin and other "internationals" working in and around the Mostar Gymnasium learned not to use the term "integration" when dealing with local people. Sabrina, an international volunteer working at Mostar Gymnasium explains:

> I would like to be involved in helping to create joint extracurricular activities at the school, because this is our [United World Colleges][33] mission as well—integration! It is integration that we want . . . we always talk amongst ourselves about integrated students and integrated classes at the Gymnasium. But integration is a rude word out here. When we talk about our project and mission with the local students and teachers, we explain it without using that word because we feel the people won't react well to it. We avoid the word "integration," as if it were some terrible disease.

Following this transformation, the OSCE Education Office changed its discourse when talking to the local groups' representatives, shifting from a concern with integration to reunification or the return of Bosniaks to the school. At the same time, they retained the focus on integration when talking to the outside donors. I asked Martin about this change and tension between "local" and "international" agendas:

Azra: When do you use the word "integration" in your work?
Martin: We tend not to use "integration" . . . not any more . . . actually we use it when we present the project to the donor community, but in the local context and when talking to local officials we use "unification" of the two schools. We just avoid the term "integration"—it has too much baggage. And as soon as you mention the word . . . I mean, it could be the integration of the curriculum, or the integration of classrooms, I mean . . . it's too much, it's too open-ended. We say "unification." I would even say that we usually say "administrative unification." I think it's much more specific and doesn't allow for manipulation and misunderstanding of the term.

Therefore, the OSCE used the integrationist discourse when applying for money from the reconciliation-motivated and integration-driven donor community, such as in the instance of the empty computer lab. However, when faced by the response of the ethnonational communities on the ground, which used the politics of group rights to support their quest for segmental autonomy, exclusion from the Bosnia-Herzegovina peoplehood, and demands for national self-preservation, the discourse of integration was transformed into the policy of "administrative unification," while obscuring the equivocal, unexpected, contradicting implications of this shift (Mosse 2005:19). For example, these shifting and competing discourses had profound effects, such as materialization of the empty lab and emergence of a neither segregated nor integrated school. As a result, administrative unification retained the "return of Bosniaks" component of the formal integrationist discourse but dropped, at least temporarily, the "common curriculum" and "integrated classroom" ambitions.

In addition, Martin, the OSCE, and the rest of the international field had learned from this two-year negotiation that they had to listen far more attentively to the local communities. After several months of heated negotiations and little progress, the OSCE leadership realized that the issue of an integrated school could not be resolved solely on political grounds. Instead, the negotiation had to enter the realm of society and culture and address the everyday concerns of broader communities. Martin explains: "What we have learned is that this is a social problem . . . it is like . . . you cannot be so out of step with the people's attitudes. . . . You can be slightly, maybe one step ahead, but you cannot be two steps ahead. And that is what we tried to do."

This quote hints at the political reality in postwar Bosnia-Herzegovina: the state torn between integration and segregation, and between ideologies of cultural homogeneity and political plurality, where "administrative unification" serves as a primary sociopolitical model for crude organizing of ethnic peoples and territories. These examples show how one of the main goals of the Dayton Peace Agreement, that of creating a viable political structure in which three equal, power-sharing, ethnically bounded groups are integrated within a common nation-state, remains, in practice, highly unrealistic. In everyday life, this vision of egalitarianism and ethnic pluralism, at least among the larger portion of Mostar's divided citizenry, has been translated into enduring, profound fears of assimilation into an unwanted and vague Bosnian-Herzegovinian nation. This resistance led to the creation of a new spatial and social organization of the school and its people, and this order became a powerful metaphor for the vacuum that characterizes the Bosnian state.

Success?

The clash between the interventionists' goal and commitment to a liberal, unified, and rigidly construed multicultural state, and the local performance of difference based on the ideas of cultural preservation and ethnic isolation reveals multiple tensions at the heart of the peace-building and state-making project; it demonstrates the constitutive tensions between transnational governmentality and politics of the governed, as well as related frictions between state and nation, citizenship and group identity, and inclusion and exclusion within democratic state-making in the age of international humanitarian interventions.

A large amount of cultural autonomy assigned to the ethnic groups in Dayton creates potential obstacles for integration of a nation-state in a postwar setting. Moreover, the story of the reunified school illustrates how consociational democracy and its principle of ethnic power-sharing can generate an antidemocratic environment prone to intolerance and isolation. This political and social milieu can deepen and legitimize the nationalist quest for self-exclusion of an ethnic group from the nation, and lead to the detachment of citizens from a common state. These processes further instigate emptying the nation of its followers and the state of its citizens.

Regardless of the political and social turmoil accompanying reunification of the school, the OSCE celebrated the official reunification of the Mostar Gymnasium as a great success. It succeeded in returning Bosniaks to the building, and establishing common leadership, after all. Martin explains:

> It is done! Last year was tricky. It worked. Students know now they will see the other kids in the hallway. Teachers know they will meet teachers of other ethnic groups there as well. . . . If segregation is about stereotypes and prejudices, they will start confronting this a lot now. . . . They will coexist. True, not fully unified, but not segregated, either.

Martin's celebration is understandable since the act of official administrative reunification concluded two years of heavy negotiations between the OSCE and the local political communities, especially Croats. At the same time, the finalization of the official political negotiations opened up new spaces at the reunified school for the expression of segregation and popular anxieties rising from a fear of proximity. Troubled by the politicization and passionate reactions around the integration of the Mostar Gymnasium and concerned about being portrayed as supporters of segregated education, the OSCE decided not to negotiate integration, at least for a while, of any other schools in Bosnia-Herzegovina.[34] Thus, for OSCE, the project of integration via education was essentially over at the time of the official reunification of the Mostar Gymnasium. For Mostarians who anxiously anticipated shared spaces, however, the struggle—the poetics and pragmatics of living together—had only begun.

Chapter 2

Cartography of Peace-Building

Mapping the School

As the previous chapter demonstrated, the school reunification policies embodied ethnic divisions and reemployed ethnic categories in order to examine and fix the social reality at the Mostar Gymnasium. For instance, in the aftermath of the negotiations with the ethnonational leaders and community that led to the transformation of "integration" into "reunification" of the school, the OSCE and the other international actors included in the reunification efforts have continually relied on the ethnic ideologies of identity as an a priori condition for the reunification of the school. What this means in practice is that management, evaluation, and regrouping of teachers and students were implemented based on the ethnic principle, and explained as necessary for peaceful coexistence. This approach becomes especially visible in the context of "map-making."

Creating a blueprint for the reunified school is a profoundly political task, since "it is not merely about drawing maps: it is the making of worlds" (Harley 1990:16). In a postwar context, map-making embodies multiple visions, ideologies, hopes, and anxieties that become the foundation of peace-building and state-making efforts. Paying attention to the role of cartography at the Mostar Gymnasium reveals the narrow logic of peace-building and state-making efforts in Bosnia-Herzegovina.

From the very first day of my fieldwork, I was overwhelmed by the ethnic conceptualization of the school's geography. The understanding of social space in terms of ethnic equilibrium powerfully shapes movement, experiences, and interactions at the school. At times, I also felt that the ethnicization of space at the school dominated my (and others') speech, if not my capacity for thought. Even though the ethnic categories were not always mentioned in everyday discourse in the school, the terms designating difference were frequently used, such as "they" and "us" (Čorkalo et al. 2004:155). Our conversations consistently included spatial indexicals that inserted ethnic bipolarity into our speech and framed our thinking, such as "our side/their side," or "our children/their children." I felt that even if I could think beyond this bipolarity (which I hoped I could), the register of language that would enable me to express my thoughts was missing in the divided city and the reunified school. As a consequence, every time someone asked me where I lived in Mostar, I felt frustrated because I had to say that I lived on the east, Bosniak side, since that was the only legitimate way to talk about the geography of the city and to be understood by its inhabitants.

The precision of the ethnic symmetry in the geography of the Mostar Gymnasium is ubiquitous. For instance, the Croat classrooms are marked with Roman (grade) numbers and lowercase English alphabet letters (e.g., I-a, II-b, III-c, IV-a) to mark a specific class of a specific grade. The Federal curriculum (predominantly Bosniak) classrooms are marked with Arabic numbers and Roman (grade) numbers (e.g., I-2, II-3, IV-2). So, if one said III-1 or II-a, everyone at the school would know whether the person is referring to Croat or Bosniak students and to which curriculum. There are plaques with class numbers on the doorway of each classroom. During the short breaks between classes, students (especially those who do not smoke) typically stand in ethnically homogeneous groups in the hallway in front of their classroom, while gazing at the students of the different group standing in front of their classrooms, at a safe distance.

In order to avoid total segregation, however, the OSCE and the management of the school decided to alternate Croat and Federal classrooms, so the classroom sequence is Croat–Federal–Croat–Federal–Croat, etc. This process of spatial governmentality at the school reduces potentially dynamic social life to conceptions of homogeneous ethnic territory, thereby reducing complexity and contingency. The only time the sequence breaks down is in the case of the general purpose rooms, such as the library, computer lab, gym, student council room, student duty room, and teachers' room. But even within these spaces, the ethnic distribution is often preserved. For example, the teachers' room is located at the center of the second floor. It is a clean, nicely lit room, decorated with several tall green plants. The room borders the administration and the principal's (Croat) offices on one side and with the vice-principal's (Bosniak) office on the other. In the room itself, there is a large wooden table, with ten to twenty-five plain chairs around it. From the first day on, the teachers "naturally" divided up around the table: the Federal curriculum teachers sit on the left side, and the Croat teachers sit on the right. The only Bosniak teacher who teaches in the Croat curriculum frequently sits between the two groups. This teacher often tried to initiate dialogue between the two sides.

Sometimes, the teachers who taught only a few classes at the school were not immediately aware of ethnic segregation and they "made a mistake" by sitting at the wrong side of the table, as one teacher explained: "At the beginning, I sat on the wrong side. Who cares? Everyone at the other side of the table gave me looks. Because, you know, there are two sides of the table." The tension between the two sides of the table was easily felt, and was manifested as whispering and short exchanges in low voices among the teachers on either side of the table, but rarely across the divide. More recently, several more experienced teachers who used to teach together before the war have started to exchange words over the invisible wall in the middle of the table. In addition, several younger teachers who despise the division intentionally sit on the "wrong" side. The words of exchange are uttered in an artificially loud voice, indexing something unnatural and daring about the act of communication. Regardless of these small signs of progress, the tension is present and easily perceptible in the teachers' room, as Nadja explained: "We will never mix in the teachers' room. *Why?* Because there is a habit in the people! Since the first day when we sat down [separately], we kept that habit. And it continues like that today—we sit on one side, and they [Croat teachers] sit on the other."[1]

When I returned to the field in the summer of 2012, I reminded Nadja of her comment. She laughed and said, "You remember everything, don't you. . . . Well, we [Bosniak and Croat teachers] can talk about more issues now, for sure. Still, the divisions persist. They are most visible when we discuss issues related to nation and ethnicity . . . and language. Yes the language stuff is difficult. About that, we cannot talk about and probably will never be able to, for as long as the country is divided according to ethnicity." The power of Nadja's comment became clearer to me later that week when I was invited to join the faculty to celebrate the so-called *Dan škole* or the "Day of the School." After a short, joined student performance at the school, we strolled to the Old City where we had a four-course meal. The restaurant owner, mindful of his space, organized the tables in two

Figure 2. The Day of the School lunch—two curricula at two tables, May 2012. Photo by the author.

long, separate rows. Reenacting the embodied seating habits visible in the school teachers' room, the teachers separated according to the two curricula—all teachers from the Croat curriculum at one table, and the teachers in the Federal curriculum at the other. Only Nadja sat at "the Croat table," and she was soon joined by Ismet, the Bosniak principal at the time. Nadja signaled to me to come to her seat, and when I did, she said, "See, things have improved, as I told you. But look how we are sitting. People still have *podjelu u glavama* [division in heads—the embodied politics of ghettoization]." The effects of *podjela u glavama* were especially visible in Ismet's sweaty face. He worried about the quality of service and food at this restaurant, deeply nestled in the Bosniak part of town. Later, he confessed to me: "You have to be nervous. I felt like I was sitting on needles. You saw me come over to your table [I was sitting at the table with the Croat curriculum teachers and Nada, the vice-principal] asking if everything was OK . . . because, if something is not OK, they will complain, and it will immediately become ethnicized. Why did we go to the restaurant on his side? Look how bad the soup is, or . . . whatever."

These embodied divisions solidify around the issues of "culture" (mostly language) and "structure" (cartography) put in place in 2004. Sitting arrangements are only one instance of the embodiment and naturalization of ethnic spatialization at the school and beyond. For example, the class books—the large notebooks for each class in school with the names of students and their grades—are also divided based on the curriculum. The Croat ones are black and horizontally positioned on a small table next to the door of the teachers' room (so that teachers can grab the one they need for the next class on the way out), while the Federal ones are dark red and vertically positioned on a narrow shelf next to the table.

The employment strategy for the main school bodies, such as the school management and the school board, is defined by the school's statute, and it is also based on the principle of ethnic symmetry. This approach to the school's management strongly resembles the way the Bosnian state functions as a whole. For example, since the principal at the time of my fieldwork was a Croat, the vice-principal had to be a Bosniak. The school's secretary was a Bosniak. The administrator for finances was a Croat. The president of the school board was a Bosniak, with equal numbers of Bosniak and Croat representatives on the board. The teachers were almost exclusively ethnically divided, with four non-Croats teaching in the Croat curriculum (three from a mixed marriage background), and one Serb[2] teaching in the Federal curriculum. Those from the mixed marriages who were teaching in the Croat curriculum mostly identified with Croats.

The Serb teacher in the Federal curriculum taught English language. This was seen as less controversial than if she taught, for example, Bosnian. Similarly, at the time of my fieldwork, the only Bosniak teacher who taught in the Croat curriculum was a German language teacher. Only one teacher, the information technology instructor, who also happened to be a Serb, taught in both curricula. The only aspect of the school where the employment strategy based on ethnic symmetry is collapsing is in the less powerful positions such as the cleaning women, four Bosniak and one Croat.

The school year is organized differently for the two curricula, since they follow different ethnoreligious holidays. The beginning date of the school year is the same, but the official holidays and breaks are different: the students in the Croat curriculum finish their fall semester right before Christmas, since most Croats are Catholics and celebrate Christmas. They start the spring semester during the second week of January. The Federal curriculum does not have Christmas break, but ends the fall semester in early

January and begins the spring semester at the end of January or beginning of February. In this curriculum, there are several holidays linked to Islam and the month-long observation of Ramadan, which are not observed in the Croat curriculum.

The senior proms are also organized separately. During the year of my research in Mostar, the seniors in the Croat curriculum celebrated their prom at the end of March at the Hotel Ero on the Croat side, where the national anthem of the Republic of Croatia marked the beginning of the evening. The seniors in the Federal curriculum celebrated their prom at the end of May in the Hotel Bistrol on the east side, with no anthem, just, as one student remarked, "pop and rock music blasting." Several Bosniak students and teachers said that the choice of the Croatian anthem was offensive, and that it undermined the efforts for unification of the school, city, and state. When I approached Nada, the principal of the school, with these comments, she responded that the statements were exaggerated and the anthem only showed the appreciation of the Bosnian Croats to their *domovina* (homeland), Croatia.

Puzzled by the overwhelming ethnic fragmentation of the school's space and population achieved in the name of "liberal peace" (Duffield 2001:9–15), progress, and modernization (Ferguson 1994; Mosse 2005; Scott 1998), I asked Martin, the main Mostar OSCE education officer, to explain how the organization of the school space came into existence. He responded:

> Because . . . there is so much scope for manipulation, political manipulation, on either side, on any issue, but really any issue, even the most obscure, that just everything had to be meticulously orchestrated. And leaving anything to the spontaneous and ad hoc would simply not work. The atmosphere was such that people were looking; they were pointing fingers . . . aaa . . . that any issue would have created, hmm, tension. And we had to be clearer than clear, somehow.
>
> Azra: Is this a permanent way you see the school?
>
> Martin: I mean, the way we set it up, uh, it is not formally defined like that, it was in agreement with Darko and Ismet [principal and vice-principal at the time] that this is the way we would structure the classrooms . . . that these are the classrooms that different curricula would have . . . Nada [new principal] now also introduced the

[unintelligible] system. It is completely fluid. Over the past twelve months, eighteen months, if anyone would propose changing the system, we would have had a serious problem.
Azra: Why?
Martin: Because, the way it is set up at the moment shows complete neutrality, and any changes could be misconstrued. We are reaching the point now where I think practical steps and pedagogical needs seem more important than ethnic consideration. Ethnic consideration is becoming less important, since students and teachers are starting to interact with each other. When we set the school up 18 months ago, when the society thought this was impossible and that the students should stay separated . . . this step, that you are critical of now, seemed like a great progress. You can look at this ethnically sanitized situation and say, "Okay, the situation normalized, maybe it is a time to make progress again. . . ." But it might not go anywhere. Why? Because, you have to stay in step with the attitude of the people, maybe just slightly ahead . . . if we do not get the structures, the curricula that would be fit for joint classes, I cannot see how we could do anything further . . . for as long as Croats are feeling an endangered minority there is no way they will sit in joint classrooms.

This discussion unveils multiple visions of the school, city, and state by those in charge of their reunification. Martin was irritated that I found ethnic demarcation troubling. His introductory words demonstrate the popular understanding of Bosnia-Herzegovina sociality and politics held by the "internationals" in Bosnia-Herzegovina, even those who have lived in the country for many years. This approach established ethnonationalist groups as bound, fixed, and stable categories of analysis and social life, despite their demonstrated elasticity and contingency (Gilbert 2008). Martin thought that ethnic symmetry and segregation were the best way to secure peaceful coexistence and to limit political manipulation and nationalization of the space. His thinking about reunification was at first highly instrumental.

During our many discussions, however, Martin revealed a much more sophisticated and savvy understanding of local politics and competing visions of the school and Bosnia-Herzegovina. For example, he stressed the temporary nature of the process of the school's integration; he saw ethnic divisions as necessary at this point in time, but he envisioned the future when those could be overcome with some political adjustments. He also recognized how constraining ethnic territorial segregation can be to those who do not feel comfortable being isolated in their "ethnic boxes" and who either have memories (teachers) or hear the stories (students) about past interconnectedness during the Tito-imposed ideology of Brotherhood and Unity.[3] Therefore, in his concluding words, Martin hinted at increasing cross-ethnic interactions at the school, which, in his opinion, could lead to more profound trans- and supra-ethnic relationships.

But Martin's positive attitude was limited by the very nature of Dayton Agreement nationalism (Ćurak 2004), which does not inspire or support a political vision of heterogeneous Bosnia and Bosnians, but prefers to recognize the Bosnia-Herzegovina state as a sum of its three ethnic parts. Therefore, I had trouble seeing the future direction of this early progress, given the ethnically structured nature of the school space and limitations put on students' spontaneous cross-ethnic interactions, at the school and beyond. In addition, Martin's articulated hopes reveal the aforementioned myth of Bosnian multiculturalism and the unrealistic expectations of contemporary Bosnians—Martin hinted that with time, the students and teachers were going to develop meaningful relationships, organically and "simply," because now they work and study in close proximity to each other. These expectations glorify a particular, imagined, and romanticized notion of Bosnian multiculturalism, and they relieve the international actors of obligations for deeper involvement (Coles 2007; Gilbert 2008). Finally, I was discouraged by OSCE's decision to stop its quest for integration of other "two-schools-under-one-roof" in the country.[4] This decision by the OSCE leadership was made to avoid an emerging reputation of being responsible for the creation of a new type of "integrated" educational institution in Bosnia-Herzegovina—the one that favors "separate and (un)equal" teachers and students.

No-Man's-Land

During my fieldwork at the Mostar Gymnasium, some of the school's teachers and students agreed with the ethnic distribution of the space, and voiced wishes for separate teachers' rooms for the two curricula. Those who said these things loudly were in the minority, however. Those who openly argued for the full integration of students and teachers were even fewer in number. These teachers insisted on organizing common activities for students from both curricula. They sometimes faced resistance by their coworkers who were not eager to integrate. For example, the information technology teacher organized a computer-based extracurricular activity for students from both curricula, so that they could actually use the fancy computer lab. Since this Serb teacher taught in both curricula, and given that the OSCE really wanted to see the computers used by students, this initiative was acceptable to the management and Croat political leaders. On the other hand, a teacher who insisted on the unification of her very popular extracurricular activities was threatened by a politically engaged teacher with a reputation of being a hard-core nationalist. One day he stopped the prointegration teacher in the hallway and told her that if she did not terminate her demands he would announce to the public that she socialized with her students outside of school. While the OSCE supported the prointegration teacher, they did so quietly, trying to avoid any conflicts at the school.

While some teachers told me that they supported integration, they typically stayed passive about their support, not attempting to organize joined activities. Several students attempted to cross the ethnic divide but were often discouraged by their disapproving professors. Most students in the Croat curriculum supported segregation of curricula but opposed an enforced equilibrium in all segments of the school's life, as Marijan explains: "Simply by emphasizing these things, by telling us that there have to be *x* number of students from this side and the same from the other side, they [the OSCE and the school's management] create and enforce the problem of segregation. They should just let us be!"

Some employees at the school also criticized the primacy of ethnic ideology over efficiency. In the words of Jadranka:

In order to make sure that we are all perfectly distributed, our work suffers. For example, I do finances, Janja does curricula development, and Selma is a secretary. And we all share one room. Our work suffers because we do not serve the same kind of clientele . . . but the OSCE had to have a Croat and a Muslim in the same room, even if it does not make any sense, professionally.

Finally, there are those who disagreed with the segregation on moral grounds, and who voiced their nostalgia for the system that in their opinion nurtured true diversity. One teacher, Adil, told me that he felt "too liberal" for the consociational model of democracy. He explained to me that in a true democracy people are treated as equal, regardless of their ethnic or other background. He also explained that the existing model in Bosnia-Herzegovina made equality among individuals impossible, and that instead of respect, consociationalism provoked ignorance, hatred, and isolation.

On a crisp day in March 2006, Adil met me at a restaurant located at the bank of the Ljutica River in the divided town of Uskok, from which he commuted to Mostar every working day of the week. As we enjoyed the specialty of the house, an eel stew, we commented on the history of coexistence in Bosnia-Herzegovina. His words were full of sorrow when he uttered:

> When people ask me if the Mostar Gymnasium is a unified school, I tell them that I am ashamed that I work there. *Why?* Well, because I do not want to give up my essential upbringing and my main approach to life . . . it is not natural to separate children from their young age, and tell them stories. I think that the beauty of living is in differences and diversity. And now, if a child learns in the elementary school that Croats go here and Bosniaks go there, and if that continues, unfortunately, in high school, and at the university . . . I think we will create *degenerike* [degeneracy in youth], young people who will not be ready to be creative members of any society.

Adil links consociational democracy to the collapse of social order and the production of democratically incompetent youth, who experience ethnic divisions as natural. These words and previous examples demonstrate resistance to an all-encompassing division of the school space based on the principle of ethnic equilibrium and supposedly, integration. Another profound commentary on the ubiquitous spatialization of ethnicity at the school came from Mario, a student at the school. I capture it in the following vignette.

On a rainy day in November 2005, I joined Mario in the duty room after second period. Students who were "on duty" were free from class the day they performed this task. They had a small room next to the main entrance, since one of their obligations was to observe and document who came into the school. Ideally, these students would make a record of where the school visitors were going, but Mario did not do it diligently. The room was small, made of plywood. The only pieces of furniture were an old desk and a wobbly chair. Both were embroidered with various drawings and messages students wrote to each other. Mario and I chatted casually until Mario suddenly jumped off the desk on which he was sitting and said: "Wanna see something cool—I will show you *ničiju zemlju* (no-man's-land)." I felt that something exciting was about to happen. Mario laughed and explained to me that he created a no-man's-land between his classroom and the Federal classroom next door. Not Croat, not Bosniak, no one's! Of course I wanted to see it! I ran upstairs to the teacher's room to grab my camera. I bumped into Ismet, the Bosniak vice-principal, who said: "What is going on?" I heard myself reply: "Do you want to see the no-man's-land?" Intrigued, he joined me on the adventure. I saw Mario standing next to his classroom with another student. The "land" was located between two third grade classrooms, III-1 (Federal) and III-a (Croat). There were decorative red lines on the gray floor, one next to each classroom, which perfectly framed the space between the two rooms. "Here it is," Mario said, not showing much concern that I was accompanied by Ismet. For a few minutes we admired this piece of unattractive grayish floor.

Suddenly, the Bosniak vice-principal stepped into the "land" and signaled to Mario to join him; after a second of hesitation, Mario jumped in, a little shyly, and they shook hands, acting important, while posing for my camera. In the photograph, the vice-principal stands in the middle of the "land" and appears confident in his performance, while the student, standing on the margin of the "land," looks a little surprised by the developments and seems somewhat reluctant in front of the vice-principal and my camera.

As I look at their smiling faces and shaking hands captured in my pictures, I think of the student and the vice-principal becoming "border crossers" (Feuerverger 2001:xiii; see also Palmberger 2013), individuals who challenge and redefine the limitations of "ethnic geography" at the school. Their hand-shaking is metadiscursive—it is a commentary on the politics of map-making that produced ubiquitous ethnic segregation of the school, the city, and the state.

This event illustrates how the careful planning of spatial organization of people and territory in postwar Bosnia-Herzegovina relies on the logic of spatial governmentality. This spatial governmentality provides the main framework both for the policies of peace-building and state-making, and, more specifically, for the arrangement of the school's territory, including

Figure 3. Border-crossers, fall 2005. Photo by the author.

the management and regulation of ethnically conceived school populations. This "singular cartographic delineation of territory" (Crampton 1996:353) has brought a particular school into being where certain features of belonging, such as an interethnic student body, became "unmappable" (Campbell 1999:401).

But lived territory is not a map. As the no man's territory illustrates, everyday life at the school is messy, tense, and at times located in spatial cracks spontaneously created in between the neatly drawn lines of the school's territorial plan. Therefore, the reunification of the school is a powerful instance of the tension between abstract space conceived through the dominant discourse of policy makers (McCann 1999) and the practices of the people that engage with these spaces through their resourcefulness and performances (Lefebvre 1991). As a result, any interpretation of the spatial negotiations at the Mostar Gymnasium requires untangling and denaturalizing the nexus between the identifications and practices of students and teachers, and the ethnic geography of the school.

Claiming the Walls

The problem of (de)emphasizing ethnicity under the umbrella of integration becomes especially visible in the analysis of the decorations of the school. While there is a profound ethnic division of the space and curricula, there are no markers of ethnic belonging decorating the school's hallways. There are no posters, signs, or writings symbolizing ethnic nationhood. This is the result of the OSCE order that all ethnic identification of the school should be removed. As a result, all the symbols of Croat nationalism, identity, and history that used to decorate the school prior to reunification were removed before the Bosniaks returned to the building, under strict monitoring by the OSCE.[5]

The walls are not completely bare, however. There are several framed posters and photographs hanging on the freshly painted wall in the main hallway, next to the duty room. These are mostly pictures of the Mostar Gymnasium before the war and emblems of the city of Mostar, the Federation of Bosnia-Herzegovina, and the Bosnia-Herzegovina state. This lack of ethnonational imaginary is striking in comparison to the rest of Mostar, which is encumbered with ethnoreligious symbols marking its streets and hills, such as the images of churches, crosses, mosques, and flags.

There are numerous boards on the walls in the hallways, however, hosting temporary student exhibits, such as recent news about extracurricular activities, information about school trips, and the student council's announcements. All the official announcements are advertised in either the Croatian or the Bosnian language, or in both, if they are announcing calls for the same position. These advertisements in mutually understandable languages are regularly displayed next to each other.

In addition, the artwork related to Ramadan, Christmas, and celebrated Croat and Bosniak authors and artists is put on some of the larger boards in the hallways. The decision to take down these sensitive displays is a political statement and the doorman usually waits for a signal from the principal or vice-principal to remove particular objects. Proof that these exhibits are really sensitive is that some work would occasionally disappear "overnight." This happened with the Ramadan exhibit in 2006. Investigation into what happened with the items was minimal in order to avoid further interethnic tension that was, according to the vice-principal, already present and significant. The Bosniak language teacher who prepared the exhibit with her students complained about the incident to the other teachers in her curriculum and to me, however. This incident demonstrated the fragile nature of reunification and the tension that instigates acts of reclaiming the space from "the other side," subversively.

While the ethnic groups are not allowed to use the walls to express their ethnonational belonging, the OSCE uses the walls to hang multiple plaques in recognition of international donations received for the reconstruction of the school. These plaques celebrate the contributions of governments that donated the money for the library, labs, floors, heating system, and so on. They are strategically placed over the entrance doors of different rooms or in the hallways, signaling ownership of place via political framing of targeted donations. These ornaments add flavor and political significance to the projects of transnational governmentality and the internationally supervised state-making and cartography of peace-building at the school.

Sociology of Transnational Governmentality

Claiming the walls of the new school is not the only way in which international presence frames and structures the life in and around the school, however. One day as I was chatting with the secretary, I casually looked out the window as several army trucks pulled up and parked at the square in front of the school. I felt anxious—who are they and why are they here? Then I saw a Spanish flag on one of the vehicles' doors. I was even more confused, but somewhat relieved. "Ah, to su Španci" ("Oh, those are the Spaniards"), said the secretary, who seemed far less concerned, as she slowly walked to the window. Several dozen soldiers jumped out of the back of the trucks and formed a straight line in front of the monument in the middle of the square. They saluted the monument and shortly after, they left.

The square in front of the school, the secretary explained, is popularly known as the Spanish Square. Before the war, this was a major intersection and the beginning of a long pedestrian promenade. At the time of my research, it was a ghostly strip of land, framed by skeletons of burned buildings, and decorated by a large chess field, several benches, and a few young trees. This piece of land was the key point of the war front line, and most of the buildings in its vicinity were completely destroyed, some of which remain wraithlike today. After the Dayton Peace Agreement was signed, a Spanish patrol was set to guard the frontline, since the Spaniards were the main part of the NATO force stationed in Mostar (D'Alessio and Gobetti

Figure 4. Spanish soldiers at the Spanish Square, fall 2005. Photo by the author.

2006). The Spanish army established the monument to remember the sacrifices of its soldiers who died in the Mostar vicinity. The monument was erected by the Spanish army, without an authorization by local authorities (2006). The site also unofficially attained the name Spanish Square, that is, *Španski trg* for the Bosniaks and *Španjolski trg* for the Croats (2006).

These examples show the visible public display of the presence of the "intervention apparatus" at the school and beyond, which inserts "international" versus "local" asymmetry, plurality, and heterogeneity. These wall decorations and soldier-performances are signs of power "that have force, that get interpreted and reinterpreted, and feed back further significance into the system" (Mbembe 1992:8). Furthermore, while the plaques, the physical presence, and the millions invested in the reconstruction of the school clearly demonstrate that the "international community" is neither an outsider nor unbiased in the politics of Bosnia-Herzegovina, their authority to mediate in a context defined by hostile ethnic difference derives from their power to claim noninvolvement (Gilbert 2008:17, 18).

These visible forms of claiming ownership of (local) spaces and people capture well how the international institutions representing global governance demand attention to their particular forms of mobilization, justification, and rewards, thus thickening and multiplying their points of engagement and control (Duffield 2001:9, 11).

Populating the School

In the summer of 2004, four months after the legal reunification of the school, two months before the beginning of the school year, during the international frenzy around the reopening of the bridge, I met separately with the principal and vice-principal of the reunified school. The first principal of the reunited school received me at his recently renovated office at the school, which was under heavy construction in summer 2004. He voiced multiple concerns in regard to the possible dangers emerging from the students' physical proximity, especially because of the history of occasional violence at the school in the years following the war. The fact that the school was located at the borderline made it especially susceptible to violence, since it was easily accessible from both sides of the city. In addition, it was at the time the only populated public building at the center of the boulevard.

The acts of school-related violence happened in the past and included throwing stones at the building, robbery, and one especially hostile act by a group of young Bosniaks. After hearing that one of their Bosniak friends had been attacked by a group of Croat youth in Kantarevac—a sports complex behind the school on the Croat side of the boulevard—these young men quickly formed a group and set off for the school with two pit bulls. After breaking into the school, they entered one classroom where class was in progress and began beating up a number of Croat students and their teacher. The teachers and students at the school often recall this event, as Zana remembers: "Each side blamed the other. I do not know who started it, but from the boulevard there came rocks flying. . . . I do not know if it came from Mahala, I don't know where they came from. For that whole year the police guarded the school, from a car, like a police patrol." This history of physical violence at the school, in addition to the pressures from the political leadership, the local communities, and the OSCE, made the employees, including the school principal, anxious: "Kids will have different classes but they will intermingle during the breaks between classes . . . we have to react if there is some word spoken that can be politicized into a conflict. We have to be ready to suppress it."

When I came back to Mostar in the summer of 2005 to begin my long-term research, I met with the principal and vice-principal in order to learn about the events during the first year of reunification. Since my last visit, the Croat principal had been replaced in April 2005 by Nada, a younger and more energetic principal. We met at his new office at the Institute for Education in west Mostar, where he was now working as the physics education advisor. As we talked, he remembered the first days at the reunified school, his inability to resist integration, and the disagreement of the Croat community with his actions:

> It was a really hard feeling. Both Ismet [the vice-principal] and I spent all the time at the school—we literally slept there. The first day, as I was walking to the school—I always came in early, right after the doorman Stevo—I was thinking: *what if we do not succeed?* At first, we were all on duty—no one spent time at the teachers' room . . . we all walked up and down the hallways, monitoring interactions among students. At first, kids looked at each other in a shy and suspicious way, but slowly they got to know each other. At the same time they [Croat community] blamed me for the reunification: *How could I allow it to happen?* The attacks arrived especially strongly from two teachers, and from some parents and students . . . they were angry. Media also tried to intensify the situation. Once, a journalist who is also a teacher at this school came to make an interview with me and he started accusing me of allowing the reunification to take place. Under the influence of some professors and parents, the Croat kids refused to cooperate at first. One group of kids took a school desk in front of the school and organized a referendum against the return of Bosniaks to the school. They came to talk to me, two bad students, who are bad examples to the others. They told me that they wanted a referendum. I told them that the principal does not sign a referendum and that underage students cannot vote at any referendum. . . . Those were delivery pains. I have deep feelings that political parties, at least one person from each side, orchestrated all this. This school was always multiethnic.

> There were always students of Serb and Bosniak ethnicity [in addition to Croats] at this school, while the school in Mahala did not have any other students [but Bosniaks]. Politics wanted to unite the school. Even if I wanted to bring an arsenal of weapons and stand at the door, they would succeed in doing it. I was just a puppet in this game.

This quote shows the heaviness of negotiations involved in the reunification of the school. Here, the former principal emphasizes that the unification was a result of an intricate political deal between the international actors and ethnonationalist elites on both sides. In addition, he stresses that reunification was not a genuine process of people coming together. He justifies his acceptance of reunification to the wider Croat community by pointing at the politicians who made him give in, and who pronounced him incapable of juggling the competing interests of the Croat community on the one side and the wider political pressures for integration on the other. He believed he was a scapegoat in the process of accepting the return of Bosniaks.

On the other side, many Bosniak students and teachers complained about power asymmetries at the school, regardless of the official equilibrium. They told me that they had to "swallow" much symbolic and structural violence during the first year of reunification. They accepted this situation in order to meet the main goal—to complete the return of all Bosniak students to the Mostar Gymnasium. The return was deeply important for this community since the school has a special place in the lives of many Mostarians. Bosniaks felt that they were unjustly forced out of "their" school and everything it used to stand for, including prosperity, coexistence, progress, and excellence.

The return itself, however, was full of obstacles. Numerous Bosniak students told me about a particular situation that occurred in the middle of the first year of reunification, as Sara remembers:

> Teachers told us to be patient. But it was not easy, because the Croat side was dominating the space, and they provoked us. For example, we came back from the winter break to find terrible things written on our blackboard and the walls of our classrooms, including the "Arbeit Macht Frei!"[6] sign that was written in Auschwitz. Also, they draw their *Ustaša*[7] symbols on our walls . . . you know . . . the U

with the cross in the middle. At first we went crazy, we felt scared and angry, and we wanted the media to come and see what happened. Our Bosnian language professor helped us write a statement for the media and the OSCE. But then our principal,[8] Ismet, told us to calm down, not to respond to their provocations, because we had to think about the rest of the students from our school who were still in Mahala. So nothing happened, and we let it slide. But if we did something like that to them, I can only imagine what they would do—it would be all over TV, and we would be punished!

Another Bosniak student remembers a different incident that, in her opinion, showed the lived asymmetries and dominance at the school, where "the Croat side was more privileged":

During the first year, they [Croats] did everything to make us feel that we do not belong here, that this school is not really ours. For example, right before their Christmas holidays, they shortened their classes, while our classes remained the regular length. So the problem arose about the school bell that signals the end of the class period. They had the bell adjusted to their short class periods, while we had to look at our watches and calculate the time. How is this fair? If they [Croat management] changed the time of the class periods for those few days, why did we all have to suffer, why did they impose different schedules? They only wanted to show their dominance.

Other students, who were still in Mahala during the first year of reunification, also remembered the challenges their teachers were facing having to teach at two different locations. Merima remembers: "It was really hard on our teachers to teach a few classes here, and then go over to Stara Gimnazija, to teach a few classes. Sometimes they were impatient, and we knew that something was going on at the Stara that made them this way. So, we did not complain."

Even though the students in the Federal curriculum that I interacted with expressed great satisfaction about their return to the Mostar Gymnasium where many of their family and friends went before the war, most of them also emphasized that something was lost with this move: intimacy, warmth, an easygoing attitude, special relationships with the teachers, and a relaxed atmosphere in the ethnically homogeneous *sredina* [surrounding] in Mahala.

Reunification was hard for many Croat students as well. Several told me how nice it was to have the school for themselves prior to the reunification, and how intimate and cozy it was before the Bosniaks returned:

> Azra: How was it to go to school before the Bosniaks returned?
> Andrej: Somehow, we all felt more connected. There were only four classes in one shift. You knew everyone from your class and all the others, like we were all from one village or something. So when [smoking] in the bathroom, you knew everyone, who had a brother, who had a sister, who was a good student, who was dating whom. . . . It was a small space, two bathrooms and four classrooms. Everything around that little area on the ground floor was blocked and we could not go upstairs—it was in ruins.
> Azra: And do you remember how it was when the Bosniaks returned?
> Andrej: I do not know—I expected there would be some conflict, but . . . I do not know, nothing happened . . . I just remember the first day we looked at each other as if the others were aliens . . . in the hallway, you would walk by, and the heads were turning, checking you out. I remember when they first came, we were already . . . I mean . . . you go to the bathroom, I remember . . . a group of boys, five or six of them, if they had to go to the bathroom, three to four other guys would go with the guy who had to go, because of the fear, you know. On the one side, you know, we were already here, *na našem* (on our own territory), and then they arrived, and they felt scared.

Another Croat student remembers conflicts, tensions, and uncertainties during the first year of joint schooling:

> There were no problems, even though we expected them. Actually, there was one thing, around Christmas. Tanja and I were going down the hall on the third floor . . . and this girl and I were walking, and this one guy, I really do not remember who it was . . . and there was this Christmas poster on the wall, and the two of us were passing, and he said, "Hello Christmases, can I celebrate Christmas with

you?" I turned around and without thinking, I said: "No, you cannot, two Bajrams[9] are enough for you!" The guy just looked at me . . . he did not say anything. Later on I felt a bit guilty, but I understood it as a provocation. Maybe it was not . . . I do not know.

Regardless of these and many other uncertainties, tensions, suspicions, obstructions, imbalances, and provocations in and around the school, *škola je preživjela* (the school survived) its first year of reunification. This endurance came as a surprise to many distrustful citizens of Mostar on both sides, who expected more violence to take place upon reunification. Some of these skeptics commented that "the school survived" exactly because it was not "truly" unified, but it was a political façade for an order still reminiscent of segregation.

The proximity of joined schooling created a public space for the reevaluation of ethnic homogeneity, regional identity, and intimacy. This was an opportunity to challenge the division of the city and to reintroduce the principles of interconnectedness and solidarity among the youth in Mostar. The politics of ethnic symmetry at the school and its dynamic of "negative peace," however, created the ethos of ethnically "separate and (un)equal" teachers and students. The vision of the school as an absolute ethnic equilibrium, in spite of experienced asymmetries, in which the Croat (student, classroom, sign, etc.) stands next to the Bosniak (student, classroom, sign, etc.), limited more spontaneous movement and interaction. The visible and invisible walls between ethnic communities at the school made every interaction across the ethnic boundary unusual, risky, and exaggerated, visible in behaviors such as loud speech across the divided table in the teachers' room or performative, cross-ethnic hand-shaking in the "no-man's-land." In this way, ironically, practices of border-crossing often accentuated the firmness of the borders themselves, causing continuous reethnicization of the school life.

Zooming Out

It is well known that states produce and reify categories within "improvement" policies and projects aiming to address discrimination and inequities based on these same categorical distinctions, such as race, caste, ethnicity, and class (Scott 1998). Furthermore, throughout the world, identity groups clash over such issues as language rights, federalism and regional autonomy, political representation, religious freedom, education curriculum, land claims, immigration and naturalization policy, and national symbols such as the choice of national anthem or public holidays (Kymlicka 1995:1). What accentuates this struggle in Bosnia-Herzegovina is the authoritative role of the international actors in state-making, and their complicated relations to the ethnonational groups, which experience themselves as differently positioned in relation to power; the reification of ethnic demarcation is generated both by the local ethnonationalist political elites and by the internationally run organizations and agencies, which had a mandate to overcome ethnic divisions. Moreover, the conceptualization of Bosnia-Herzegovina as a persistent ethnic issue based on the unquestioned link between territory and ethnicity requires a certain form of ethnic segregation, even under the umbrella of unification. Furthermore, by bringing the two mutually exclusive impulses together, the quest for unification and the struggle for partition, integration retained and even exacerbated the tension it hoped to overcome.

The cartography of the Mostar Gymnasium illuminates the extreme demarcation of ethnicity and profound ethnicization of everyday life, which continued to deepen under the umbrella of consociational democracy. Martin and the rest of the OSCE understood that "genuine" unification entails more than the mathematical antithesis of monoculturalism and homogeneity. They were aware of the fact that historically, people in Bosnia-Herzegovina shared many aspects of economic and social life, despite religious and ethnic differences. Under this long-standing local sensibility of interconnectedness, ethnoreligious difference was lived and negotiated on a daily basis. This ambiguity and fluidity of identity, and the appreciation and historical exposure to difference, have not been incorporated into the consociational model of state-making, however. Rather, its narrow script shaped and gave context to the horizons of integration of the school. Instead of integration, under the cartography of cultural incommensurability, interethnic and nonethnic interconnectedness became unmappable.

The creation of no-man's-land by a student at the school challenged this ethnic partition as a necessary foundation of the reunified school. Regardless of its marginality, the effort and creativity that led to the creation of the "land" provide a chance for rethinking ethnic cartography at the school. This space that mediates essentializing ethnicization and that creates cracks in ethnic territories presents an opportunity for a dialogue in the heterogeneous public sphere and envisions a mode of representation that accommodates and fosters transethnic conversation and pluralism. In addition, it suggests a prospect for a more complex understanding of the relationship between space, place, and identity (Lefebvre 1991; Massey 1994).

Mario, the student who created the no-man's-land, is not alone. A number of people in post-Dayton Bosnia-Herzegovina feel trapped in their ethnic identities and imprisoned within the structures of the poorly considered, dysfunctional state with countless layers of corrupt administration and without a clear vision for the future. Their frustrations with the fragmented country, however, remained uncultivated, silenced, and politically up for grabs during my fieldwork. These dissatisfied citizens, whose (a)political voices are perpetually disjointed and silenced by the overpowering ethnonationalist discourse and the consociational model that safeguards it, remind us that group boundaries are blurry and that "particular community identification does not exhaust the various layers of selfhood of a person" (Chatterjee 1998:280).

These instances of "spontaneous" and performed border-crossing in the hallways could not find recognition under the state-making script that relies on the war-produced ethnicization of peoples and places, and classifies citizens into determinate ethnic communities. Because of their positive immediate outcomes (i.e., the return of Bosniaks to the school), these arrangements are hard to critique or change. The positive aspects of this process are clear, but its dangers stay hidden in the years of the postwar social reconstruction. The risk is that both the Dayton Peace Agreement and the ethnicization of everyday life at the school and beyond are not temporary conditions, as was first imagined. They have become permanent political solutions that have continued over two decades of "democratic" transformations, fostering the anger, disillusionment, and estrangement of numerous young Bosnians and Herzegovinians from the nation and the Dayton state to which they officially belong.

Chapter 3

Bathroom Mixing

On a beautiful day in spring 2006, Amna comes up to me, hiding one of her fists behind her back: "Hajmo se miješati" (Let's go and mix), she says. She opens her fist and I see a cigarette, its long, elegant body rolling up and down her palm. She grabs my hand and leads me to the bathroom at the end of the crowded hallway, away from the teachers' views. We open the door and find ourselves enveloped in smoke so overwhelming it blocks the smell of urine.

I stop, unable to see or breathe, letting my eyes adjust to the smoke. I barely distinguish the sinks attached to the wall—they are covered with cigarette butts on the wet surfaces. Water from the pipes gently drips on the butts, causing them to expand. A yellowish cleaning sponge awkwardly rests on the frame of the second sink, as if dreading its future.

I feel Amna's hand pulling my elbow; I follow her lead, trying not to touch the cold, damp walls. I recognize voices, but I fail to decipher the words spoken. We enter the second room, which has a window. Finally, I can breathe again. Living in the United States for the last nine years has made my lungs "weak," unable to tolerate the cigarette smoke, the signature of Bosnian public spaces. Amna stops next to Igor, hugs him,[1] and says: "I like to 'park' next to these Croats. I visit them more than they visit me." Three more students, who are smoking, join us. One of them says: "Amna, would you ever marry a Croat?" She replies swiftly, her voice rising above the smoke: "Sure, but he would need to convert to Islam first." Damjan says: "No problem, teach me some verses from the Qur'an." I jump in: "Marijan said yesterday that he would marry a Muslim girl." Marijan replies, promptly. "Sure, but only if she is infertile." The whole group laugh. Amna and Marijan hug tenderly.

Figure 5. Bathroom smoking during recess, spring 2006. Photo by the author.

The bell rings, signaling the end of recess. The bathroom empties of students who passionately inhale the last bits of smoke before they toss the butts in the sinks. The students go away, leaving me in the company of the grubby sponge and swollen butts. I lean against the window, gasping for the fresh air rolling down from the surrounding hills. I catch myself patting the camera resting in my hands while thinking, "Is this school bathroom the only place in Mostar in which mixing happens these days?"

The importance of public bathrooms for the production of identities, subjectivities, and political projects has been documented by numerous scholars.[2] Pushing the school bathroom to the forefront of discussion about a postwar society illuminates how internationally guided state-making policies reinforce war-generated ethnic homogenization of territory that historically never existed as uniform (Hammel 1997). This unique postwar spatial governmentality progressively generates social orders and identifications that are increasingly produced through governance of ethnically conceived spaces. In the context of the school, the spatial governmentality therein limits opportunities for a transethnic social order to (re)emerge. Furthermore, the focus on smoking—one of the key social practices of interethnic sociality in prewar Bosnia-Herzegovina—links the practices of bathroom smoking to the long-standing history of mixing as a form of public sociality in Bosnia-Herzegovina and shows how the current sociopolitical model spatially discourages the continuance of this tradition.

Mixing

Theories of mixing have been an important part of scholarly discussions on the nature of relationships and contact between individuals and groups in different sociocultural settings. Lévi-Strauss's (1969) famous thesis on the "exchange of women," which produces social structures of debt/reciprocity and group alliances, provoked an ongoing debate about the nature, structure, and function of the "mixed marriage" phenomenon in anthropology and beyond. In addition, Barth's seminal work on the character of "ethnic boundaries that persist despite a flow of personnel across them" (Barth 1969:9) initiated multiple works on the notions of ethnicity, identity, and group boundaries that continue into the present day. Recent interest in globalization in general, and global and local dynamics in particular, has spurred additional research, notably on the notions of mimicry, interstice, hybridity, and liminality (Bhabha 2004), theories of liquidity (Bauman 2000, 2003), examinations of "mêlée" (Nancy 2000), and explorations of mestizaje, callaloo, creolization, and multiculturalism (Khan 2004). All these works show, in one way or another, how mixing, when intertwined with histories and hierarchies of colonialism, imperialism, and resistance, becomes a powerful site for the interpretation and evaluation of relationships between individuals and groups in diverse social, political, and cultural contexts.

To speak of mixing at all is to enter a realm of hesitancy and unease for many Bosnians. My own reluctance echoes Jean-Luc Nancy's embarrassment and reservation when, in 1993, he was asked to write the "Eulogy for Mêlée"[3] dedicated to the besieged Bosnian capital of Sarajevo. Nancy, troubled by the task, suggests that the best eulogy for mêlée would be the one that is not written, since the notion [of the mélange or a mixture] itself could not even be discerned or identified (2000:147).

Talk about mixing saturates vernacular discourses in Bosnia-Herzegovina today. As an ethnographer, I felt obliged to pay attention to the pervasiveness of discourses of mixing, regardless of my own anxieties related to the political and scholarly discussions and manipulations of mixing, as an indicator of Bosnian plurality, culture, and society. My discomfort with mixing is twofold: the first emanates from the common idea that if there is mixing, there have to be some "real" standing entities and "substantial identities" (Nancy 2000:147) that enter into the mixing process. In the case of Bosnia-Herzegovina, these subjects are conceived as three dominant, constituent Bosnian peoples: Bosnian Muslims, Serbs, and Croats. Thus, ironically, the focus on mixing frequently reifies the ethnoreligious groups as substantial identities regardless of their proven elasticity, changeability, and fluidity (Gilbert 2008).

This tension became especially clear to me in my multiple conversations with those students who mix the most in the school bathroom and who despise the term *miješanje*. Their resistance is not directed to the processes of mixing, but they struggle with the term itself. They see the idiom mixing as restraining, historically loaded, and superficial. One day, as I was chatting with Damijan in front of the school, I mentioned mixing, and he snapped at me: "I hate that word, as we are some trash and now we are all mixed together." Melita, who was sometimes referred to as "the mixing queen," showed her dislike of the general attitude toward mixing by putting it into a historical and comparative context: "that sounds to me like America in the '50s, like 'mixing of races,' as if we are not people. And now, fifty years later, we made nation [ethnonational identity] into something that prohibits integrated classrooms." Similarly to Melita, Jasenko mentioned the racialized connotation of mixing: "To me, that is all nonsense, as if we are two races and now we need to mix." Regardless of their problematic use of the register of race, these profound verbalizations of resistances to the increasingly more visible discourses of mixing are still limited in Mostar; *miješanje* remains one of the most popular terms used nonchalantly in the everyday jargon in Mostar, so that even the individuals who resist the term continuously use it in everyday speech.

The second aspect of my discomfort with mixing stems from the treatment of mixing in much of the scholarship on the Balkans—in most of these works, mixing is either romanticized as a long-standing, uniquely Bosnian multicultural social order, or depicted as competing and disputed statistical representations of mixed marriages.[4] While deeply related, these two discourses of mixing are not identical, however. They have been used interchangeably by different scholars, often adding to the confusion and idealization of mixing in Bosnia-Herzegovina.

Postwar Bosnia-Herzegovina is an exceptionally fruitful context in which to examine mixing as an enduring and modern form of public (and, at times, private) intimacy and as a social practice generative of new, postwar subjectivities. These emerging and constantly negotiated relations, identifications, discriminations, hopes, and resistances develop in the context of extreme ethnic and territorial demarcation. Therefore, bathroom mixing at the Mostar Gymnasium is interwoven with ethnonational politics and the consociational vision of democracy. Furthermore, practices of mixing, which are composed of uncanny and frail human bonds (Bauman 2003), and which are being continuously articulated and negotiated in the school bathroom, engender finite communities of "bathroom smokers." These "political communities" where students come together and smoke together are productive of new intimacies that reveal the persistence, possibilities, and limitations of mixing as a form of sociality and popular politics in the postwar country.

Sociality and Sensibility

The term *miješanje* (*mešanje* in Serbian), or "mixing," has at least a fifty-year tradition in the studies of ex-Yugoslavia. It is a word in the Bosnian and Croat languages that is often translated into English as "(to) mix, mingle, and stir."[5] As a form of sociality, mixing in Bosnia-Herzegovina has been documented by several anthropologists, especially those interested in rural areas (Bringa 1995; Lockwood 1975). These ethnographic accounts analyze public spaces of interethnic exchange and sociality, such as markets (Lockwood 1975), and private spaces, such as homes (Bringa 1995). These works point at the persistence of ethnic boundaries, but they also hint at the contextual and fluid nature of ethnonational identifications, and they suggest that "interethnic relations were based on stable rules of reciprocity that were nonetheless negotiated on a day-to-day basis" (Bougarel, Helms, and Duijzings 2007:16).

Everyday life in "the mixed regions" (most of prewar Bosnia-Herzegovina) incorporated the cult of *komšiluk*, or "neighborhoodliness," which included coffee and smoking visits, "sweet visits" (*na slatko*), visits "for joy" (*na radost*), and visits "for sorrow" (*na žalost*) at someone's death (Bringa 1995). Good neighbors, regardless of their ethnoreligious backgrounds, formed the most intimate part of one's cultural, social, and economic well-being; and *komšiluk* included a significant moral dimension (Sorabji 1995; Henig 2012). The ethnic division and social prohibition of intermarriage remained the main social rule, however, which existed alongside *komšiluk* and other mixing practices. In other words, the Bosnian rural population almost never married across ethnic lines, and practices of mixing simultaneously verified and challenged ethnic divisions.

The situation was different in the cities, however, especially during Yugoslav times. In a number of these urban centers, mixing incorporated neighborhood intimacy, awareness, and acceptance of "the other" as part of one's habitus. This also resulted in an increasing number of mixed marriages, indexing that this type of social, intermingling was becoming more socially acceptable. As a result, mixing practices created a unique form of sensibility in Bosnia-Herzegovina. This common, everyday multiculturality was linked to the Yugoslav notions of socialist modernity, humanism, and progress, and to cosmopolitan worldviews. At the same time, this receptivity to mixing relied on the (Orientalist) idea of Bosnia-Herzegovina's traditional, close-knit, overlapping, hospitable, unruly, and warm social order. This tradition-inspired yet modern cultural awareness, which required daily negotiation of diverse perspectives and identities, generated transethnic affiliations and identifications, which Bringa describes as "a particular and shared moral environment" (1995:32), and Ivan Lovrenović calls "the Bosnian experience" (2001:209).[6]

This unique sensibility, built on the recognition of and respect for ethnoreligious difference as part of one's most intimate environment, and on continuous, daily negotiated tensions between different ethnoreligious groups, was severely crippled by the war when the clash between the lived culture of interconnectedness and prevailing ethnic nationalisms forced unmixing of peoples whose coexistence was opposed to nationalist ideologies (Hayden 1996). The internationally implemented consociational model of democracy and spatial governmentality embody this ideology, solidified through discourses of "ancient ethnic hatreds" and produced via war-generated ethnonational divisions and ideologies of nonmixing. This further discouraged development of transethnic peoplehood in Bosnia-Herzegovina. At the same time, the context of ethnonationalism made mixing practices hypervisible and often exaggerated, as evident in the bathroom vignette when Amna invited me to "go and mix." This explicit invitation to mix would have been inappropriate in the prewar Bosnia-Herzegovina when people interacted more frequently and less hesitantly across ethno-religious differences.[7]

The shrinking scope and meanings of mixing in Bosnia-Herzegovina are especially palpable in the once diverse and today deeply segregated city of Mostar, where mixing ceased to be a popular form of public sociality.[8] The urban sensibility and everyday life changed drastically in the last fifteen to twenty years, as one of the longest inhabitants of Mostar and the most experienced worker at the Mostar Gymnasium explains:

Janja: What we had before was *život* [life].
Azra: And what do we have today?
Janja: Haaaa, *suživot* [coexistence], maybe better to say *životarenje* [survival from one day to the next, without a clear purpose or vision, just making one's ends meet].

In this context of *životarenje*, new generations of youth are coming of age, unaware of "the fine Bosnian multiplicity of perspectives" (I. Lovrenović 2001: 210). These youth are nurtured by the local ideologies of cultural fundamentalism and incommensurability, and the consociational political model that safeguards them. As a result, mixing, in its urban Yugoslav form, appears unmappable under the existing contours of consociational democracy. However, in the spatial "cracks" between ethnic territories, such as *ničija zemlja* (no-man's-land) located between ethnically segregated classrooms, or the bathroom, youth are (re)producing and reframing the long-standing practices of mixing, thus signaling both continuities with and ruptures from the past practices of mixing. For instance, in the bathroom vignette with which I began this chapter, students at the Mostar Gymnasium are (re)turning to social smoking in the gaps between ethnic territories. These bathroom practices of mixing are historically informed and geographically restricted, as Tanja explains: "but mixing [in the bathroom] is not enough, because . . . it would take time [to build friendship], but we will be around the school only for a bit more, and then we go to our side and they go to theirs. How can we build long-lasting friendships when we do not even have a space to drink coffee together?" The students' complaints about the absence of spaces for common smoking and coffee drinking beyond the bathroom hint at the spatial limitations for mixing and the order it stood for to (re)emerge. The absence of additional spaces for interethnic public sociality in Mostar turns the school bathroom into a unique place where students are mapping and discursively exaggerating prewar practices of mixing, such as smoking, onto the bathroom space.

Bathroom Ethnography

Bathrooms, as spaces of deliberate mixing at the school, emerge spontaneously and often with banned actions. The reading of this "extra-academic architecture" (Devine 1996) can possibly tell us more than life in classrooms about youth's challenges of spatial governmentality. Bathroom mixing is a testimony of students' "membership" in the mixed smoking community, which consolidates shared collective space in which cultural intimacy unfolds, and promotes loyalties to the principles of shared identity, such as "truculent defiance of authority" (Neofotistos 2010:303). Most of the students who consciously sought bathroom mixing were also engaged in a handful of joined activities at the school, such as student council and the debate club. Regardless of these joined practices, most students experienced bathroom mixing as more unifying. Commenting on the increasing intermingling in the bathroom, one student stated enthusiastically: "Smoking doesn't kill, it unites!"

I stumbled on bathroom mixing accidentally during a short recess several weeks into my fieldwork. The teachers' bathroom was always locked, and I forgot to take the key from the teachers' room, so I decided to use the students' bathroom. I was surprised to see many familiar faces lined up against the damp wall, enveloped in smoke. They cheered when they saw me, showing their acceptance. After this initiation, I frequented the bathroom regularly. I spent many hours inhaling illegally produced smoke in one of the two second-floor bathrooms, where seniors, the only students on that floor, had a quick smoke several times a day during the five-minute recesses. I never saw students use the toilets for their intended purpose during bathroom mixing; students as a rule avoided using bathrooms for elimination during recess. Bodily needs were suspended in order to provide a subversive and marginalized, private and public space for mixing to emerge. Any needed elimination was accomplished outside recess; students frequently asked teachers during classes if they might be excused to go to the bathroom. By creating the bathroom space as both "private" and "public," students were able to experiment with ethnic identities through smoking, making the toilets into a unique space of sociality and consumption.

Slowly the bathroom emerged as the central place for mixing, as is captured in the text message I received from a student:

> Where are you? Today [in the bathroom] everyone was there, Ana, Marijana, Ivan, and Jelica, and many students from our classroom . . . and we talked to them, and made jokes together. It was so cool! I was sad when the bell rang [indicating the end of recess]. The bathroom rules! Greetings from the best school in the world!

With no adults present, the bathroom became a place of subversion, experimentation, risk, and playfulness. It was the only place in the school for hanging out; sharing a cigarette; flooding the sink and toilet bowls; and discussing classroom work, fashion, music, and dating. These practices generated contingent and precarious feelings of interconnectedness and recognition.

More than a space for hanging out, the bathroom, and the illicit smoking pursued therein, constituted a unique space that enabled experimentation with ethnoreligious identity. For example, during one recess, Mario, wearing a shirt with "Croatia" written on it, mockingly recounted the verses from the Qur'an that Amna had tried to teach to him. When I asked him about this contradiction, he said that he was "fooling around in the bathroom, not like I did it in class or something." The marginalized space of the bathroom allowed for experimentation and playfulness that, according to the student, could not happen in the official, ethnicized setting of the classroom. The toilets emerged as a secluded space that encouraged otherwise restricted experimentation with one's identity and where students displayed seemingly contradictory behaviors. For example, one time during recess, a Croat student and self-proclaimed nationalist shared a cigarette with a Bosniak student who, one year earlier, had stormed into a Croat school and insulted the students and teachers. When I specifically asked them about this, they just shrugged their shoulders. This (lack of) response reminded me of a situation during my fieldwork in North Belfast. In March 2006, I met two high school students who spent time together at an integrated (Protestant and Catholic) school yet engaged in violence against each other across the peace line in the afternoons. When I asked them how they could be friends in the morning and enemies in the afternoon, they said that it was "normal." This particular cultural logic is a vernacular response to the consociational model that assumes concurrent integration and segregation of peoples and territories. In addition, it is a powerful commentary on the complexity embedded in everyday negotiations of shared histories and diverging sociopolitical identities.

On multiple occasions at the school bathroom, experimentation with ethnicity emerged from flirting between the youth. A Bosniak girl, who mentioned that she would never date a Croat, gave a warm hug to a Croat student, in front of me and the others. When I asked her about this, she said that "superficial flirting [in the bathroom] is OK, but serious dating [outside the bathroom] is not." The quote echoes the ideas presented in the opening vignette, where Marijan said he would marry a Muslim girl, but only if she were infertile. In addition to showing how the power of ideology works through social agents, these responses index the changing nature of mixing in Bosnia-Herzegovina, where mixing is increasingly seen as a risky, subversive yet highly visible practice, in need of constant policing and regulation, since it transgresses or threatens to transgress the political orders of cultural purity and segmental autonomy of the three main ethnic groups.

Spaces of mixing are so limited at the reunified school that several students who wanted to mix went to the bathroom even though they did not smoke, only "to hang out with them." Some students were so eager to meet students "from the other side" in spaces other than bathrooms that they asked me for help, with statements such as: "I cannot just go to their classroom and say: 'Here I am.' Would you please introduce me to the guys from IV-c [the Croat curriculum classroom next door]?" While these bathroom opportunities open new spaces for communication and relationships across ethnic divides, these interactions simultaneously bring about memories of violence and unresolved wrongdoings in the recent past, which reinforce isolation.

Mixing and Violence

The school reunification provided an opportunity for youth to explore new domains of social relationships by interacting with the students of the other ethnic group whom they otherwise had no opportunity to meet. While some students, mostly those who considered themselves to be "urban" and "cool," seized this opportunity and entered, however hesitantly, the spaces of bathroom mixing, for other students it increased anxieties. The new proximity often initiated the tearing apart of badly sealed wounds from the recent war, which then shaped student behavior, often subconsciously. For example, Anisa, who was three years old when she was first imprisoned and then forced to walk for twenty miles to freedom, explained: "I do not know . . . I cannot establish any real contact with them. I am not capable, not yet. I have some feeling, undefined, which I never had before . . . is it fear, or mistrust, this or that, I simply feel uncomfortable and all I can do is say 'hello' to them."

This student's experience shows the effects of spatial governmentality, which brings students into proximity to each other, but does not encourage meaningful interactions among them. Instead, the logic of cultural incommensurability, and the silence and lack of vision for a common future, create a climate of mistrust and fear among youth whose wounds from the recent war have not even begun to heal. The consociational model of "safe" coexistence at the school does not address the conflict and living asymmetries. As a result, there are no clear school policies that work to engage students in meaningful cross-ethnic activities; that is left to the students to negotiate.

While some students say "hello" and maybe even start a conversation, others project verbal or physical violence in the shared space of mixing. One day, Melita, "the mixing queen," approached me visibly shaken: "You will not believe what just happened to me . . . I walked in front of their classroom. . . . I looked at them, and one of them told me *mrš* (piss off)! I froze." This exchange, like many others, was left unaddressed in the environment of multiple and conflicting agendas and expectations of reunification.

Similarly, school trips, excursions, and seminars that have for their main goal bringing together students of different ethnic groups to help them confront the stereotypes can easily become spaces where tensions from the unresolved past are invoked and dealt with in unique ways. Amna remembers: "I went to the United States with Igor [Croat student] and Jasna [Serb student]. We had the best time, and we became friends. We are still good friends and we spend time together. While in the United States, we called each other *balijkuša*, *četnikuša*, and *ustaša*.[9] Our American hosts did not know that we were joking and they were all worried."

This quote suggests one of the ways in which students who opt to communicate across ethnic divisions are dealing with the violent past. Feeling overwhelmed by their war experiences and ethnicized identities, students of different ethnic groups transform the labels of exclusion into material for teasing and jokes. In this case, the appropriation and transformation of hateful language into youth slang enables the emergence of a fragile, temporary solidarity among youth. The combination of foolishness, fear, and ethnonational identification, which marked the youth's behavior, left their American hosts threatened and confused. This short-term solidarity, cultural intimacy, and sense of groupness that emerge from the transformation and humoring of hateful speech reduced the heaviness of the situation, even if they did not fully eliminate but rather reproduced the tension. For example, Amna confessed to me that she did not mind joking like this, but she also told me it bothered her when Igor expressed his loyalty to Croatia at the expense of his Bosnian-Herzegovinian identity. Rather, the three students appropriated the position of knowers, and thus of superiority, while emphasizing their own marginality.

Similarly to students, some teachers experienced seminars away from Mostar as both a possibility for rebuilding trust and an opportunity to revisit the violent past. Nermina explained her experience at one of the seminars organized for the teachers of both curricula in Neum, a small and impoverished Herzegovinian coastal town. Here, the terror of the past came not from confronting the teachers of the other curriculum, but from the presence of other guests at the hotel, which organizers from an international organization did not take into account when they planned the seminar:

> and the second to the last time we went to a seminar . . . I cannot remember exactly . . . but the name was I think . . . The Croat War Veterans. They also stayed at the hotel at which we were staying. You cannot imagine the scene . . . when we arrived, they were in those black shirts, on which it was written *Za dom spremni* ["Ready for the Homeland," the main slogan of the Croatian Defense Forces during the wars in Croatia and Bosnia-Herzegovina], and they were holding signs . . . all cripples, in wheelchairs, without eyes, deformed, with scars marking their faces . . . initially I felt empathy . . . but [raises her voice], how deep their *Ustašluk* [*Ustaša* sentiment] goes?! They started screaming *balija* and cursing *Allah*,

> *Muhamed* . . . ten years passed since then [since the war], Azra, but all that stayed deep inside of them [unintelligible] . . . and some of the professors from the Croat curriculum felt uncomfortable because of the situation. Azra, that night we were too scared to go out, because they [Croat War Veterans] reserved the main part of the hotel. We circled around the hotel to avoid them. Until four or five in the morning they sang and played music, only *Ustaša* songs. . . . Every hair on my body was erect . . . so much fear, so much negative energy . . . so many years have passed, so much was forgotten, but they . . . still think like in 1993—crippled but ready to fight, for that something, I do not know what, for some idea of theirs. That is that *duh Ustaštva* [*Ustaša* spirit] I was telling you about.

This exposure to the wider context saturated with ethnonationalism both threatened the teachers and brought a sense of solidarity among them, since some teachers from the Croat curriculum openly showed that they were made uncomfortable and distanced themselves from *duh Ustaštva*.

These examples show the complexity of integration in a divided society. Martin, the rest of the OSCE, and other international actors involved propagated reconciliation among the Mostar students and teachers, while acknowledging and institutionalizing the right of groups to be ethnically isolated. Caught in this political and social limbo, the students and teachers at the school were left to balance the larger political and social climate, the transnational governmentality, and their own aspirations.

Bathroom Graffiti

In addition to instances of verbal violence, the conflict manifested itself in the form of drawings and graffiti that students wrote to each other on the bathroom walls. These drawings were a product of solitary, subversive activity that took place during class, or when only students from one curriculum were present at the school. The messages were numerous, including the *Ustaša* signs engraved in the bathroom walls or chairs and notes such as *Balije, Bog vas jebo* (*Balije*, let God fuck you). One common inscription on the walls had to do with soccer. The walls exhibited graffiti such as "Red Army" and "Ultras," which symbolize the supporters of the Velež soccer team (Bosniak-dominated) and Zrinjski (Croat-dominated team) respectively.[10]

I was immediately intrigued by these messages on the school's carefully guarded architecture, its skin, "where the verbal and the written connect" (Miklavcic 2008:448). One of the ways to explain the use of graffiti in the school is to see them as the constant negotiation of exclusion and inclusion. Here the encounter with the ethnic other is not verbally mediated, but expressed in visual signs. The messages I mentioned above, such as the *Ustaša* signs, mark the territory of the school as "ours," while the school management is left to wipe out these messages, healing the scars in a way that allows for the hate to be erased and the future to be rewritten (449). These messages often provoke anger or sadness in those who are their designated recipients. These feelings do not usually escalate into larger conflicts, however, since they stay captured behind the doors of the bathrooms, where youth are left to negotiate tensions that have been historically an intricate part of everyday life in Bosnia-Herzegovina.

While the school produced some, albeit limited, fearful, and bathroom-contained, opportunities for spontaneous practices of interethnic public sociality, the larger context remained saturated with ethnicized spatial segregation, nationalism, and ethnicization of everyday life. Therefore, the school's integration and bathroom mixing have to be seen in the context of pervasive social, political, and territorial segregation, as Ismet, the vice-principal, was quick to point out to me: "They [the OSCE, some local politicians, and the general public] expect a lot from us, and we are doing our best. . . . but let's be realistic! How much can we achieve when everything below us [elementary schools, neighborhoods, . . .] and everything above us [FBiH, Bosnia-Herzegovina] remains totally divided!" It is this larger context of (un)mixing—including coffee drinking—in which practices of bathroom mixing need to be situated and interpreted.

Coffee/Mixing/Nation

Having a coffee with family and friends is one of the favorite leisure-time activities among all generations in Bosnia-Herzegovina and its diaspora (see Croegaert 2011; Helms 2010; Stefansson 2010). For example, the UN and OIA[11] study showed that 78 percent of youth in Bosnia-Herzegovina spend their free time in coffee shops (OIA 2005:2). In Bosnia-Herzegovina, having coffee with someone means much more than just "having a coffee"—it stands for intimacy, trust building, and routine, all signs of (potential) friendship. Having a coffee with someone from "the other side" would therefore signal one's readiness to challenge the postwar divisions, the attempt to cross over the boundaries of divide, or even to reestablish the old relationships. The following statement of Nada, the school's principal, demonstrates the symbolism attached to coffee drinking: "When I was thinking about taking this job, the [education] minister called me in and said: 'Do not take the job if you are not ready to have a coffee with Ismet [Bosniak vice-principal].'"

To call someone on the phone and ask them to come over for coffee, or to meet a person in town and say "let's go for coffee," are common expressions of sociocultural intimacy, friendship, and family relations that existed in many regions of the former Yugoslavia before the war and still continue today. However, during the time of my research these invitations for coffee rarely happened across ethnic divides. One teacher, after I asked her if she ever meets for coffee with teachers from the other curriculum, passionately replied: "Do you know what it means to have a coffee with someone? I carefully pick who I can have coffee with!"

Students at the school mentioned that having coffee with students from the other curriculum with whom they socialized in the bathroom was something they desired but was hard to organize due to the ethnically divided places of public sociality. But even if the students managed to go for coffee together, as some did, these coffees could not easily evolve into a "true" friendship, partially because of the restricted time of the high school schooling, and the lack of a larger context that would nurture nonethnic socialization.

The limited opportunities for coffee drinking and the development of cross-ethnic intimacies and bonds led many students and teachers to stress that mixing today does not lead to true friendship, as it did in the past. Rather, these new interactions among ethnically divided individuals stop at the level of a superficial friendship, as Nermina explains:

> Seminars also connected people, because after the official seminar we would go for coffee, drink coffee together. But, when we come back to Mostar, no one goes to coffee with anyone else. No one wants that. Because seminars . . . they are not about true friendships.
> Azra: What is true friendship for you?

Nermina: True friendship is when I have a need to call you and have coffee with you, and that I do not have any secrets in front of you, and that I celebrate New Year's and birthday parties with that person and . . . that you can talk about anything, in a relaxed manner with that person . . . Because, with them [Croats] I can talk about a lamp, how nice it is, or about cosmetics, and stuff like that . . . but about politics and the war you cannot talk to them, because our opinions differ. Because, there are three truths [the Serb, the Croat, and the Bosniak truth] here now, and you have one *narod* (nation, people) whose 8,000 people were slaughtered in Srebrenica, but that very same narod killed 100 Croats in Drežnica,[12] and everyone looks at their truth and pain.

This quote illustrates multiple dimensions and limitations of postwar mixing and the growing estrangement among ethnically conceived populations in Mostar. This distancing is promoted by the war-destruction and postwar lack of spaces of cross-ethnic public sociality where joint smoking and coffee drinking, as core practices of prewar mixing, could take place. Advancing these practices is discouraged by the tripartite nexus of spatial governmentality, tenacious official politics of ethnic nationalisms, and ethnicization of everyday life in Mostar.

This larger context of (un)mixing made the school bathroom truly unique—in this subversive space, students consciously disciplined their bodies in order to engage in creation of a "smoking community" and a dialogue across (ethnic) difference. Youth's willingness to engage in these practices made visible the tension at the heart of postwar spatial governmentality—the absence of shared geography in the city where youth could drink coffee, smoke, and continue to learn about each other by confronting the past and engaging in a dialogue about a shared future. Regardless of the marginal nature of bathroom mixing, ethnic boundaries and ethnic identifications that have been twisted this way challenge the consociational model of ethnically separated groups, even if temporarily. This membership in the "bathroom community" is thus more extensive than "simple" student solidarity against the authority (Devine 1996). In other words, these subversive and politically uncultivated practices of bathroom mixing subtly work away at the constricted and constricting ethnopolitical logic and spatial governmentality at the school. At the same time, these playfully executed, resistant cultural practices are not separable from the history of mixing and the context of segregation and violence in which they materialize, to which they eventually refer, and with which they stay entwined. In this way, bathroom mixing is both a transformation of the traditional practices of mixing and a commentary on the suffocating nature and profound limitations of the current sociopolitical order.

New interactions among students within the bathroom walls, however, do not destroy the barriers between youth and do not create a long-lasting sense of groupness. More likely, these interactions both challenge and reassert existing ethnic identities. Furthermore, the contact across ethnic lines gives rise to competing feelings of memories of violence, narratives of victimhood and fear on the one side, and a hint of enthusiasm and hope for some form of shared future on the other. In the context of consociationalism, mixing practices emerge as bathroom-contained, socially undesirable, and politically uncultivated forms of sociality and politics.

And yet, the restricted opportunity for spontaneous interaction in the bathroom provides a minimal but promising prospect for the acknowledgement of "the other"; it offers a space for deepening social sensibility and democratic possibility, even if imperfect and provisional. The school bathroom, regardless of its malodorous and grimy setting, is a unique, dynamic, and heterogeneous social sphere, produced in the cracks between ethnic territories. In this unique space, mixing as a long-standing practice of public solidarity continues, albeit changed, alongside consociational democracy. As a result, the school bathroom at the first reunified school is possibly the most productive place for grasping how students maneuver, more or less successfully, the complexities of ethnic identifications, nationalist aspirations, spatial governmentality, and consociational democracy.

PART II

Disintegrating the Nation

Chapter 4

Poetics of Nationhood

In early October 2005, I attended a three-day workshop organized by the Mostar branches of OSCE and the Nansen Dialogue Center.[1] The workshop brought together a large number of student representatives in an attempt to initiate a Union of Student Councils in Herzegovina.[2] For many of these seventeen- and eighteen-year-olds, this was a rare opportunity to spend a prolonged period of time with students from other ethnic groups.

The location of the workshop was Neum, once a nice coastal town on the Adriatic Sea. Today, Neum is the only noteworthy town on the Bosnia-Herzegovina coast. Bosnia-Herzegovina encompasses twenty-three kilometers of the Adriatic seashore, the section of the coast squeezed between two parts of the Croatian shoreline. Unlike the nearby glamorous Croatian cities of Dubrovnik and Split, Neum is a depressed and lifeless town. Most of the buildings and hotels were built during the socialist era in the fashion appropriate for that time: large, cold, uniform, seemingly functional gray buildings. At the time of the workshop, besides their communist heritage, these buildings displayed bullet holes from the recent war that were especially visible when illuminated by the late October sun. Only the sea, which I could see stretching below the rooftops of the cascading hotels, and its crystal-clear, fluorescent waves that devotedly kissed the shore of this devastated country, brought a breeze of relief to the town and its visitors.

At the end of the second day of the conference at the Zenit hotel, I joined a group of students at the table for dinner. The tables were covered with clean pink tablecloths, on top of which were smaller, square-shaped blue napkins. I chose the chair between Mima and Lana, whom I had befriended earlier that day. I could hardly recognize them; they had changed into their party clothes and put on heavy makeup. The waiter took

Figure 6. Workshop in Neum, fall 2005. Photo by author.

our order; the two girls requested a regional specialty, the "mixed meat" dish. Mima giggled and commented: "Lana (Croat) and I (Bosniak) like to mix, so we like to order mixed meat," they laughed, as Lana added, "We *do* like it mixed."

At our table were also Sabina and Saša, both from the Republika Srpska. The five of us started nonchalantly talking about traveling, "the sore zone of cultural sensitivity" (Herzfeld 2005:x), since many Bosnian youth have never traveled outside the country due to a strict visa regime at the time and economic despair. The youth from the Republika Srpska explained to me that they had Bosnian passports, but the stamp said Republika Srpska. Next to Sabina and Saša sat Andrea and Iva from Medeno Polje, a small, homogeneously Croat, economically developed town in western Herzegovina. They joined us in conversation. Sabina and Saša were shocked to learn that Andrea and Iva had Croatian passports and not Bosnian ones. "No way," said Saša, who applied his experience from the Republika Srpska to make sense of Andrea's and Iva's situation, "you probably have Bosnia-Herzegovina passports with a Croat stamp in it." "No," I jumped in, "they have *real* Croatian passports, the same ones that people in Croatia have." Andrea and Iva felt obliged to explain the issue to Saša: "Of course we have Croat passports, we are Croats." Saša moved impatiently in his chair, which squeaked under the pressure of his body: "But you live in Bosnia-Herzegovina." Andrea interrupted him: "No, we live in Croatia. I love Croatia. My capital city is Zagreb." Saša's voice raised and he turned red in his face: "I also feel that Belgrade is in my heart, but I cannot say that it is my capital city. I live in Bosnia-Herzegovina."

We fell silent for a moment. . . .

Saša turned to his other side, to the place where Muris sat. He touched Muris's bony shoulder covered by a red shirt with a picture of Tito on its front. Muris turned to us. Saša: "Muris, where are you from?" Muris: "From Skokovi." Saša: "Besides that?" Muris: "From Bosnia-Herzegovina." Saša: "Thank you! God! In my town you cannot pass from the second into the third grade if you do not know what Bosnia-Herzegovina is and how it came about."

This lengthy field entry alludes to the clashing notions of peoplehood[3] and nationhood[4] embraced by youth in Bosnia-Herzegovina. It was at that dinner table in Neum that I realized I was observing youth coming of age as three separate ethnically and territorially divided groups of people. The physical proximity among youth during the workshop provided an ideal opportunity to observe how they interacted across the lines of politicized ethnicity. One of the things that continually surprised me was the extent of the social gap among them; two decades of living in the aftermath of forced unmixing and destruction of "the common house" powerfully shaped their group experiences. Andrea's comment at the end of our dinner captured this phenomenon: "I wish I lived during the times of Brotherhood and Unity but I did not. We had some exercise at school the other day, we had to recognize the facial characteristics of different groups of peoples, different races . . . and everyone in my class said I looked like a Serb." Then, half-embarrassed, half-excited, she added, "actually, like a Serb singer."[5] She made a short break in her speech and then concluded, with a voice echoing sincerity, "I like Serbs . . . Serbs are so exotic to me!!!"

While Andrea's statements encapsulate multiple ideas, knowledges, and views about diversity, "race," and intimacy, what interests me the most here is Andrea's concluding sentence: "Serbs are so exotic to me!" which reveals the profound sociocultural change in Bosnia-Herzegovina. For those educated in socialist Yugoslavia, exotic things were those unknown, foreign, mystical things, places, and peoples that one only imagines, essentializes, totalizes, and admires from afar, such as Pacific Islands, United States, Asia, Latin America, and Africa. We were taught (also problematically, in an orientalist fashion) that those people lived very different, foreign, and exciting lives, outside our reach or our comprehension. Following this logic, the "others" in Bosnia-Herzegovina, except maybe for the traveling Roma, could not be exotic to "us" because "they" lived next to us; we visited "them" at home, "we" played with "them" in front of our apartment buildings, and "we" shared our desks in school with "them." Through these practices we learned that the "others" were very similar (if not identical) to "us," regardless of our different-sounding names and occasional discoveries of dissimilarity, such as the time when my Serb friend's mother served her beans with delicious pork meat sausage, something people in my family and many other Muslim families rarely did. These differences were apparent to most of us, but we understood them in relation to the shared cultural idioms, values, habits, political projects, and rituals of daily life. These shared expressions existed even in those few regions in prewar Bosnia-Herzegovina that were more ethnically homogeneous, but where people often came in contact with ethnic others through schooling, trading (attending market fairs), and mandatory (for men) army service.

These conflicting yet related processes and their effects become especially visible when youth discuss their political and social affiliations, coordinates of belonging to the postwar state, and especially the interpretations, articulations, and practices that youth assign to the notion of *narod*. "Unpacking" the multiple usages and connotations of the category narod allows for a deeper understanding of the emergence, maintenance, and transformation of peoplehood, statehood, and nationhood in the context of external state-making in Bosnia-Herzegovina. It reveals youth's stance that being Bosnian, Serb, Croat, and Bosnian and Herzegovinian both enriches and restricts them. It also discloses contrasting images, sentiments, and obligations that they associate with their country, and it shows how those contribute to their views on patriotism, ethnicity, and nationalism. Youth's expressions of what Brubaker calls the "idioms of nationhood" or "thinking and talking about cultural and political belonging at the level of the nation-state" (Brubaker 1992:162) therefore illustrate how the majority of young Bosnians-Herzegovinians, lacking identification with a cohesive nation, became alienated from the state and its institutions, including the rights and responsibilities of formal citizenship.

Notes on Narod

Since the early days of my ethnographic fieldwork, I have been puzzled by the scope, contextuality, contradictions, and irony that the term narod connotes. The scope of narod is truly remarkable—as a discourse, it circulates among people of all religious, ethnic, gender, and age backgrounds. It saturates ordinary speech, ethnic and interethnic encounters on streets and markets, in public and private spaces, in rumors and popular critiques, in political campaigns and economic endeavors. The capacity of narod as an analytic term to capture both ethnic (exclusionary, homogenizing) belonging and above-ethnic (inclusionary, heterogeneous) identifications provoked my anthropological curiosity—a very similar productive tension between inclusion and exclusion, similarity and difference, unity and disunity, and centripetal and centrifugal forces, is at the very heart of all anthropological endeavors.

The majority of works that address groupness in Bosnia-Herzegovina focus on narod as an ethnic category of belonging. This is understandable since during and after the war, ethnic cleavages were politicized and ethnonationally conceptualized; homogeneous narod rooted in ethnic territories emerged as the most powerful form of identity and politics that structures perception, informs thought and experience, and organizes discourse and political action. Regardless of this prevalent meaning of narod, the ethnic dimension of narod does not capture all the meanings of the term, since it "does not exhaust the various layers of selfhood of a person" (Chatterjee 1998:280). Rather, in this wider, beyond, in-between, and below ethnicity sense, narod continues to lurk and shape discourses of identification and politics of possibility among ordinary Bosnians and Herzegovinians.

As a result of this multidimensionality, narod emerged as a popular icon of academic literature that focuses on the former Yugoslavia. Regardless of its popularity, it escapes an easy definition, since it connotes multiple, conflicting and context-dependent, meanings at once. For example, narod does not make the distinction between people and nation (Woodward 1995:30). This array of meanings that escape easy translation has been addressed by several anthropologists and other scholars of the Balkans, who warned against seeing collective identity in prewar Bosnia-Herzegovina through the prism of Western idioms of group identity. According to these scholars, transplanting "Western" terminology to the Balkan context tends to flatten and assimilate different forms of local collective identity into the

Western models of nation and ethnicity (Sorabji 1995). For example, Sorabji (87) warns against the common practice of translating the Bosnian/Croat/Serbian term narod into the English word "nation," since this leads to the simplification and misapprehension of local identity politics.

Furthermore, in the former Yugoslavia, especially during the early years of its post-World War II existence, narod formed a part of the official state's doctrine. In that context, it had two different meanings: on the one hand, it referred to all Yugoslavs as a type of collectivity, where narods were different but their difference become meaningful only in the context of their interconnectedness (see Sorabji 1995), thus including people of all nations, nationalities, and ethnic groups who fought for the liberation of the country from German and Italian occupation (Torsti 2003). In this way, narod included the popular motto "Brotherhood and Unity" and it was often associated with Narodno-Oslobodilačka Borba (The People's Liberation Movement) during World War II. As a consequence of this understanding and promotion of narod as a collectivity of all Yugoslavs, during the early years of the Yugoslav regime, there was support for the creation of a unified Yugoslav nation (Ramet 1992:51). After 1964, however, Tito started to promote a different idea of Yugoslavism—an organic unity where multiple and different groups would coexist together in harmony (Burić 2011; Ramet 1992). Understood as a synchronization of many different parts, Yugoslav narod is not a concept easily translatable into the Western idea of a nation.

In addition to indexing Yugoslav unity of diverse groups, the category *narod* was used during the Titoist regime to index six institutionalized nations (*narodi*) in Yugoslavia living side by side: Serbs, Croats, Muslims, Macedonians, Slovenians, and Montenegrins. Some scholars suggest that the success of communist leadership after 1943 stems from their willingness to recognize the separate existence of Yugoslav nations (Woodward 1995:30). These nations were different, in the official discourse, from *narodnosti* (pl.) meaning "nationalities" or "people," which included Hungarians, Albanians, Italians, and others. The main reason for the official distinction between narod and *narodnost* was that *narodnosti* did not live "wholly or mainly within the borders of Yugoslavia—most Albanians live in Albania, and most Hungarians in Hungary, and so forth" (Sorabji 1995:88).

Besides *narodi* and *narodnosti*, there was a third term in circulation, *etničke grupe* or "ethnic groups." This label was reserved for those groups that lacked their own kin-based states, such as Roma (Bieber 2005:17). This understanding of ethnicity was quite different from the official discourse today where *etničke grupe* largely replaced the idiom narod. This "replacement" was stimulated by outsiders who were trying to make sense of the "Balkan crisis"; Western media, politicians, policy-makers, and academics framed the wars of the Yugoslav secession as *ethnic wars* between *ethnic groups* (see Gagnon n.d.). For example, Gagnon (n.d.) shows how from the very beginning of the Bosnian war, every peace plan put forward by the international diplomatic community rested on the "territorialization of ethnicity and ethnicization of territory" (see also Campbell 1999). The vision of ethnic groups was also readily embraced by the regional and local conservative political elites, who used the protection of ethnic groups discourse to monopolize the political field and demobilize the opposition (Gagnon 2004; Gordy 1999). This understanding of an ethnic group linguistically remodeled and flattened multiple connotations of *narodi* into singular, territorially separated, and homogeneous ethnic groups at the expense of the heterogeneity of life projects, political subjectivities, and social relationships.

The meanings of narod are even more numerous and complicated. The Yugoslav state presented a view of all Yugoslav Serbs, regardless where they lived within Yugoslavia, as one narod, all its Croats as one narod, all its Muslims as one narod, and so forth (Sorabji 1995:89). At the same time, however, the Serbs in Serbia and Croats in Croatia experienced themselves as different from Bosnian Serbs and Bosnian Croats, whom they viewed as culturally primitive and backward, but also hospitable, easygoing, temperamental, and warm (Sorabji 1995:89). Bosnian Muslims, while employing the same pattern of differentiation, saw themselves as separate and different, meaning more advanced and developed, than Muslims living in the region of Sandžak, a territory carved at the intersection between Serbia, Montenegro, and Bosnia-Herzegovina, and mostly populated by Muslims (89). Therefore, Bosnian Serbs, Bosnian Croats, and Bosnian Muslims perceived themselves and were perceived by others as Bosnian, in addition to being members of other nations within Yugoslavia. This interconnectedness is visible in the use of the identity marker *Bosanac* (Bosnian) during the Yugoslav times. This term was used by Bosnians themselves and others in Yugoslavia when talking about the residents of Bosnia-Herzegovina (Bringa 1993:34). *Bosanac* at that time indexed not nationhood, but rather territorial identity and membership in the Yugoslav Republic of Bosnia-Herzegovina. The interconnectedness among different groups within

Bosnia-Herzegovina that the term *Bosanac* encapsulates emerged mainly due to shared history and geography, and the fact that in "prewar Bosnia the settlement patterns of the three groups were mixed in large parts of the country . . . and that Bosniaks, Serbs, [and] Croats of Bosnia speak the same language and have largely similar traditions and cultural habits" (Bieber 2005:2). The three ethnic groups coexisted together, intermingled, sharing their differences, and managing the tensions that frequently arose from living in close proximity (Bringa 1995). The shared notion *Bosanac* was thus understood as a republic-wide, *territorial* identity. The territorial overlap generated shared cultural practices and intimacies, regardless of the three groups' different memberships and identifications with larger, transrepublic ethnonational groups within Yugoslavia.

In everyday vernacular, narod also refers to "people" or "a people" (the French, the Germans, etc.) (Bringa 1993). Understood as "people," narod implies a certain level of collective identity and shared sentiment (Sorabji 1995:88), visible in the popular phrases such as "people are disappointed" or "Bosnians are very hospitable." Here narod designates a group's experiences of shared sentiment and popular politics. This notion of narod is different from the notion *običan svijet* (ordinary world, people) or *obični ljudi* (ordinary people), which designate individuals who feel a certain way, but do not imply cohesiveness or group-like characteristics (Sorabji 1995:88). Where I depart from Sorabji's otherwise brilliant discussion of narod is in the interpretation of narod as *običan svijet*. Unlike Sorabji, I understand *običan svijet* as a site of an intricate political work and negotiation. As we will see in the final part of this chapter, ordinary people utilize and emphasize precisely this unsettled, nonthreatening, and apparently apolitical notion of narod to provide a space for solidarity and "popular politics"—to emphasize common suffering of all "normal people and children" regardless of their ethnicity. As a result, narod functions as a discursive mechanism to separate oneself from *politika* (and by extension from injustice, indecency, greed, dirtiness, and corruption) and to project a glimpse of a sociopolitical and economic vision of the future which is "rid of immoral force of *politika*" (Kolind 2007:127).

Transborder Ethnic Nations

In order to better understand how youth in Bosnia-Herzegovina view and experience their country(ies) and their nation(s), I take the institutionalized ethnic categories of political belonging as the point of departure. While I am aware that the category "constituent peoples" is malleable, contested, and complicated, the level of its institutionalization in the service of statemaking, peace-building, and "progress" is overwhelming.

Today, in the era of pervasive ethnonational ideologies, boundary-making along ethnic lines is perceived as crucial for the realization of a group envisioned as a homogeneous cultural unit (I. Lovrenović 2001).[6] The ethnicization of everyday life is underscored by the politics of spatial governmentality as the foundation for consociational democracy. Implementation of these dominant visions of plurality and politics of governance leads to the constant reinsertion of separate nationhood and peoplehood, and it seals social distance created through "ethnic cleansing" during the war. These phenomena are especially visible in towns where people physically coexist, work, and go to school together. For example, in my secondary research site, the small northwestern town that I call Bijelo Brdo, the physical proximity (Bosniaks and Serbs live in homes sometimes next to each other) is diminished by what my informants called "podjela u glavi" (division in people's heads), which shapes one's exposure to diversity as secondary and yet intimately related and hegemonically connected to the homogeneous, ethnically constituted idea of groupness. This ideology of *ethnic* narod is manifested in people's movement through social space: in walking only on certain sides of streets, in frequenting only certain coffee shops, or in visiting only people of one's ethnic group at home. With time, *podjela u glavi* does not disappear but widens since it becomes habitual and embodied, even if people cross sides of divided towns more than they did immediately after the war.

A member of the school board at the Mostar Gymnasium captured this growing spatial and mental distance among ethnically conceived narods when she commented how her son "has a fear of the unknown, and he does not know their [Croat] names because he does not encounter the names from the other side of the river in everyday life. And it is not only a physical distance—it is a mental distance as well." In other words, this young man in Mostar and others similar to him walk by each other on the streets of their shared but segregated town frequently, oblivious to their connected histories and cultural similarities. This crack in social space and cultural knowledge erases the traditional and Bosnia-specific practices of mixing and the sensibility it generates. I. Lovrenović describes this sensibility as "a feeling for otherness, for different as part of the daily reality of one's most personal environment" (I. Lovrenović 2001:209). Through the war-produced ethnicization of political and social life, this "feeling for otherness" has been crippled and as a consequence, "Bosnians have ceased to be Bosnian and became just Muslims, Serbs, and Croats" (209).

Intrigued by these political changes that lead to the spatial and social separation of *Bosanci* into the three ethnic groups, I searched for conversation on this topic. One of the people who attempted to explain the workings of social distancing to me was a teacher at the Mostar Gymnasium, who commented that "despite the depth that we have—so much intermixing, interconnections in the country we share, and so many religious objects so close to each other . . . despite the shared heritage in habits, in practice, and in life, we absolutely do not know each other. This creates a gap—huge gap and mistrust." The lack of transethnic spaces of sociality, sharing, exchange, and everyday communication in Mostar creates an ideal background against which ethnic nationhood can flourish at the expense of common peoplehood.

Bosniaks: The Keepers of the Bosnian State?

I am sitting in the Bosnian language class with IV-2. The classroom is bright, absorbing the light reflected from the white rocks surrounding Mostar. It is almost too bright to keep my eyes open. The teacher is explaining the works of Meša Selimović, one of Bosnia's most famous authors. She opens the discussion by saying how Bosniak writers of that time (1960s and 1970s) wrote the most beautiful literature, much nicer than the Croat and Serb authors were creating. Amel, who is sitting in the middle row, interrupts and says:

> Teacher, may I ask you something? I found it on the Internet that Meša Selimović's family was *poturčena* [converted to Islam, "made Turkish"], and that later in his life he declared himself a Serb, and that his philosophy was Serb?
> Amna: Devil take him!
> Sandra [whose father is Muslim and whose mother is Serb]: Good job Meša!
> Teacher: Our people were *ni na nebu, ni na zemlji* ["not in the sky, not on the earth" meaning lost, in between]. Their uniqueness was not recognized. You knew deep down, in your soul, who you were,

but you had to keep your mouth shut and you had to declare your identity in one of the two existing categories [Serb or Croat], because the third one did not exist. When this author was writing, the Serb influence was the strongest so he declared himself a Serb. And Ivo Andrić [the Bosnia-Herzegovina Nobel prize winner, the author of the famous novel *The Bridge on the Drina*] declared himself a Serb but now Croats claim him as a Croat writer. Even Mak Dizdar . . . why did he give himself that nickname, Mak, and why did he not keep his Muslim name, Mehmedalija? Because Mak sounds Croat! Those were the circumstances under which they worked, at those times. But their works say it all. Indeed, their works were crucial so others could realize that there were *special*, third people [in Bosnia-Herzegovina]. Their works are an attempt to show to the public that they were not Serbs nor Croats, but something third, something *special*.

Adis: But you say that narod did not know if it was *na nebu ili na zemlji, ni tamo ni 'vamo* [not here not there]. So why do not we study them as Yugoslav writers if they declared to be that? Why do we claim their work?

Sandra applauds.

Teacher: We do not allege anything. That work belongs to the literature of the Bosniak people. Croats and Serbs, they are the ones who claim the works of others, because they say that Andrić is a Serb or a Croat writer but he is a Bosnian writer, his work talks about Bosnia-Herzegovina people.

Amna: But teacher, how does it happen that a man is reduced to something . . . Bosnia is what we should use in this case, we should not use Bosniak. Because today Bosniak means Muslim, Croat means Catholic and Serb means Orthodox . . .

Teacher: But Bosniak does not mean Muslim!

Amna: But that is what it became, and what are those people who are none of the three?

Teacher: How would you call them?

Amna: Well, you will laugh now, teacher, but, I do not know, maybe BosHerc [slang for Bosnia(n) Heart].

Laughter.

This anecdote captures, among many other things, the changing content of the Bosniak narod. The fluidity between Bosnia and Bosniak is clearly demonstrated by the teacher's explanation where she calls Andrić a Bosnian writer whose work fits under the corpus of Bosniak literature, but it cannot fit under the rubric of Croat literature. Here, the Bosnian-Herzegovinian identity and the Bosniak identity are equated, leaving the combination of simultaneous Bosnian Croat and Bosnia-Herzegovina identity unanswered. When confronted by the students who want to probe, complicate, resist, and resolve these tensions, the teacher uses the story of past inequalities to explain the unique nature of Bosniak identity and its special importance for Bosnian literature.

This instance of conflation between Bosniak and Bosnian is not isolated. There is a growing perception among many, primarily non-Bosniak citizens in Bosnia-Herzegovina that, in reality, Bosnia-Herzegovina is a true homeland only for Bosniaks, and not for its other constituent people. As Tamara told me, "that is only normal since both Croats and Serbs have their 'real' homelands, Croatia and the Republika Srpska, respectively, while Bosniaks only have Bosnia-Herzegovina." A slightly different explanation but one that reflects the same thinking pattern, was provided by a Bosniak American high-school student I met in Syracuse, New York, in the spring of 2011. This young man became a refugee at age one, when in 1995, he was forced to flee from his eastern Bosnian town, together with his family, relatives, and other town residents. While nostalgically talking about Bosnia, he concluded: "When I think of Bosnia, I think Bosniak . . . because that is who the real Bosnians are . . . the Bosniaks. And Serbs and Croats in Bosnia, well, hmm, they are something like immigrants there."

This view of Bosnia-Herzegovina as not being a true homeland to more than half of its population powerfully shapes the contours of the Bosnia-Herzegovina state, which emerges as politically and emotionally deserted by its non-Bosniak youth citizens. In addition, the "true" homelands of Croat and Serb youth in Bosnia-Herzegovina, Croatia and the Republika Srpska respectively, are often imagined in terms of Croat and Serb nationhood. These nations stretch across the existing territorial boundaries of Bosnia-Herzegovina, thus frequently incorporating the sections of Bosnian territory in which Bosnian Croats and Bosnian Serbs live, leaving behind only a *fildžan*[7] state for Bosniaks.

Open identifications of the Croat and Serb students with their external homelands created anger and disbelief among the Bosniak students in Bijelo Brdo. Those students told me that the "other" youth were brainwashed by their parents and teachers and that they suffered, as a consequence, some *poremećaj* (disturbance) in their political views and emotions. These students expressed disappointment in their Serb and Croat friends at the school, and they repeatedly stressed that Bosnia-Herzegovina is a multiethnic country that belongs to all three peoples and others who live in it.

All the students whom I interviewed and who self-identified as Bosniaks said that Bosnia-Herzegovina was their *domovina* (homeland), that they had no other home, and that regardless of its many problems and the fact that they would want to leave it if they could, they still loved it dearly. In their response to my question "What does Bosnia-Herzegovina mean to you?" Bosniak students typically wrote: "Bosnia-Herzegovina is the country in which I live, it is my domovina. Different peoples have lived here for centuries, including Muslims, Serbs, Croats, Gypsies . . . I love my country and proudly say that I am *Bosanka* [Bosnian for female]."

Bosniak students in general expressed deep devotion to Bosnia-Herzegovina. What underscored this attitude was an idea that what really makes Bosnia-Herzegovina special is its Bosniak flavor. Under this worldview, the special domain of Bosnia-Herzegovina, understood as a crossroad of three constituent, equal peoples, is its Bosniak element, which is articulated in its *Baščaršija*,[8] its traditional architecture, its *Sevdah*,[9] and a special type of Islam born at the crossroad of east and west. Without these elements Bosnia would be, as one youth told me, yet another Christian country in Europe. This perception of a special place of Bosniaks within Bosnia-Herzegovina is also captured and analyzed by Torsti (2003), who writes that in the Bosnian history text book, there were two levels of the "we" group: "the territorially-defined Bosnian nation, and the ethnically-defined Muslim nation . . . and a common construction of the book served to present an event or occurrence first from the Bosnian point of view, and then particularly from the point of view of *Muslims, who were seen as true Bosnians* defending common values and so forth" (252, emphasis added).

The additional element of apparent Bosniak uniqueness is related to the recent war experience. This feeling is often supported by statistics; numerically, the majority of the war victims were the Bosniaks. This sense of victimhood generates a stance among the Bosniak population that they deserve to be in charge of the state in order to, among other things, prevent history from repeating itself. This attitude is clearly expressed by Sabina, a student from Bijelo Brdo, who complained that "in my town, there are constant fights [between Serbs and Bosniaks], especially during the religious holidays. In the eyes of [Serb] individuals you see hate, *they would slaughter us, if they could.* It is good that we are still the majority here because if they outnumber us, *loše nam se piše* [bad destiny is awaiting us]!"

Sabina criticizes continuous divisions and mistrust among the two peoples sharing this small, devastated town. Her fears and suspicions about the other ethnic group's motivations are only lessened by the fact that Bosniaks are the majority in her town and her country. Furthermore, Sabina believes that for the sake of their survival, Bosniaks have to be in the majority. Therefore, the attitude of "equal constituent people" is complex: the idioms of multiculturalism among the Bosniaks rest on the notion of *ravnopravnost* or "having the same rights"—Torsti coins this Bosniak attitude as "pannationalism" or nationalism that can include several nations without competition among them (Torsti 2003:244). This notion of pannationalism is strikingly similar to Tito's vision of harmonious Yugoslavism as constituted by different but equal, united, and harmonious, *narodi* and *narodnosti*. At the same time, the idea of *ravnopravnost* also allows for Bosniak dominance. This justification of (moral and political) superiority of Bosniaks among *ravnopravni narodi* (equal nations) is common among the majority of ordinary Bosniaks and especially among Bosniak politicians and government officials. This apparent right to be in control is threefold: it is justified by decades of nonrecognition in the former Yugoslavia, by the disproportionate suffering of Bosniaks during the recent war, and by the special input that Bosniaks contribute to the Bosnia-Herzegovina cultural landscape and *merhametli* social life.[10]

This position of Bosniak superiority within Bosnia-Herzegovina is rejected by many young, urban "Bosniaks," who feel bitter about the contours and substance of their Bosniak identity. One of these youth, Emil, once told me impatiently: "*Nemoj mi, molim te, tog Bošnjakluka!*" (Please, do not bother me with that Bosniakhood). A few years later, in August 2008, I was walking around Sarajevo with a group of friends. It was getting cold, so we took a cab home. The radio in the cab was on, and we caught the end of the news, announcing the most recent success of Bosnia-Herzegovina cinematography; the local film and its director, a young Bosnian woman, won a prestigious award at an international film festival. Visibly annoyed, one of my friends commented: "Listen, please, they called her *Bošnjakinja* (feminine for *Bošnjak*)! Remember how we used to joke about that term when it became popular in the 1990s. We would see each other on the street and say jokingly, '*Šta ima Bošnjaci*' (What's up, Bosniaks)? Horrible! Look what happened—we are surrounded by millions of Bosniaks!"

There is a profound anxiety among numerous people in Bosnia-Herzegovina, Bosniaks and others, that the country is becoming increasingly Bosniak. The capital of Bosnia-Herzegovina, Sarajevo, as one of the frequently celebrated symbols of ethnic coexistence and multiculturalism in Europe (sometimes referred to as "the European Jerusalem"), is becoming, those critics suggest, a Bosniak city. This rising discomfort about the possible transformation of the multiconfessional city into a Bosniak, Muslim-dominated one does not explain the other groups' detachment from their native country, but it makes it simpler and easier to articulate and defend, and gives it more power to manifest itself abundantly. The fact that more and more Serbs and Croats are leaving Sarajevo for their "true homelands" or the regions within Bosnia-Herzegovina where they are in the majority is commonly explained as a reaction to Sarajevo becoming increasingly Bosniak.

Croatia Is My Homeland

One day in spring 2006, I decided to skip the third class and spend some time with the students "on duty." There were three young men sitting in the small room next to the main entrance; two of them were on duty today, the third one skipped most classes. I joined them at the moment when they were discussing *ekskurzija* or the main school excursion, which usually takes place at the end of the junior or the beginning of the senior year of high school. The trip involves seven days of travel to some exotic country (often Greece for Serbs, Spain or France for Croats, and Turkey for Bosniaks). I asked the student from the Croat curriculum why they postponed their trip to France. He explained that there were some problems with French visas. I was confused since most Croats have passports of the Republic of Croatia, the citizens of which needed no visa to visit France. I shared my confusion with the student, who further explained: "Most of us have Croat passports, but my passport expired, and it takes two months to have it renewed in Zagreb. So, because I needed it fast, I got myself the Muslim passport!"

This incident shows that for this student, Bosnia-Herzegovina and its symbols, such as its passport, are experienced as Muslim (Bosniak). Tomislav, a Croat student living in west Mostar summarizes this attitude by saying: "No one can feel Bosnia as their own state but Bosniaks. It is one shitty country, without any perspective." Interestingly, Tomislav's comment hints at the fact that the main reason for his detachment from the state is not necessarily his loyalty to Croatia, but the fact that Bosnia-Herzegovina cannot offer him any perspective for a successful future. Tomislav's friend Ivo was less descriptive when answering my question "What does Bosnia-Herzegovina mean to you?" He "simply" said: "Nothing at all."

In addition to being equated with Bosniaks, Bosnia-Herzegovina was seen as something confusing, underdeveloped, backward, and unneeded for the majority of young Herzegovina Croats whom I befriended during my fieldwork. For example, Vanja said: "How can I have two nationalities? It is weird, that thing about identity—I go to Sarajevo and they tell me 'You are a Bosnian Catholic, not a Croat [Catholic]!' But I am not [a Bosnian Catholic], I am a Croat Catholic!"[11] Vanja's friend Marijana listened carefully while Vanja explained her confusion to me. Then she concluded: "Yes, that Bosnia-Herzegovina . . . is something . . . that Bosnian identity is not developed, it is not clear to us what it is."

The Croat youth I befriended, when talking about Bosnia-Herzegovina, spoke about the country as if it was a remote entity they never "feel," "see," or "live"; as something they do not often encounter in their lives. The Croatia-oriented education, services, and opportunities they received from that state, and the relative prosperity of Croatia, direct Croat youth toward Croatia, and leave their relationship to Bosnia-Herzegovina vague and undeveloped. In history classes, these students primarily studied events important for the country of Croatia, and the world events were explained and discussed from the Croat point of view. In geography class, until recently,[12] students in the Croat curriculum studied only the regions, currency, anthem, and borders of Croatia, mentioning Bosnia-Herzegovina only as its neighboring country. Knowledge of Bosnia-Herzegovina's history and geography among Croat youth, especially those from western Herzegovina, is for the most part absent.[13] This became noticeable during our dinner in Neum, when I had an opportunity to talk with the youth of the three groups simultaneously.

> Andrea smiles and says: We do not know anything about it [Bosnia-Herzegovina]. We have straight As in school, maybe that is a problem . . . they do not teach us about that stuff in school, they only teach us about Croatia and Croat narod.
> Azra: So what do you know about Bosnia-Herzegovina?

Poetics of Nationhood   121

Iva: Well, nothing really . . . actually I do know that there are three entities[14] and that there are Serbs, Muslims, and Croats living in it.
Azra: If Croats live in Herzegovina, where do the others live?
Andrea: They live in the north, and they are . . . as I imagine it now in my head, they are all mixed there. I think they live in this corner—she gestures as if pointing at the corner of the heart-shaped country on an imaginary picture in the air above her head. For example, today was the first time that I heard that Republika Srpska exists in Herzegovina. Oh, I am shocked! I am not sure what Republika Srpska is and where it is. I had no clue it was in Bosnia-Herzegovina. Maybe they did cover that in the second grade [U.S. tenth grade], but I was living in Zagreb then. But, we in Medeno Polje, study about Croatia, its poetry, history . . .
Iva: I do not know anything about it. In geography class we only learn about some industry, but I do not know the name of the hill near Medeno [Polje].

Andrea recites all the geographic regions in Croatia, with no hesitation or confusion. She knows her regions. Satisfied with her performance, Andrea turns to me, her face smiling, her cheeks pink, and her eyes full of excitement.

Later than night, Andrea and Iva told me that Croat youth are in possession of Croat passports and that the majority of them do not think about applying for a Bosnia-Herzegovina passport: "Who needs that one, you need a visa everywhere you go!" Croat students told me. Most of them, including my new friends Andrea and Iva, planned to attend the universities in Croatia, or if they could not afford them, in west Mostar. Sanja, a Croat student from Mostar, was the only one among hundreds of Croat students I met during my fieldwork who told me that she would like to study in Sarajevo. Sanja was on Bosnia-Herzegovina's junior karate team and she represented the colors of that country in numerous international competitions. She admitted that, at first, she wanted to be on the Croat karate team, but it did not work out. Now, she told me, she is grateful to be on the Bosnia-Herzegovina team.[15]

Sometimes, to attend international workshops, Croat students had to balance their loyalties, at least officially, between Bosnia-Herzegovina and

Croatia. From time to time several students were chosen by different international organizations to be the Croat youth representatives of Bosnia-Herzegovina at international events, and for that purpose they have to travel on Bosnia-Herzegovina passports with other youth from that country. Many Croat students found this annoying and bureaucratically complicated since they needed to first obtain a Bosnia-Herzegovina passport and then apply for visas, while they need no visas for many countries when traveling with Croatian travel documents. In addition, a problem arose when these students were expected to represent Bosnia-Herzegovina at these gatherings. Marijana explains:

> Marijana: You ask me where I belong . . . that question is very complex. When we went to Amerika [United States] on a trip, we knew exactly when we *had to* say that we were from Bosnia-Herzegovina and when we *could* say that we were from Croatia.
> Azra: Is that not confusing?
> Marijana: Well, it is. It is very complex. I am *Hrvatica* [a Croat woman], *Hercegovka* [woman from Herzegovina] and a citizen of Bosnia-Herzegovina. And who am I really, I do not know how to call that . . .
> Azra: Bosnia-Herzegovina?
> Marijana: Yeah, everyone in our group was saying that. But only Bosniaks feel Bosnia as their domovina, because they do not have another domovina as the Serbs and we do. When we were in the United States, for example, Sajra from Zenica wanted to show to our hosts the type of flag we had before this new flag. And she took out of her suitcase the flag with the lilies.[16] Then Aleksandar from Banja Luka took out the flag of Serbia and he said: "This is our flag." It was so tense . . . I have another example for you. During our stay in the United States, our hosts took us to some cave where you could write on the walls. We all hurriedly signed our names. Dejan, you know him, was in there forever, engraving something into the rock. I came up to him and I saw that he wrote CROATIA in big, capital letters. When the others saw what he did, they started to shout: "Why did you do that? Aren't we all here together because we are from Bosnia-Herzegovina?" We are, but that is how he feels.

Marijana's story hints at a profound social maneuvering necessary for multiple representations of identification in different contexts. In addition, this quote shows multileveled idioms of peoplehood and nationhood employed by Croat youth in Bosnia-Herzegovina. In addition to the attachment to the Croatian state, this student introduces another level of identity, the regional and territorial Herzegovinian sense of belonging. Andrea's remark, "When people meet me, they say: 'Oh, you are from Bosnia,' but I correct them, 'No, I am a Croat from Herzegovina,'" also hints at this regional identity that many Herzegovinians feel as their strongest sense of belonging. Most people in Mostar complained that the international staff, the world media, and the Bosniaks often said Bosnia when they meant Bosnia and Herzegovina.[17]

The majority of students in Herzegovina thought that the constant omission of Herzegovina from the country's name by non-Herzegovinians was one aspect of discrimination against Croats in Bosnia-Herzegovina. Soon after I arrived in Mostar, I realized that Herzegovinians see themselves as distinct from the Bosnians in the north. During my first visit to the school in Mostar, I was immediately identified as Bosniak [ethnic identity] and as *Bosanka* [indexing geographic identity], meaning not Herzegovinian, and I had some trouble adjusting to this division; people who geographically belong to Bosnia, as I do, often mean Bosnia-Herzegovina when they say Bosnia, and they do not see, at least not initially, the use of this abbreviation as exclusion of Herzegovina from the name and meaning of the country.

Even though Herzegovina had always included ethnic Serbs, Croats, and Muslims, young Croats in Mostar and especially in western Herzegovina[18] often invoked their Herzegovinian identity as a homogeneously Croat identity. For those who equated Herzegovina with Croat, any exposure to non-Croats in Herzegovina arrived as a shock, as Andrea's earlier comment, "Oh, I am shocked! I am not sure what Republika Srpska is and where it is. I had no clue it was in [Bosnia-]Herzegovina," so powerfully demonstrates.

Another student, after I probed him about his identification with Croatia, said: "Maybe it is best to say that I am Herzegovinian, and that Herzegovina is my true homeland." I asked him to explain Herzegovina as domovina in the context of Bosnia-Herzegovina. He continued: "You see we, Herzegovinians, are different [than Bosnians]. We are more progressive, we like to work, we have more money, and our land is more beautiful. Look at these rivers, these rocks. And Bosnia . . . that is in the north and I perceive it as backward, almost socialist, you know what I mean, underdeveloped, with old factories, poor people, and somehow gray." This idea of "backward, socialist and gray Bosnia in the north," adds to the feeling of embarrassment that Croat youth feel in relation to the Bosnia-Herzegovina state, as Hrvoje described: "Here, on our side of Mostar [west Mostar] they say: 'Croatia is my homeland.' In reality, Bosnia-Herzegovina is our homeland, but we are ashamed to say it." After several moments of silence, Hrvoje continued: "When I am on the chat room on the Internet, I say I am from Croatia. But I am really from Bosnia-Herzegovina. . . . Everyone knows where Croatia is. If you say Bosnia-Herzegovina, well . . . it is true everyone knows it, but they think of the war and of us as *fukare*.[19] So I say Croatia."

In addition to the deep feelings of embarrassment, some students explained their detachment from Bosnia-Herzegovina as a result of the anti-Croat sentiment in Bosniak-dominated Bosnia-Herzegovina. Ivica clarified this position: "We, Croats in Bosnia-Herzegovina, are discriminated against. We do not have our rights. We are not allowed to have a TV station in our language, but only to watch the ones in Bosniak or Serbian languages.[20] Our leaders are always discriminated. " Ivica's friend Helena agreed with Ivica: "That is true. The people in power always attack Croat politicians—why is it always they who are in prisons, in The Hague?[21] That is not fair." Both of these young women favored the Croat statehood over the Bosnia-Herzegovina one, even if they realized that they were not "really" from Croatia. Ivica explained this identification in historical terms, when she commented: "And historically, we were always directed toward Croatia. During the war we all thought that Herceg-Bosna[22] would become part of Croatia and many people still think that. We belong to the same narod, we should be all treated the same!" And then, she concluded: "Uh, I am ashamed; I do not know the president of Bosnia-Herzegovina. That is the truth. But I do know all the Croat things."

This quote encapsulates multiple meanings, practices, and approaches that Croat youth exhibited toward the state in which they live (Bosnia-Herzegovina) and toward the state they consider to be their true homeland (Croatia). Their education, both in school and at home, was directed toward the state of Croatia. Ivica, Marijana, Helena, and Hrvoje, like most other Croat students, knew very well the Croat flag, regions, currency, and anthem. The Croat anthem was an especially powerful and emblematic symbol of Croathood for the Croat youth in Bosnia-Herzegovina. As Katarina told me, "When I hear *Lijepu našu* (Our Beautiful [Homeland], the

Croat anthem) I get goose bumps! I do not feel anything when I hear the Bosnia-Herzegovina one . . . actually I do not know what it sounds like!"[23]

Even though Croats are one of the three constituent people in Bosnia-Herzegovina, they experience themselves as an endangered minority who need the protection of the Croatian state. Therefore young Croats look to Croatia for statehood and citizenship, which explains their constant identification with the Croat state. It is the statehood that is the essence of the Croat students' attachment to Croatia. Torsti's study confirms this conclusion: "The Croat history book *Povijest* emphasized *the importance of the state* for Croats . . . who enjoyed a long state tradition since the 9th century [and it stated] that life under Serb occupation in the first Yugoslavia was such a tragedy that the Croats were ready to accept any kind of a state, even the NDH *Ustaša* state.[24] . . . Thus one characteristic defining the representation of the auto-stereotype of nation in *Povijest* can be defined *as a right to a state*" (Torsti 2003:245, emphasis added).

This combination of minimal education about Bosnia-Herzegovina, the extensive education about Croatia, home upbringing, feeling of shame and social discrimination, right to hold dual citizenship, and a real and imagined Bosniak dominance in the Bosnia-Herzegovina state produces Croat youth who often feel indifferent and detached from the country in which they live. At the same time, these youth emphasize the importance of Bosnian Croats as a political community within Bosnia-Herzegovina, crucial for the survival, progress, and protection of the Croat nationhood. This bundle of identifications creates a strong connection between the Croat youth in Bosnia-Herzegovina and what they feel to be their true homeland, Croatia.

Belgrade Is in My Heart

The duality of citizenship in Bosnia-Herzegovina means a great deal for young Serbs in Bosnia-Herzegovina, providing for an opportunity to experience and encounter the state in everyday life. For example, the Serb students I befriended during the workshop in Neum were proud of the stamp in their passport that indexed their belonging to the Republika Srpska, as Saša stressed to me during the dinner. All the Serb students that I interviewed experienced the Republika Srpska as their true state. The Republika

Srpska, which is officially part of the larger, Bosnia-Herzegovina state, exists legally and in practice as a real state with its governmental institutions, symbols, education, and its clear boundaries. The students from Banja Luka (capital of the Republika Srpska) whom I befriended in Neum understood the Republika Srpska as a state upon which a larger, unwanted Bosnia-Herzegovina state was imposed. This collision between the "imposed" and "true" homelands and identifications continues to be the underlying reason for tensions and frictions that become visible when wider social circumstances spark divisions among youth, as I witnessed during my research in Bijelo Brdo.

In the ethnically mixed III-g (U.S. eleventh grade) class in Bijelo Brdo, students had friendly relations with each other. Even though the youth almost uniformly shared desks with students of their own ethnic groups (there are two exceptions, however), the students in class developed easy-going relationships. When in 2005, the Bosnia-Herzegovina soccer team was playing against Serbia's soccer team, a large number of young males from the Republika Srpska went to Serbia to cheer the Serb team. The president of the Republika Srpska, Miroslav Dodik, made a public statement that he only supports the Bosnia-Herzegovina team when it plays against Turkey, suggesting that he only dislikes "Turks" more than "Bosniaks." This wider social tension erupted in the small town's high school and manifested itself among Serb and Bosniak students in III-g. The issue caused a serious fight and frictions among students. Biljana recalled:

> The Muslim students told us: "What did you do to us in Belgrade!" ... But nobody from Bijelo Brdo was in Belgrade when they [the Serb soccer fans] were saying those things [*Nož, Žica, Srebrenica* (Knife, Wire, Srebrenica)]![25] The big fight followed in class. ... The Muslim [students] did not understand that they [the Serbs] feel that those [Serbs in Serbia] are their narod, their faith ... that's it, you are of the same faith [as them] and you have to support them.

In addition to illustrating the fragile nature of postwar coexistence among ethnically mixed students in divided towns of Bosnia-Herzegovina, this incident demonstrates how the Serb narod functions as a transborder, ethnoreligious community of faith, which encompasses Serbs in Serbia, Montenegro, and Croatia, while depicting parts of Bosnia-Herzegovina that are not in the Republika Srpska as foreign. This attitude is skillfully captured by the most popular Bosnian diaspora writer, Aleksandar Hemon, in his short story "Nataša u Inostranstvu" or "Nataša Abroad," which is based on a true event. In the story, his cousin's ten-year-old daughter Nataša, who lives in the capital of the Republika Srpska, Banja Luka, comes to visit the author in Sarajevo for the first time. After doing his best to impress Nataša by showing her the unique places in and around Sarajevo, Hemon sorrowfully but straightforwardly concludes:

> Nataša liked Sarajevo very much. It is a bigger city than Banja Luka, it has more shops, bars, and tourists, but she feels, she said, like she is in a "foreign country": the buildings are different, there are many mosques and Muslims (that do not exist in Banja Luka, do they?[26]), the names of streets are different (Ferhadija, for example, just like that mosque which is no more in Banja Luka), etc. From the position of an average child from Banja Luka, Sarajevo is a foreign land. Thanks to the efforts of Radovan Karadžić[27] and his successors who sit on the top of the Dayton state which they tried to destroy recently, Nataša is cut off from history and experience, not only from the country in which she lives, but from her own family as well—I am that uncle from the far away foreign land. (Hemon 2005:1)

Hemon's story provides a moving reaction to the effects of the ethnonational model that shapes the contemporary situation where Bosnia emerges as a foreign land and a place abroad for the new generations coming of age in the Republika Srpska. Discourses that produce an illusion of "weak integration and choreography of minimal tolerance" present themselves as the existing order, while there "in Banja Luka, children are being taught that Bosnia never was and that she never will be, that Bosnia is . . . somewhere abroad" (Husanović 2006:61, my translation).

The roots of this attitude can be found in the centralized education in the Republika Srpska, where history instruction emphasizes only two types of state attachment: Republika Srpska, and the Yugoslav (Serb), leaving Bosnia-Herzegovina out of the picture (Torsti 2003). Yugoslavism in these books is equated with Serbhood; "the Serb nation was portrayed as constructing and taking care of Yugoslavia for the sake of the common good and the suffering of Yugoslavia and Serbia were presented as synonymous" (246).

In addition to the identification with the Republika Srpska, the young Serbs I interviewed felt a very strong attachment to the idea of the Serb narod, which transgresses the boundaries of history and geography. This transhistoric, transgeographic, ethnically defined notion of Serbian narod is built on the long-lasting myth of the valiant Serb people and their heroic past. For example, Torsti (2003: 246) shows how in *Istorija* (a history textbook) used in Republika Srpska, the central idea was the one of Serb people's victimhood (246), which connected the Serb narod in all regions of the world.

The situation among the Serb youth who live in the FBiH was more complicated. I spent much time discussing the ideas of *država* and *narod* (state and nationhood) with the Serb youth in Bijelo Brdo, many of whom said that they feel Bosnia-Herzegovina to be their domovina. However, they all supported the Serbian soccer team when it played against the Bosnia-Herzegovina soccer team, because they felt that they had an obligation to support their faith and their narod, thus pointing at the disjunctive tension between the state and the nation (Appadurai 1996). The power of Serb narod and its precedence over the Bosnia-Herzegovina state introduces irony; simultaneous attachment and detachment of Serb youth from Bosnia-Herzegovina. Similar to the experience of Croat youth, the disconnect young Serbs in the FBiH expressed in relation to Bosnia-Herzegovina was articulated by Dragana as the emotion of shame: "Imagine you live in a country for which you are ashamed to admit that you live in.... You live in Bosnia-Herzegovina, do not know its anthem, you are ashamed about its soccer representation's performances; they are always at the bottom." This sense of embarrassment, also iconic of the Croat youth's experience of the Bosnian state, points at uneasy similarity between the Croat and Serb youth living in Bosnia-Herzegovina, whose detachment from the Bosnian state is equally strong, even if shaped by different discourses.

The strongest state-level affiliation among the Serb youth in FBiH is still with the Republika Srpska, even though they live in FBiH. Most of the Serb youth in Bijelo Brdo spent their refugee years in Derventa, a small town in Republika Srpska, where they were educated in Serb history, Orthodox religion, and the Cyrillic alphabet according to the centralized curriculum in the Republika Srpska.

None of my field sites were in the Republika Srpska, so my ethnographic knowledge of that region is limited. The following anecdote I owe to a

Poetics of Nationhood 129

fellow anthropologist who conducted research in several elementary schools in the Republika Srpska. During one observation of classroom instruction in third grade elementary school, the anthropologist joined a group of five girls who had a task to find the railway tracks in Bosnia-Herzegovina on the map of the country. The girls sat in a circle around a table, surrounding the map from all sides. The girls, who were sitting close to the bottom/south of the map, started looking for railway tracks in the FBiH. One of the girls closer to the top (north) of the map, thus covering the territory of the Republika Srpska, looked at the first group and said: "Do not look at that, *to je tuđe* [that is, others']."[28]

This diagnostic event shows that unlike the Croat youth who until recently did not study Bosnia-Herzegovina except as one of Croatia's neighbors, the Serb students included Bosnia-Herzegovina in their studies. Their focal point was limited, however, and it pertained only to the Republika Srpska, while Bosnia-Herzegovina was used only as a framework that enabled the Republika Srpska to exist. Under this paradigm, the Dayton Peace Agreement was interpreted not as an agreement that brought peace to Bosnia-Herzegovina, but as an agreement that established the Republika Srpska. Therefore, for the Serb youth, Bosnia-Herzegovina embodied an unwanted and vacant state, which was imposed on their "real" state, the Republika Srpska. In addition, Bosnia-Herzegovina was perceived as the main obstruction to the Serb narod living in one state of Greater Serbia.

The three examples show how in contemporary Bosnia-Herzegovina the sociocultural and economic similarities have been overshadowed by the politics of ethnic narod, which is the predominant way to experience and regulate self-determination, identification, peoplehood, and nationhood. While the youth of the three ethnic groups have had different understandings of their narod and their state, they all projected, to a different extent, an ethnic emphasis of political and national belonging, leading to the further unmixing of formerly multiethnic communities, and generating a Bosnia-Herzegovina empty of its young citizens. This detachment from the state was underscored by the mixed feelings of discrimination, lack of opportunities, and shame many youth feel in regard to the state in which they live.

At the same time, an element of the transethnic interconnectedness, created through centuries of multileveled forms of coexistence and shared economic predicament in the lived present, continued to linger in everyday speech and practice, in curiosity about difference and coexistence. I witnessed this one night in Neum. I was awakened from sleep at 2:45 a.m. by noise from a room on my floor of the hotel. After unsuccessfully trying to fall back to sleep, I followed the noise and ended up among students squeezed in a hotel room. When I entered the room, the youth applauded while inviting me into the room. Quickly, I screened the room and realized that there were youth from many different areas of Bosnia-Herzegovina present, lying and sitting next to each other on the beds, floors, and chairs, talking nonstop in the dim light of a hotel lamp.

I expected to encounter much alcohol and talking about sex, typical of young and unobserved youth of their age under these circumstances. While the talk about sex was not absent, and there was some alcohol in circulation, I was surprised that the youth mostly wanted to talk about the other groups' religious practices. The workshop took place during the month of Ramadan and several Muslim youth were fasting, which intrigued their newly made friends from other ethnoreligious backgrounds. Lively discussion developed for more than an hour, until it vanished with the first beams of sunlight resting on our sleep-deprived faces.

The interest in the question of different religions points at several interconnected things, including the increased importance of religion in the lives of the Bosnian youth today, which is evident in a great demonstration of knowledge about their own religious practices. The questions they posed to the others, however, signaled limited knowledge about other religious practices in Bosnia-Herzegovina, while still indexing some historic commonality and recognition of each other. For example, many Croat and Serb youth did not know what Ramadan was and how the fast was observed. While I was surprised by their lack of knowledge of the "other," I was moved by their empathy and genuine interest in each other as young people belonging to different groups with a significant amount of shared history and geography. Intrigued by the persistence of these commonalities and limited mixing practices, in the final part of this chapter I probe behind the facades of ethnonational unity in order to explore the possibilities and the limits of narod as a creative form of dissent (Herzfeld 2005:1).

Narod Is Not to Blame

On a cold winter day in 2006, I went skiing with the students from the Croat curriculum at the Mostar Gymnasium at a nearby ski resort called Blidinje. After a whole day of skiing and absorbing the whiteness of the quiet mountain range, our bus brought us back to Mostar, where it stopped at Rondo circle, in the center of west Mostar. I watched the students as they got off the bus and disappeared into the cold, rainy night. I was the only one who stayed on the bus, besides Nusret, the bus driver. Nusret was a Bosniak who, like me, lived on the east side of the divided city, and he offered to give me a ride home. Temporary solidarity emerged between this man and me "simply" because of the side of town we lived on. In Mostar, the location of one's home represents much more than urban geography; it tells people "who you are." As we were traveling across the boulevard, which currently divides the city, the bus driver told me his war stories. He spent the whole war in Mostar, and at the beginning of the war he fought against the Serb-dominated JNA. Then the war against Hrvatsko Vijeće Obrane (Croatian Defense Council) started "so I [Nusret] was right here, at the boulevard, at the first frontline." I asked him how he felt now, ten years later, driving the Croat youth. He responded: "Come on, narod is not to blame. Those were abnormal times, and everyone was abnormal. But it is not children's and normal people's responsibility. Politics is to blame." I did not give up: "Which politics?" Nusret paused for a second, and then said: "*I naša i strana*" [both ours and foreign] . . . and narod, narod has to suffer it all." I did not let it go: "Come on, who is that narod of yours?" He looked at me, while turning the bus toward Tekija, where I lived, and said confidently: "*Narod, to ti je, moja Azra, običan svijet*" (Narod, that is, my Azra, common folk).

The vignette captures some additional complexities of narod—an ambiguous, polyvalent category of nationhood and an important dimension of micropolitics in postwar Bosnia-Herzegovina. For example, Nusret uses narod to separate "ordinary people" from *politika* (politics) and politicians, both "ours and foreign."[29] In Nusret's statements, politicians, regardless of their country of origin, ethnicity, and party affiliations, are all grouped together in a bundle of untrustworthy, compromised, greed-driven, career-oriented people. These unreliable leaders are sharply opposed, at least in Nusret's discourse,[30] to narod—decent people of any ethnic background, who experience similar hardships regardless of their different ethnicities.

Nusret's narod-centered words and actions provide a critique of the current political and economic establishment, without necessarily "talking politics." Furthermore, Nusret's utterances demonstrate how ordinary Bosnians create "gaps" between and beyond dominant, ethnicized political discourses in order to recapture their (and others') dignity, sociality, political agency, economic necessity, and sense of moral order. This discursive and strategic usage of transethnic narod to create solidarity and establish bridges across war-divided ethnicities is only seemingly in stark opposition to ethnicity-specific employments of narod; rather, the two discourses are tangentially intertwined and mutually constitutive. Furthermore, these multiple connotations of narod are not a reflection of the lack of analytic terminology; rather, they mirror the extent to which these meanings and tactics are overlapping, "interwoven and hard to separate, even for people themselves" (Kolind 2007:137).

This transethnic narod is not a fully formed, observable, and objective category of belonging in need of academic rescue and rediscovery. In addition, narod is not a simple icon of togetherness, ethnicity, or an apolitical expression of tangible cultural commonality. Rather, the narod that Nusret invokes is best understood as a discursive, transient category without a politically articulated essence. As such, it eludes appropriation into a fixed political agenda, while simultaneously challenging and reinserting the existing pervasiveness of ethnicity in contemporary Bosnia-Herzegovina. What is more, this persistent yet marginal discourse of transethnic narod is being absorbed, flattened, and manipulated by local ethnonationalist discourses, "multicultural" liberal opportunisms (see Arsenijević 2007; Hajdarpašić 2008; Kurtović 2011), and the internationally inserted consociational model of democracy. Yet, it continues to linger and complexly inform everyday lives, practices, and political actions of Bosnians and Herzegovinians.

The transethnic sensibility that the notion of narod embodies has been noted and addressed by several scholars of the region (see, for example, Bringa 1993; I. Lovrenović; Markowitz 2010; Torsti 2003), and it is usually explained as a "cultural phenomenon" stripped of political significance. Here, however, I argue that this form of transethnic narod is indeed *political*, since it is within this discursive "unsettling in-betweenness" (Pickering 2009:167) that territorially segregated Bosnians come together and act together in order to appropriate, negotiate, and transform identifications and socialities available to them. In other words, under the discursive banner of narod, people of all ethnic groups complain about the injustices and problems they face in everyday life, including issues of health and wealth, continuing nationalism, problems of *zajednički život* (life together), uncivility (Neofotistos 2012), indecency (Kolind 2007), disillusionment, poverty, corruption, and political rigidity, that shape their postwar lives. Therefore, transethnic narod is generative of political agency and social sensibility—people use narod as a "counter-discourse" (Kolind 2007:127). As a result, it is possible to say that narod, as a discursive critique of society and politics, as a space of escape and negotiation, and a stance of a "withdrawal" from *politika* (Helms 2007; Kolind 2007), is indeed metapolitical.

Enacting Transethnic Narod

Transethnic narod, as I understand it here, is a malleable discursive space of interconnectedness between, above, and beyond ethnically divided citizenry. This narod is not a group or a fixed category, and it has not been included in the postwar Bosnian political mosaic. And yet, people regularly "do things" with this noncohesive discourse; it is revealed in social, political, and economic practices such as talk about "common mentality," strategic avoidance of sensitive topics, expressions of political discontent, and complaints about economic hardships.

For example, numerous informants told me that people in Bosnia-Herzegovina have one *zajednički mentalitet* or "common mentality." When asked what this common mentality meant, Zora, an employee at the school, summarized it for me: "Ma sve ti je to u suštini isti narod, samo što se neki mole Isusu a neki Alahu" (These are, in essence, all the same people; it is just that some pray to Jesus and some to Allah). When probed, Zora explained that this cohesion emerged from a common ethnocultural and biological origin; in other words, all Bosnians and Herzegovinians are ethnic Slavs who have inhabited the mountainous parts of the Balkan Peninsula for centuries and share the same "blood." Later, however, these people converted to different religions, Zora explained. She emphasized this shared blood at the expense of more recent ethnoreligious transformations, which were glossed over, minimized, and trivialized.

Similarly to Zora, Harun, a student at the Mostar Gymnasium, stressed the common language and mentality of all Bosnians and Herzegovinians. Unlike Zora, however, he framed his comment about common origins as a critique of those Mostarians who, for reasons of ethnic divisions and nationalism, refuse to see and endorse this shared "essence." One cold October night in 2006, in a semimagical setting of Mostar's Old City, Harun engaged in a monologue in order to explain this "essence" to me. He concluded: "For example, I do not understand some people around here . . . how can you like better someone from the other side of Drina [the river that separates Bosnia-Herzegovina from Serbia], who has a different mentality, who speaks differently?" While this statement could be read as a testimony of the ubiquity of ethnic separateness, Harun's ideas are more complex. Harun believes that all Mostarians, and by extension, all Bosnians and Herzegovinians, have a common mentality and that they used to share the same way of speaking before the war. This unique and historically shaped commonality unites all Mostarians despite their different ethnonational signatures and recent attempts to separate the three official languages: Bosnian, Serbian, and Croatian. Harun stressed that even today, after several decades of language segregation and manipulation, Mostarians speak with the same dialect, even if their vocabulary differs, and that "anyone anywhere in the country can tell the unique Mostar way of speaking, regardless of which side the person comes from." For Harun, those Mostarians who prefer to emphasize what he sees as a "shallow" ethnonational belonging to Serb, Croat, or Bosniak groups and languages, over a joint (understood as deeper and truer, thus more authentic) overarching and underlying Bosnian "common mentality" and way of speaking, are traitors and weak individuals.[31]

To complicate things farther, narod can be used as a way to circumvent difficult subjects when people who have different war experiences and understandings of recent history come in contact with each other. The use of narod as an "avoidance" strategy is political, in an anthropological, thus broad and contextual, sense of politics: it is an effective tool for people to negotiate present-day power relations and differences, to deal with the badly sealed wounds from the recent past, and to demand dignity and respect in complicated everyday encounters. Therefore, this "avoidance" is in itself a reflection of careful social work and political sensibility. This became especially clear to me when Draga, a teacher at the Mostar Gymnasium, explained the relationships between Croat and Bosniak faculty members at the Mostar Gymnasium:

> With them [Croat teachers at the school] I can talk about some things, such as teachers' low salaries . . . but about politics and the war you cannot talk to them, because our opinions differ. *Narod je napaćen i zasićen od politike. Narodu treba da malo prodiše* [Ordinary people are exhausted and saturated with politics. Narod needs a little bit of a breathing room]. And that is OK [not to talk politics] for now, because we all want to be *civilizirani* (civilized).

This avoidance of talking about politics in face-to-face interethnic encounters is cautious, strategic, and calculated, and it requires much social and political knowledge and savvy. People like Draga, who spend much of their work time in the "mixed" context of the Mostar Gymnasium, constantly assess their fragile and heterogeneous living environment to insert and guard their and others' security, civility, and dignity (also see Kolind 2007; Neofotistos 2012).

In addition to being a way to avoid potential conflict in ethnically "mixed," face-to-face situations, discourses of transethnic narod emerge as a space where ordinary Bosnians and Herzegovinians, regardless of their ethnic signature, jointly express their political cynicism and critique. The skepticism and discontent with which ordinary Bosnians and Herzegovinians approach politics is captured in the popular statement *Politika je kurva* (Politics is a whore). This phrase is commonly used to emphasize the immoral, fickle, gendered, and corrupt nature of political deal-making (Helms 2007:236).[32] Narod is depicted as being on the margins of this immoral political universe, but deeply influenced by international and local political actions. In this way, articulations of transethnic peoplehood offer a space for Bosnians to discursively distance themselves from the dirtiness of *politika*, while also being able to engage in counterdiscourses. In the words of Edina, an employee at the Pedagogical Institute in east Mostar: "Those political parties only divide narod. What narod, you ask? All of those from whose backs the politicians, *naši i strani* [ours and foreign], live. Narod are Serbs, and Croats, and Muslims, all of us who suffer and whose children do not know what to do about their lives." Zemka, another employee adds: "Yes, narod is all of us."

Similarly to Nusret's remarks, Edina's and Zemka's comments provide much insight into ordinary people's frustration with politicians, both domestic and international. These individuals intentionally suspend differences between the two groups, while blaming all elites for exploiting narod for their political gains. Thus, Edina, Zemka, and Nusret are not "blaming the Croat or Serb other, but the politicians" (Kolind 2007:126). Narod here is constituted of members of all ethnic groups, Serbs, Croats, Bosniaks, and Others, who are responding to the political maneuvering by becoming followers and victims of the corrupt regime. Narod is thus excluded from the benefits of the war and financial gains, which renders it "clean" from dirty political agendas, yet marginal and victimized, and contributing to its own oppression. Thus by carving out a space "outside" politics, ordinary people create a counterdiscourse: a metadiscursive space of political solidarity and critique, and a search for dignity.

While "on the ground" one often hears that there are poor, *napaćen narod* (narod exhausted by suffering) on the one side, and rich ethnonational criminal elites on the other. In this context, the political elites are all the same, regardless of their ethnic mark, since they use the existing ethnic divisions to mask their economic maneuvering, nepotism, and hegemony. Lana, an employee at the Mostar Gymnasium, explains further: "and when they say it is all about nationalism, it is not—it is about who is rich, who has relatives, connections, not about nationalism. It is about money, but they [the rich, the mafia, the politicians] mask our eyes with the talk of nationalism." Similarly to Lana, some youth distinguished between the rich on the one side, and the poor of all ethnic groups on the other. Filip, a student at the Mostar Gymnasium, explains:

> When I started coming to Mostar, since you know I am from the village nearby, I only came to this [Croat west] side, because it is warmer to me, I mean closer to my heart. I was angry before, when I would hear that some Croat lost his close relatives, I would be blaming those from the other side. But then I met some of them [Bosniaks] from the other side when they came to school. That was new to me—I did not know any Muslims before, and now I am friends with Harun [Bosniak student], as you know. I realized they are people like me, that he is just like me. I realized that it is not his fault that some Croat lost his family member, and that it is not my fault that someone from the other side lost their relatives. You know. . . . At the end stays only poor narod.
> Azra: Who is the poor narod?
> Filip: Poor narod are Croats, Serbs, and Muslims, you and me, and kids who will be born tomorrow. I am the first one . . . I am not guilty for who I am, or my friend Harun . . . we are not guilty for the war that happened.
> Azra: Who is doing injustice to narod?
> Filip: Politicians, the people who are in power now. They are just looking for where they can steal something, and they only want to start fights among narod, and then to reconcile narod again, as if nothing happened.

Poetics of Nationhood   137

The words of Filip, the bus driver, the school's employee, and the employees at the Pedagogical Institute encapsulate the meanings of narod where ethnic identity becomes only one of its many components. For example, in its broader, economic sense, narod is explained in a Marxist way: narod are all the people who were tricked by the war, regardless of which side they come from, and who suffer economic and political injustices orchestrated by the elites above, including the "internationals." Marijana, a teacher at the Mostar Gymnasium, explained this to me during my visit to Mostar in June 2012: "Narod cannot be the politicians . . . well, narod are all normal people in this Bosnia and Herzegovina of ours." When I asked her what "normal" meant in this context, Gordana, Marijana's coworker, interrupted: "Normal narod is the middle class!" Narod is cynical and disenchanted, impatient and unrepresented, moral, victimized and resilient. It is a mass of economically deprived and politically marginal people, "including you and me," who inertly, exhausted by war, blinded by the ethnic ideology and unscrupulous behavior of those in power, complain and await a better future.

Interestingly, Filip, Nusret, and Edina also linguistically group together "narod and children." This construction allows for narod to be equated with children, and thus to take on childlike characteristics. This positions narod away from the "adult" politics, into a morally, economically, and politically better future, free of any responsibility for the recent war. This "escape" from accountability and engagement is usually deepened by ordinary people's tendency to invoke and blame some vague *Oni* (They) for narod's and children's collective misfortune—my informants continually stressed that "It was not narod and children's fault" but that "*Oni su krivi za sve*" (They are guilty for everything). When I asked who "they" were, people would shrug their shoulders or simply say: "Politicians." This conclusion is in agreement with Kolind's findings in the war-devastated town of Stolac,[33] where the Muslim returnees stressed that society is not functioning because of the lack of political will, and that if politicians would only sit down and get their act together, many problems would be resolved (Kolind 2007:126–27).

This discourse of lazy and greed-driven dirty and criminal politics provides a way to distance narod, and by extension oneself, at least for now, from a direct responsibility and political engagement with the structures of Dayton. The four everyday discourses employed by ordinary Bosnians and Herzegovinians that were analyzed in this section are metapolitical, since they engage in a discursive critique of the core issues at the heart of political, social, and economic problems in contemporary Bosnia-Herzegovina. While these stories point at the limited yet palpable discursive spaces for cross-ethnic expression and identification, nowhere is this more visible than in the case of "mixed" marriages and their families. To these people and their stories we now turn.

Chapter 5

Invisible Citizens

Unrecognized Baby

On a rainy day in October 2005, I visited my favorite Bosnian pie shop located in the heart of Mostar's famed Old City. Davorka, the bright-faced and fast-talking owner of the shop, was there. Since I was the only customer at the time, Davorka kept me company. Soon, we started talking about her life.

> I am in a mixed marriage—my husband is Muslim and I am Croat. When I got pregnant, it was just at the beginning of the war. I was on the Croat side then, and I gave birth there in 1993. When I gave birth, they [Croat hospital officials] did not want to issue a birth certificate to my Ajra because her father was Muslim [living on the other side]. Imagine! I came to this side when there was still no water or electricity. It was so hard, but I wanted to be together with my husband. Only three months after her birth, Ajra was finally registered in the books on this [east] side. And after the war, I went back to the west side and they told me I could not register her in their books, because I was supposed to do it back then when she was born! So, [in their books] there is just information about the baby girl being born, with a blank space where her name should be.

The story of the unrecognized baby illustrates the incongruity between nationalist visions and lived realities that led to the extreme bloodshed and forceful unmixing of historically intermixed regions within the former Yugoslavia (Hayden 1996). Davorka's words reveal how memories and practices of forced unmixing penetrate, shape, and mold the most intimate relationships, including marriages, romantic encounters, and long-term friendships in Bosnia-Herzegovina. By questioning how certain forms of love and friendship became unmappable, she reflects on the larger forces and fields of unmixing, thus revealing multiple obstacles that people in mixed marriages have endured since the beginning of the war in Mostar and the rest of the state. These "invisible citizens"[1] suffered most visibly when the ethos of a multiethnic, cosmopolitan society was forcibly replaced during the war by an ideology of ethnically homogeneous people and territories. The experiences of Davorka and others in a similar situation reveal that the vision of peace-building and state-making in Bosnia-Herzegovina (spatially) discourages long-standing, supraethnic forms of mixing, citizenship, and nationhood. These ideologies of unmixing continue to powerfully inform the politics of belonging in postwar Bosnia-Herzegovina.

In my meditations on Davorka's story, which captures some effects of unmixing, I rely on Aisha Khan's (2004) discussion of mixing in the context of Trinidad. Following Khan, I understand mixing to be "as much about the conversation of boundaries and essences as their subversion" (12), where mixing discourses and practices emerge as both constitutive and destabilizing of categories of ethnicity. Thus, the notions of mixing "animate the very categories that are supposed to give rise to them" (4), allowing for their symbolic boundary-maintenance (Barth 1969; Douglas 1966). More specifically, in the Bosnian context, discourses, ideologies, and practices of (un)mixing give power and significance to ethnic categories, such as "Croat," "Serb," or "Bosniak," while transforming those who "dare to mix" into socially marginalized, politically unrecognized citizens. Furthermore, the prevalent ethnonationalist ideology of ethnic purity, protected by the consociational model of democracy, presumes that ethnic mixing produces culturally hybrid youth, "whose lack of inheritance of a clearly defined identity makes ethnic distinctions vague and therefore, logic goes, socially invisible and politically ineffective" (Khan 2004:14). It also makes them socially and spatially unmappable.

Interestingly, the spread of discourses of mixing in contemporary Bosnia-Herzegovina, either in the form of "fear of impurity" (Douglas 1966) or as popular reflections on the common (and, in the discourses of nostalgia, better) Yugoslav past, convert the politically excluded practices of mixing and mixed marriages into hypervisible social and cultural discourses and subjectivities.[2] In this way, mixed families operate as uncanny phenomena in Bosnia-Herzegovina—"anomalies" (Bringa 2003) and "abjects" (Kristeva 1982)—present but excluded individuals, familiar yet othered subjects, people apart but still essential for the formulations, articulations, and transformations of ethnic categories. Under the framework of spatial governmentality, mixed families are forced into "abjected spaces" and "no-man's-lands," which develop in cracks between ethnically conceived territories. In these spatial, emotional, sensory, and ideological ruptures, mixing continues to detach, differentiate, and moor ethnic differences and hold in suspension social agents.[3] The experiences of these spatially and ideologically excluded citizen-subjects and their continuous mixing practices powerfully reveal not only the effects of the "ethnic wars," but, ironically, the limitations of peace-making in postwar Bosnia-Herzegovina. In order to illuminate the ironies of new development and liberal peace (Duffield 2001), here I bring together, connect, and analyze the intersection between two already discussed themes: (un)mixing and narod, as they converge in the institution of mixed marriage.

Narod and Mixing

The Yugoslav regime saw practices of mixing, and especially mixed marriages, as intimately yet problematically related to the Yugoslav state-building project. The attitude of the Yugoslav government toward mixed marriages was deeply ambiguous, with no coherent policy toward this phenomenon. The communist party leaders started addressing mixed marriages as either a problem or a solution only after the polarization of ethnoreligious relations, especially during the Croatian Spring (a political and nationalist movement in Croatia in the 1970s) or during the national awakening of Bosnian Muslims.[4]

One of the most important interventions of Tito's regime was the construction of a category of Yugoslav nationhood. This category labeled as "Yugoslav, ethnically undeclared" appeared for the first time in the 1953 census (Ramet 2006:287), and it allowed mixed families and others (including some unrecognized groups) to circumscribe ethnic and republic-level identifications and to embrace a panethnic Yugoslav identity. In addition, it signaled "democratic" (equal) political representation, a cosmopolitan worldview, and a particular Yugoslav and socialist modernity (Bringa 2003).

The notion of narod was reduced and flattened, however, by ethnic nationalism and the consociational model of democracy, during and after the war. This is especially visible in the techniques of governmentality, such as the production of census categories in Bosnia-Herzegovina. For example, the 1991 prewar census listed 25 possible categories of either narod or *narodnosti*. This is in stark contrast to only four categories available during the FBiH[5] census in 2003—Bosniaks, Croats, Serbs, and Others—where all *narodnosti* have been lumped into an ambiguous othering category *Ostali* (Others) (Markowitz 2007:46; Jansen 2005).

As a consequence of these changes, at the time of my fieldwork narod in the ethnic sense was the only politically visible/official coordinate of belonging. This problematic, internationally safeguarded vision of postwar Bosnia-Herzegovina was often rejected and understood as too simplistic and rigid by ordinary people, especially those who find themselves boxed into the category "minority"—people who, according to their ethnicity, live in the "wrong" part of the state (Pickering 2009), and those Bosnians of "ambiguous social identity" who, in a new divided Bosnia-Herzegovina of ethnically pure regions, have no place (Bringa 2003:173). This political and social regime leaves transethnic forms of peoplehood and mixing politically unrecognized and socially discouraged, albeit alive in the context of everyday micropolitics. The elimination of the spaces for transethnic forms of interaction and identification causes much frustration among numerous Bosnians and Herzegovinians, those citizens who embraced and embodied the Yugoslav ideas of Brotherhood and Unity and who chose to enter mixed marriages. After the violent collapse of the Yugoslav regime, however, these same mixed families found themselves in "no-man's-land," squeezed between the two sides of their now ethnically divided country. In this context it is worth recalling the words of Sanja, a child from a mixed marriage, whose words represent an instance of spatially expressed structural nostalgia, "an edenic order—a time before time—in which the balanced perfection of social relations has not yet suffered the decay that affects everything human" (Herzfeld 2005:147). Consider, one more time, Sanja's comment:

> Let me tell you how it is . . . it is like you had one big house, where you moved around freely. In that house you had your own room, but you spent much time in the living room, visiting with other people. Or you [would] go and see them in their own rooms, which always stayed unlocked. You loved that house . . . now, there is no

living room . . . the space where it used to be is destroyed and neglected, covered in shit and dirt. No one goes there anymore. And people . . . they do not leave their rooms, which are locked at all times. . . . But we all remember how we once had a house.

The war-orchestrated annihilation of the "common house" was reified through the state-building model, creating a sanitized and fragile political context where Sanja and other "mixed citizens" were transformed from "Tito's children" into "Tito's orphans"—people "without a nation and eventually without the state" (Bringa 2003:174). This firm installation of sociopolitical segregation works in practice to cement ethnic animosity, promote a culture of nonmixing, and emphasize territorial segregation at the expense of historical interconnectedness and, by extension, the possibility of lived multiethnicity and panethnic peoplehood (also see Kolind 2007). As a result, the former Yugoslav mixed families and transethnic forms of peoplehood were transformed into spatially unmappable, bureaucratically invisible, socially marginalized (anti)citizens.

Spatial Unmappability

Before the war, Mostar had a reputation of nurturing a relatively high number of mixed families. Many older inhabitants of Mostar mention this fact, especially when recalling the "good old times of social intermingling," often saying that up to half of all marriages in Mostar were mixed.[6]

The people in Mostar told me that almost all mixed families lived in Mostar's urban core. Samir explains: "That phenomenon [mixed marriages], it existed in *gradska sredina* [urban surroundings], in *čaršija* [bazaar, Old City], but in those suburban, *seoskim sredinama* [village surroundings], that phenomenon was, we can say, unknown." Today, however, there are almost no mixed marriages taking place in the city, and mixing is commonly approached suspiciously and resentfully, as Nino explains: "The only thing common to Croats and Muslims is that they hate mixed marriages, because both sides see them as traitors. They did not pick a side, and everything and everyone in this city pressures you to do so" (Nino Zelenika cited in Matejčić 2009). Most of the mixed families left Mostar for other regions of the country, or more commonly, for foreign lands willing to accept refugees from Bosnia-Herzegovina. Those who stayed behind had to face drastic changes in Mostar's ethos from a place that accepted mixed marriages to a place that stigmatizes and spatially excludes those who "dare to mix."

Spatial governmentality of ethnicity, generated by the war and solidified by the consociational model of democracy, abolishes the shared public spaces that are the key element of mixing, common peoplehood, and the possibility of genuine democracy in Bosnia-Herzegovina. This absence of heterogeneous social spaces, in which common Bosnian peoplehood—the demos—could develop, is vividly criticized by twenty-five-year-old Nino, whose father is Croat and mother is Bosniak. Nino explains the lack of social and political spaces for mixed families in the segregated city when he comments that "people like us, living in mixed families, could only take the middle ground—and in the middle lies the river" (Nino Zelenika cited in Matejčić 2009). While Nino focuses on the spatial metaphor of the river into which one is forced but which one cannot inhabit, his words are also a critique of the political (consociational democracy) and ideological (cultural fundamentalism/ethnic purity) models that produce spatial divisions and exclude (by forcing them into the river) those who are unwilling or unable to take sides.

Some Mostarians openly rebel against this spatial unmappability. Goran, a young man from a mixed marriage of a Serb father who left the family when Goran was a baby, and a Croat mother, often complained about the lack of space for him to live a "normal life." Here, normal stands for mixing—constant and unmarked movement, openness to "the other," interaction, intersection, and intermingling. On one occasion, Goran half-jokingly and half-tragically commented: "Today in Mostar it is easier to be a bastard than to be a child from a mixed marriage. And imagine being in my situation—I am a mixed bastard." His comment is fueled with dark humor that both reveals and attempts to diminish the heaviness of his situation. He often jokes that he is neither Serb nor Croat, but, since there is "really no Bosnia," he has to be a Muslim. When I would ask him to meet me for coffee, he would say "Hoću, ali ako ćemo kod naših, kod Muslimana" (I will if we are going to our, Muslim side).

Goran is an unusual figure in the heavily ethnicized Mostar landscape, against which he openly rebels. He frequently complains that regardless of his predominantly Croat upbringing, he could not stand what he calls "the Fascist politics" of the Croat leadership during the war. Because of his views and actions, one day in 1993, in the midst of heavy fighting, Goran was forced to cross to the other, east side and started living *kod Muslimana* (with Muslims).[7] His mother and sister stayed behind on the west side and were frequently harassed by those Croats who called Goran a traitor and a coward. He still lives in Mostar, hoping to continue his studies abroad, while feeling socially trapped between the two sides, both of which are suspicious of his "normal ways" and his overt practices and dispositions.

Bureaucratic Invisibility

On a gloomy day in November 2006, I was watching TV with a relative in Bihać. My friend took a sip of the thick Bosnian coffee and commented on the show we were watching: "He is a *napolica* [halfy]." Seeing my puzzled face, she laughed and continued, "This boy on TV . . . this is a show about religious education at day cares in Sarajevo, where they divide up children [according to ethnicity/religion]. . . . I know this boy, his dad is Croat, his mom is Muslim, and now she [the mother] talks about how she does not have a day care in Sarajevo to send her child to."

This was the first time I heard the word *napolica*[8] used to describe a child from an ethnoreligiously mixed marriage. I would later hear the term more often, especially in the Bihać region, and frequently among older generations. The simultaneous synergy and fissure the term implied, in addition to the fact that the *napolica* boy allegedly had no day care to attend in the celebrated multiethnic city of Sarajevo, were puzzling. It also revealed that those who embody mixing do not fit into the contemporary ethnic Bosniak-Croat-Serb grid, thus suffering from the consequence of institutional ethnicization.

Similarly to the mother of the *napolica* boy in Sarajevo, Davorka, whom we met in the opening vignette, feels spatially and socially caught between the two sides of her divided city of Mostar, belonging, in her words, *ni tamo, ni 'vamo* (neither here nor there). Even more critically, Davorka's daughter Ajra does not fit bureaucratically into the consociational model of democratization, which legitimizes a nationalist vision of Bosnian peoples and places as ethnically "pure." In other words, little Ajra and the *napolica* boy are left "unnamable" (de Certeau 1984) and uncountable, by state institutions that obey the logic of ethnic citizenship. Cultural forces of "practical kinship" (Das 1995)[9] accommodate Davorka's daughter by absorbing her, following the rules of patriarchy, into her father's ethnic group. However, for Davorka and other people in similar situations, the tension is not resolved through the forces of practical kinship either; they continue to struggle for social and political recognition in the segregated city. This recognition, which during Yugoslav times arrived in the form of legally recognized Yugoslav citizenship/peoplehood, is absent from the political horizon in postwar Bosnia-Herzegovina since, under the current political establishment, Bosnians politically exist only as Bosniaks, Serbs, and Croats. This political vacuum of supraethnic national identity causes continuous frustration. Igor, a young teacher from Bijelo Brdo, explains his frustration with the absence of the supraethnic national category:

> What can I say when someone asks me who I am? I cannot say that I am *Ostali* since it sounds like I am Bulgarian, Eskimo, or something... hmm... like I am not from here, like I am some foreigner, *k'o da sam zalutao* [as if I lost my way].... As you know, my dad is Muslim and my mom is Croat. I grew up in Croatia and I know more about Christmas than about Ramadan, because my dad did not care about it [Islam], to teach me and my sister. When people ask me who I am, I cannot say that I am Muslim because I know less about Islam than about other religions. But what else can I say. ... If that fucking Bosnian nation existed, it would be so much easier.

The frustrations articulated by the mother of the *napolica* boy, Sanja, Goran, Davorka, and Igor, who found themselves boxed into the unmappable, unrecognized, and invisible *Ostali*, or absorbed, via rules of practical citizenship, into their father's ethnic collectivity, point at the tyranny of spatial governmentality and cultural fundamentalism that excludes and renders bureaucratically invisible forms of mixing—mixed bodily dispositions, affective states, ethical projects, and sensibilities in contemporary Bosnia-Herzegovina.

Discrimination and Resilience

One cold Sunday afternoon I was enjoying a cup of tea at the local bookstore overlooking the new "Old" Bridge. Spontaneously, I entered into a dialogue with the only two other people at the shop, Predrag and Marija. We started talking about what it is like to live in Mostar after the war, and soon I learned that both Predrag and Marija were children from mixed marriages. An exciting dialogue developed, which I recorded in my notebook as soon as I left the bookstore. The following interchange is reconstructed from my notes:

Azra: So, how is it to be a child from a mixed marriage in Mostar today?
Predrag: Do not ask. Terrible. Most of the people in mixed marriages were forced to leave, regardless of which side they lived in. It is still bad today.
Azra: How is it bad?
Predrag: I am a student at the University and for example, I know for sure I should have gotten a 10 (an A) and I got a 7 (a C). As soon as someone at the University sees my name, the same thing happens again. And then, I am half Catholic on my mom's side, and half Montenegrin on my dad's side, and I was dating a Muslim girl, who was from the Old City. And after a few days [of dating] she said to me: "I have to break up with you." I was surprised, but I replied: "Okay, but tell me why." She told me: "Because you are Predrag and if my parents find that out, my dad will slaughter me, stab me with a knife." And she was from the Old City!!! Or later, I had another, Catholic girlfriend from the other side [laughs at himself for the use of this term] and we went out only once. First she said the prayer before we ate. I suffered through that. But then she started questioning me; would I marry in a church and would I agree to be baptized. She works for Caritas,[10] she goes to church every day, but I know more about the Catholic religion than she does. And that is how it is around here.
Azra: Where do you go out?
Marija: In my group of friends you can find anything, there are girls with huge crosses around their necks, but that is because of religion, not because of nationalism. We go to Abrašević,[11] and as you know, *everyone* goes there.
Predrag: There are no places, not one place. Go to Staro Veležovo [a part of west Mostar with many pubs and coffee shops] and you will not find one person from this side.
Marija: Yes, you can find them there. And during the war too—on the one hand, Croats were forcing Muslims out, while on the other

hand, some Croat neighbors were helping and hiding these same people. Those are paradoxes, but it is true. Not even we, the people of Mostar, understand this. I do not want to focus on the dark things only as everyone else in this city does. I refuse to live like that, but I am upset that in this city everyone wants to put me in a box. And I do not want to be categorized.
Predrag, jokingly: Just tell me who is your *ćaća* [slang for father] and I will categorize you.
We all laugh.
Marija: Why do you care about my *ćaća, ja sam ja* [I am my own person].

I provide this lengthy transcript of my conversation with two young Mostarians, both children from mixed marriages, to better show what they have to face on a daily basis in the divided city. As they learn to survive in this hostile social environment, they either criticize the changes that have taken place, in the case of Predrag, or they try to find and nourish an oasis of coexistence, as does Marija. In these struggles for survival, Predrag and Marija reflect on the changes in their environment as they experience them on their own skin. For example, Predrag is astonished and hurt by the fear-driven "closed-mindedness" of his first, Muslim girlfriend, especially because she came from the Old City. The Old City represents, for Predrag and numerous others, the core of the cosmopolitan urban spirit that embraced and nurtured mixing for decades before the war. He feels that his girlfriend, but also her whole neighborhood and urban Mostar, betrayed him. Then he criticizes the superficial religiosity of his second, Catholic girlfriend, by saying that he knows more about her religion than she does, but, ironically, she is the one who tests him to see if he is a good enough Catholic. Finally, Predrag brings up the limitations of spatial governmentality, which eliminate public space for ethnically mixed Bosnian-Herzegovinian citizens. Instead, these individuals have to constantly move between the sides, continually being rejected by both, or being absorbed into one ethnic box based on, in most cases, their *ćaća*'s ethnicity.

Marija, on the other hand, took a different approach to the situation—by choosing to surround herself with likeminded people who hang out together at the cultural center Abrašević. Protected by the walls of "the mixing-friendly" center, and supported by her diverse group of friends, she looks for opportunities to resist the ethnicization of everyday life by helping

Mostar and its young people rejuvenate and reinvent themselves as multicultural, cosmopolitan citizens. This unique space of the cultural center is viewed suspiciously by numerous Mostarians, however:

> The Mostar cultural center Abrašević looks like any alternative youth gathering in Europe—a relaxed atmosphere, cool music and cheap beer. Still, you enter Abrašević as if entering a marked space, as if you are going to the meeting of some despised sect, so that you have to check carefully before you sneak inside. . . . [L]ocal people know that Abrašević is at the boundary between the Muslim and Croat parts of the city, and that the children of mixed marriages [go there], and generally suspicious types who want to revive "brotherhood and unity." (Matejčić 2009)

In addition to being seen as an alternative and marginalized space[12] some Mostarians like to stress that Abrašević could not survive without external help, support, and donations. While these claims are not easy to prove, international organizations do tend to favor centers that promote the politics of integration, tolerance, and mixing. Furthermore, they recognize people who are ready to "mix" and those in mixed marriages as enlightened cosmopolitans who are "highly self-aware, who succeeded in building a strong sense of self regardless of the pressure from collective identity" (Ljiljana Gehrecke quoted in Matejčić 2009). This quote captures the dominant and conflicting rhetoric generated by many international staff I met during my research. In the eyes of numerous internationals, locals who enter mixed marriages or consciously choose to mix by attending events and activities at Abrašević are more mature, cosmopolitan, multicultural, open-minded, and democratic citizens. Ironically, by installing the crude and mixing-unfriendly consociational model of democracy, the international political machine legitimized, expanded, and solidified the ideologies of ethnic purity, and engraved spatial boundaries between the three main groups, thus contributing to the political and social marginalization of mixing in contemporary Bosnia-Herzegovina. In this way, despite its reconciliatory and cosmopolitan rhetoric, the "international community" assisted in the creation of a sociopolitical environment in which practices, dispositions, subjectivities, and sensibilities of mixing stay spatially unmappable, politically overlooked, bureaucratically invisible, politically irrelevant, socially discriminated, and romantically unimaginable.

Love Unmixed

The majority of students I befriended had clearly defined views on mixing, which indicates that their families, friends, teachers, and wider ethno-national community transmitted unambiguous messages to them in terms of who to date and marry. The moments of romantic mixing in the school's bathroom, late night intimacies in the hotel room in Neum, and other spaces of cross-ethnic exploration and sensibility are left intentionally unnoticed and limited spatially and temporally by the state that was built on the postulates of spatial governmentality and by the norms of ethno-national cultural intimacy. Teachers often reproduced these scripts; for example, Ferhad, the Islamic religion teacher in the Federal curriculum, told me that he advises his students against mixed marriages. He often tells his students the story about his aunt, Catholic Ljilja, the wife of his *rahmetli amidža* Ahmo (deceased uncle Ahmo, God rest his soul): Ferhad explained that his aunt's "answer to that question, when she was advising her children and children of her sister was: 'Do not do what I did.' And that is what I say to my students." After seeing my puzzled facial expression, he continued to explain his words and teachings, by placing them in the larger social context: "Regardless of all the similarities in the mentality of the people, in their way of life, but . . . they [mixed marriages] are not a solution. They are more of a problem, both for the married couple and for their children. It is even a bigger problem for their children because of the reactions of the surroundings in which they live." He continued by stressing the importance of endogamy, or marrying into one's social group, as a sign of the acknowledgment of the "other": "I do direct my students to look at cultural and religious identity of a person when they choose the marriage partner. Choosing the partner from your own religious community is the best way to also spark recognition and the respect of the other." He stopped, thought for a moment, and concluded by framing his views as truly democratic, concerned with respect for difference and free choice: "True, we do live in the world of a free choice; everyone is free to do what he wants and wishes. And if someone stresses their freedom to support mixed marriages, then they should not take away from me my right to suggest nonmixing to my students."

A Croat teacher at the Mostar Gymnasium, herself married to a Serb, echoed Ferhad's story of the Catholic aunt very closely:

I said to my husband that I would do the same thing again [marry him] and that I am not sorry about what I did. But I would not recommend it to others. Every community has its own problems, and one has to adjust himself to that community and in that process give up a part of himself. Every additional pressure on the community [unintelligible] . . . if a person can avoid it he should, because there are too many problems anyhow. I say all this to my students; it is wise to run away from temptations and challenges. Unfortunately, my husband and I did not have children, but if we did, how would we name him? Lazar [Serb name] or Ante [Croat name]? I did not say all this just like that . . . all societal problems land on mixed marriages. For example, we could not get jobs. And we paid a high price for our ethnic identities—I suffered many insults from his side, as he did from mine.

These explicit messages about "mixing troubles," transmitted through family, community, and official public institutions such as schools, form clear rules of proper social conduct in terms of who to date and who to marry. These norms emerge as powerful discursive fields within which ethnic boundaries are tested, transgressed, and reinserted. Furthermore, in accordance with the postulates of the postwar state-making, the avoidance of mixing is framed not as an effect of ethnic nationalism and isolationism, but as a preference for cultural preservation and as a symbol of cross-cultural respect. Consider a comment by Ajna, a Bosniak student at the Mostar Gymnasium:

I do not want to mix with them, why would I? Luckily I have a boyfriend, but even if I break up with him, and find a Croat boyfriend, my mom would say: "What is in your head?" Now, you Azra, will think that we [my family] are nationalists, but I am not a nationalist . . . I just respect my culture and theirs. I mean, why would I date them and spend time with them, when I have these wonderful friends [all Bosniak]. Why would I mix with them [Croats]? I do not just date anybody.

In addition to resembling larger forces and rules of cultural intimacy, this quote also captures something that I heard many times in Mostar—

"why should I mix, it is easier not to!" Mixing involves effort, risk, and possibility of being hurt on the long road of (re)building relationships, which some youth could not or did not want to undertake.

Another aspect that discouraged dating across ethnic divides was embodied fear of public and private renunciation and exclusion, including ostracism from the most intimate of institutions, the family. An especially moving story is Berina's. During my research at the Mostar Gymnasium, Berina was seeing a young man from a mixed marriage of a Croat father and a Muslim mother. After several months of romance, Berina's parents found out about their relationship. I spent many hours with Berina and her three best friends, discussing this issue. While Berina had an excellent relationship with her parents before "the incident," the relationship changed drastically after they learned about Vedran, Berina's "mixed" boyfriend: "They told me *ili mi ili on* [pick either us or him]. But we [Vedran and Berina] love each other so much. And he is more Muslim than I am—he lives with his Muslim mother, and he respects our ways. He does not even talk to his father. He is not *really* Croat, but his name is Croat." Berina's friends were supportive but very critical of their friend. They and others in Mostar did not accept Berina's explanation that Vedran was "not really Croat." Under the influence of her parents and friends, Berina broke up with Vedran and cried about it every time I would ask her how she was. Her tears were bodily reactions to the unbearable tensions between personal desires, mixing, and the larger context of "not dating just anybody."

Other young people tried to either ignore or openly challenge ethnic segregation when dating. One day I was spending time with my main informant, Melita, and her friends, who were casually leaning against the wall in front of their classroom. Suddenly, Melita interrupted our chat and quietly said: "Look at that boy, he is soooooo cute," pointing at a young man wearing a red shirt with Che Guevara's picture in the middle of his chest. "He is cute," I agreed. Irma, Melita's closest friend, added "yes, but he is Croat," thus limiting the field of intimacy and possibility of romance. Melita looked at me, silently asking for help. Luckily for me, the bell rang and we returned to the classroom.

That afternoon, I joined Melita at her home for the family meal. I did this frequently, since Melita's parents enjoyed having people over for meals, and I very much liked their large household where people spoke loudly, interrupted each other when speaking, joked around at each other's expense, and openly displayed love and devotion to each other. On this day, we sat around the large wooden dining-room table, eating veal stew and *somun*, warm and soft Bosnian bread, and chatting about Melita's plans for continuing her education in the United States. After the meal, we moved to the living room, and sat comfortably on the leather sofa covered with pillows, enjoying the smell and taste of the famously rich Bosnian coffee. In the middle of our relaxed conversation, Melita asked her parents: "What would you do if I came home and told you that I am seeing a Croat?" After a second of silence, Melita's mother, Suzana, replied: "I would be happy because that means that he is also open-minded since he wants to date you." Families such as Melita's are rare in socially devastated, ethnically divided, postwar Mostar, in which the spirit of mixing has been altered and considerably contracted, so that it excludes dating and marrying people from other ethnic and religious communities.

Similarly to Melita, Fedja, who frequently mixed in the bathroom, decided not to sacrifice his romantic relationship for the sake of wider pressures. Fedja met Daria when he was a young boy, since the two families have been friends for a long time: "They and I, well, we do not have *podjelu u glavi* [division in a head], which is the main problem in this city today. . . . Yes, many people comment and criticize what we are doing, even the teachers, one of whom told me: 'Could you not find a nice Bosniak girl?' But we do not care; it is those people with *podjelom u glavi* that have problems." *Podjela u glavi*, or division in people's heads, which both individuals and the state, including the teachers at the school, exhibited, is an embodiment of spatial governmentlity. *Podjela u glavi* shapes one's exposure to diversity as secondary and yet intimately related and hegemonically connected to the homogeneous, ethnically constituted idea of groupness. Fedja and Daria broke up two months after the interview, however. After the breakup, Fedja confessed that their romance was not strong enough to survive the hostile, mixing-discouraging, ethnonationalism-prone environment.

Similarly to Fedja, Natalija from Bijelo Brdo chose love over ethnic ideology and she lost her best friend because of this decision. Natalija still suffers because of the failed friendship:

When Tijana came back to Bijelo Brdo, we were in the seventh grade. The two of us were the best friends, we were always together. One day we went to Ostrvica village for some gathering, and that is where she found herself a boyfriend whom she is with today. That was in June, and when I started dating Emir that September, Tijana's boyfriend did not like it, because, you know, Emir is a Muslim and all that. That bothered Tijana's boyfriend like it bothered all other Serbs. I did not want to pay attention; that simply did not interest me. And then he said to Tijana to choose between me and him, because, you know, how can I tell you, many Serbs hate me. And the two of us split right there. We still have the best friend in common. And one month after all this happened, Tijana told that friend of ours how she regrets everything that happened, and that she would like if we could again, you know.... I said that I could never be with her the same as I was before, because when I needed her the most, when it was the hardest for me, I did not have her. That was so hard to me, I loved her too much [starts to cry]. But what can I do, I cannot ... [starts to sob].

This account of a failed friendship is a powerful commentary on the ethnonational logic that assigns the labels of "danger," "impurity," and "tragedy" to cross-ethnic mixing and marriage. These powerful cultural forces penetrate and dismantle the most intimate relationships of love, mixing, and friendship in postwar Bosnia-Herzegovina, while reaffirming the power of ethnic identities. The synergy between official ethnonationalisms, informal rules of cultural intimacy, and perpetual ethnicization of everyday life, results in the spread, deepening, and solidification of unmixing, which is clearly visible in youth's responses to dating and loving the ethnic "other." This avoidance and fear of mixing locate mixing practices and subjectivities at the very margin of the society, making them into powerful abjects: socially marginalized, transgressive, subversive, and politically untrustworthy "agents of impurity," hybridity, and the morally and politically dubious socialist past.

These experiences of Bosnians whose intertwined lives became unmixed during and after the war point at the tension between individual desires and larger, obligatory frameworks of intimacy: cultural, social, and political. And yet, despite this largely mixing-unfriendly sociopolitical arrangement, mixing discourses and practices materialize as both constitutive and destabilizing of categories of ethnicity. The broader conceptions of interethnic intimacy, such as mixed marriages, are shaped as much from without as from within; and they became the basis for understanding how and why (un)official actors of ethnic ideologies have inspired to define ordinary people's most intimate acts and desires (Friedman 2008). Therefore any discussion of mixing is a discussion of simultaneously public and private forms of love, belonging, nationhood, identity, and intimacy. The key here is the Derridean notion that mixing and writing about mixing—any openness to the other—is always an infinite process that knows neither beginning nor end and, hence, also knows no "end-results" such as ethnically or spatially homogeneous populations.[13]

Chapter 6

Anti-Citizens

Since the first day of my fieldwork I was struck by how frequently the theme of corruption cropped up in the everyday conversations of my informants, revealing how an empty state became implicated in the texture of everyday minutiae (Gupta 2006:211). More specifically, I realized how discourses of corruption and morality here function as a diagnostic of anti-citizenship—a stance emerging at the intersection between transnational political economy, international practices, and local discourses (213, 226). When coupled with the war-produced ethnopolitics that seeks popular legitimacy in the name of "ethnic people," the related discourse and practice of immense corruption, and what people refer to as a "decline in morality," generate a mixture of cynicism, abandonment, resignation, and detachment of youth from their state, enhancing the nation's perpetual emptying of its young citizens.[1]

In my numerous discussions with youth, they often complained about their country having an impossibly complex bureaucracy, deep ethnic and political divisions, and a lack of accountability and transparency, which, in their opinion, leads to "massive criminalization of the state" (Transparency International 2009:1). In order to keep their political integrity and moral agency semi-intact, youth I spoke to during my fieldwork often situated the post-Dayton Bosnian situation within broader horizons of politics and imagination: for example, they assessed their current difficult situation within the larger—pre-2008 economic crisis—European context, which was imagined and discursively framed as more democratic, just, and livable. This larger context of political and social imagination created opportunities for both openness and closure, and it allowed many youth to make sense of their current situation, by diagnosing it as *nenormalna* (abnormal) and *pokvarena* (spoiled or rotten). This positionality permitted the youth to distance themselves from their unwanted state, and in the process of exercising anti-citizenship, preserve their citizen-morality.

This transformation of youth into anti-citizens initiated circulation of anxieties and discussions about youth, including the publication of the UNDP 2003 and OIA 2005 comprehensive studies on Bosnian youth attitudes. As a result, the public sphere in Bosnia-Herzegovina became permeated with talk about young people's future. These discourses were often conflicting; on the one side, a number of discussions focused on youth's agency, obligations, and ability to save the country from the disasters caused by the war and the bad leadership of older generations. On the other side, youth have been repeatedly described as lazy, lethargic, disillusioned, and more nationalistic than older generations (Freedman et al. 2004:231; but see a different discussion of Serbian youth's "lethargy" in Greenberg 2010, 2011, 2014).

The "youth situation" depicted in numerous reports, TV analysis, articles and newspapers was described as alarming, especially when the UNDP 2003 survey figures were released stating that 62 percent of youth would like to leave the country and 24 percent would like to leave the country never to come back. Another UN-sponsored report emphasized that 77 percent of youth would like to leave the country, while 92,000 young people left between 1996 and 2001, and by 2004 that number exceeded 120,000 (OIA 2005:2). Because of these startling numbers, international agencies such as UNDP and OSCE and local political elites significantly increased their focus on youth when presenting their sociopolitical programs and agendas about the future of the Bosnian state. For example, former high representative Paddy Ashdown put "youth," especially the phenomenon of brain drain, second on his priority list next to corruption.[2]

These multidimensional discourses of youth illustrate the fine line between discourses of morality and corruption as they relate to the state and citizenship. Furthermore, the ethnographically generated understandings about morality and corruption as "an optic for examining larger and more complex political issues, such as citizenship and the state" (Haller and Shore 2005:8), demonstrate that for the majority of youth, the Bosnian state and corruption are essentially synonymous. For example, youth that I befriended often spoke bitterly about their country as *država lopova* (the state of thieves) that is spinning out of control and that contains *pokvaren narod* ("rotten" people). The following exchange posted on the Internet portal *reci.ba*[3] captures this attitude: "Will the citizens of Bosnia-Herzegovina ever see their state institutions arrest thieves and distribute their illegally collected wealth to the social institutions?" Numerous and humorous responses followed, including: "We do not have that many prisons" and "Come on, people, after we arrest all the thieves, we will not have any politicians left!" The ironic stories and discourses of corruption reveal Bosnians' growing expectations and frustrated aspirations for peace and democracy. Paradoxically, while the promises of peace and democracy in Bosnia-Herzegovina rest on the notions of rule of law and a just society (Coles 2007), the practices of state-making (including the convoluted and extremely corrupt process of privatization of state and public property) reveal growing corruption in all spheres of social life, and Bosnian youths' fine skills in navigating the coordinates of a "new disorder."

New Economies of Morality

Bosnia-Herzegovina is perhaps the most corrupt country in Europe; the World Bank continually ranks it the most corrupt and "captured state"[4] in the "transitioning" Southeastern Europe and Central Asia (Blagovčanin 2012). Ordinary Bosnians also rank corruption as the fourth most important problem facing their country, after unemployment, performance of the government, and poverty (UNODC 2011:3).[5] Bosnians also routinely complain about corruption; it is possibly their favorite pastime. Corruption for them encompasses many faces and aspects, including bureaucratic corruption stemming from the nightmarishly complicated bureaucratic infrastructure inserted via the Dayton Peace Agreement; political corruption, which includes numerous forms of cronyism and nepotism; organized crime; and petty, everyday corruption (2011).[6] Ordinary people experience and describe these different spheres of corruption as deeply intertwined, often pointing at how these diverse forms often include the same actors.

Popular understanding and dissatisfaction with corruption in Bosnia-Herzegovina are not new; they have been documented throughout what is today the former Eastern Europe at least back to the socialist period. Collective fascination and irritation with what Bosnians themselves call corruption, however, have escalated throughout the country in the recent history of external state-making and introduction of a market-based economy. Intrigued by the prevalence of "corruption talk" among ordinary Bosnians,

I started paying attention to the local meanings and manifestations of corruption and its relationship to "citizen-morality," especially as lived and understood by young people.

The patterns of what many scholars would term "corruption" are part of the traditional fabric of everyday living, but this fabric is changing in ways that are often unfamiliar and challenging for the people to maneuver. I refer to these regimes as the new economies of morality. The new economies of morality incorporate the old, albeit altered norms of "proper action" and the novel rules of ethical behavior. While these multiple and overlapping economies of morality might seem conflicting to observers, for the majority of people in Bosnia-Herzegovina, they are fragments of one reality (D. J. Smith 2006). In addition, these economies generate ambiguous persons and relationships between individuals, communities, the state, and the "international community." For example, the instruments of democratization, peace-building, and state-making, such as the huge bureaucratic machine established in the aftermath of the war, are seen as key to the most extreme forms of corruption. It is widely believed that these institutions have been manipulated by local and transnational elites to grow their capital at the expense of "poor narod" regardless of narod's ethnicity (see Chapter 4).

In addition, linking discourses of morality to the externally regulated state reveals the transnational nature of corruption, since these cultural practices cannot be conceptualized as a "closed domain circumscribed by national boundaries" (Gupta 2006:213). Therefore, exploring how an empty nation and anti-citizens emerge from discourses and practices of corruption requires attention to transnational processes and the interstate system (213). In Bosnia-Herzegovina this manifests itself in the accounts of anger, frustration, and discontent with "democratization," which are made more complex by the ambiguous role of the international staff in these processes. For example, immediately after the war ended, many ordinary Bosnians hoped that the new, "democratic" social order would not be as duplicitous as communism (Heintz and Rasanayagam 2005) and that the presence of international humanitarian and military forces would disallow corruption to continue into the future. The opposite happened, however; since the end of the war and the beginning of the internationally supervised and governed (un)democratic state, war-amplified corruption escalated and became more visible and openly displayed. This caused much disillusionment about transitions to democracy and neoliberal forms of capitalism among ordinary people, who sometimes mentioned that Bosnia resembles corrupt states of Latin America, while relying on structural nostalgia (Herzfeld 2005)—the memories of communist "corruption" that was framed as legible and controllable—to critique the contemporary out-of-control forms of political and social action.

Encountering Corruption: Past and Present

During my fieldwork, ordinary people, caught in the forces generated by the new economies of morality, were ambivalent about corruption, which they found both frustrating and necessary to endure.[7] One of the most obvious indicators of the society becoming increasingly corrupt in the eyes of my informants was the fact that even "honest" (outside official politics) people engaged in and at times bragged about their shady jobs and behaviors, simply to survive, to protect their dignity, or to insert power and hierarchy, as the following field entry clearly demonstrates.

On a beautiful, sunny, slightly windy Sunday in April 2006, I met a childhood friend of mine, Anela, for breakfast. She picked me up in her car and soon we were driving out of Bihać, following the road framed by the cascades of the exceptionally beautiful Una River. As we were driving, I gazed at the river and thought of numerous times during the war when I swam in this cold, mountainous water, the noise of its magnificent waterfalls blocking the deadly detonation of nearby shelling: Una was my escape and my protector, my road to sanity. As I shared these memories with Anela, she started to drive faster, as if trying to outstrip the speed of the river's current. At a point where we did not expect patrols, a police car showed up from nowhere and stopped our car. After a typical short flirtation with us, and after he realized we were not going to try to bribe him—the classic way to resolve these situations—the policeman started to write a speeding ticket. My friend looked at him boldly. With an expression of entitlement on her face and a tone that indexed authority, she said: "You can write as much as you want. I have connections and I will never have to pay that."

This incident captures the complicated set of actions, discourses, and beliefs exhibited by ordinary Bosnians in everyday encounters with the corrupt state. Anela was very critical of the country where policemen can expect or even openly demand bribes from citizens they are allegedly protecting. At the same time, she was not hesitant to boast about her connections in high places in order to show the policemen that his behavior would not be fruitful, that he was wasting his time, and that she had better connections. What constituted "right" or "wrong" in this situation was not entirely clear, since the moral planes had been expanded, tweaked, and transformed in the postwar country. As a result, young Bosnians like Anela emerge from war destruction and postwar restructuring as active participants in the social reproduction of bribing, and as its principal actors and primary victims.

Stories about corruption, like the one depicted above, dominate political and symbolic language in the country. The accusations about corruption, bribery, and immorality are directed at the local elites, the "international community," and within—at one's community and, at times, at one's self. The practices of corruption and the commentaries that these behaviors generate provide the main context for Bosnians to imagine and create the relationship between the Dayton state and society in ways that are both similar and significantly different from the communist past; it is precisely the vanishing of the old socialist systems of "acceptable/predictable corruption" that makes these new forms of high-volume corruption hard to digest, leaving numerous citizens disoriented and disenchanted by the promises of peace and democracy. The new economies of morality thus emerge in the relation to the (imagined) socialist ones; while Yugoslav socialism operated under the ideology of "hidden" social networks,[8] postwar state-making produces overlapping, wide-ranging, ambiguous social actors and actions.

These tensions become especially visible and exacerbated during massive social crises, such as the war in Bosnia-Herzegovina. The morally vague actions were tolerated, however, as temporary side effects of war. The bigger reason for massive discontent among ordinary citizens is that the postwar state-making and peace-building further complicated and "suspended the normal" about morality even farther; these processes transfigured the social environment so that previously intolerable behaviors emerged as acceptable. As a result, the notions of right and wrong that characterize Bosnian cosmology today are conflicting, blurry, fluid, and constantly negotiated in the context of an empty state and everyday life. No clear guidelines about the "proper way" to be a moral citizen are emerging. Instead, the more clearly articulated standards of moral values that, according to my informants, existed prior to the war are diminished and constantly reshaped in order to accommodate those behaviors that would otherwise be considered as immoral (Heintz and Rasanayagam 2005:5). In the process, they show that ordinary people are not in control of their own moral actions and interpretations of these actions (Greenberg 2011). This is believed to increase general "acceptance" of corruption and a view of it as endemic to a postwar, criminal state and its "rotten" narod.

When the rules of comprehensible corruption are broken, people often experience feelings of shame and disorientation for their participation in these processes. For example, there is a widespread and long-standing practice to take a gift (including farm products and, more recently, money) to one's doctor. The rates of these transactions escalated to the point today that many people struggle to secure the "doctor money," and they have to rely on the extended family for help.[9] In November 2006, my friend's uncle was admitted to the hospital in Bihać for a prostate condition. The doctor told the family he would operate on the uncle the following day. The evening before the operation, the family got together to discuss how much they should give the doctor. They decided on 500 KM (approximately US$380, two thirds of an average monthly Bosnian salary at the time). The person delegated to give the money to the doctor was the uncle's daughter, Lamija. The following morning, Lamija went to the hospital and knocked on the door of the office. The doctor invited her in and when she tried to give him a white envelope with money, he refused and said: "They sent you, young and beautiful, to do such a dirty thing." Lamija was impressed, but also shamed and disturbed by doctor's reaction; he interrupted the semi-established rules of expected behavior related to "health and wealth" (Jašarević 2011), leaving the whole family uncertain and semiparalyzed, not knowing how to best read his rejection. Was he "really" moral, thus both respectable and deserving of pity for his naiveté, or was his reaction a signal of some sort? Was the sum inadequate? Or was perhaps Lamija too young and gender-inappropriate to engage in bribing?[10] It is precisely through these uncertainties stemming from the vanished socialist "system" of acceptable, doable, and predictable corruption, that the empty state and its questionable laws and norms come to be imagined in the eyes and lives of citizens. During communist times, citizens claim, the process of giving bribes through semi-established and self-limiting channels, public transactions, and performative gestures (Gupta 2006:216) was more or less legible. The majority of people, however, feel they are missing the cultural, social, and economic capital required to negotiate these services in the era of external state-making and neoliberal market economy. This leads to much cynicism and related detachment from the state among ordinary Bosnians, especially youth.

War Profiteers, Whores, and Bicycle Thieves

How did narod come to be seen and described as rotten and profusely corrupt? My data and personal experience imply that the intricate moral foundations of prewar Bosnian society, mostly influenced by the socialist ideology of "trust," informal networks, and state control, mixed with traditional rules of the "Bosnian way of life," changed considerably during and after the war. "War is the time that brings out the best and the worst in people," I often heard, which makes everyday existence tense, emotionally charged, and always at the edge. This fragility of life gives rise to the discursive fluidity between the notions of right and wrong. For example, the start of the war gave rise to a new socioeconomic phenomenon, the so-called international and local *ratni profiteri* or war profiteers, who made their fortune *preko noći* (overnight) by reselling food and other basic necessities to starving populations under siege in cities such as Sarajevo, Bihać, Goražde, and Tuzla. These networks of illegal trade were complex, effective, and in many ways ironic, since they involved trading with the ethnic enemy or the UN soldiers (see Nordstrom 2004). Their logic was especially visible in the regions under siege, such as my home town, Bihać.

Bihać was one of the six regions declared by the UN as "safe havens," meaning that the UN was supposed to protect the populations under siege from shelling and possible mass killings.[11] Bihać was surrounded by the Serb-dominated army forces for three and a half years, during which the inhabitants were put under a terrible regime: we could not leave the region, we had limited food supplies, and we were constantly bombed from the surrounding hills and mountains, while expecting that the Serb army could break the defense line and walk into our city any moment, causing massive destruction of buildings and bodies. These expectations created enormous psychological pressure, which, when coupled with continuous physical danger and enduring hunger, resulted in a population sealed off from the rest of the world. Our only sources of food were insufficient local farms and the UN humanitarian aid convoys that would come only sporadically, at the whim of Serb army checkpoints. The food we received was mostly canned meat (there were many rumors that the unidentified meat in cans was horse meat), beans, and flour. Women became war magicians as they created edible dishes out of these meager ingredients.

Various individuals in town (and beyond) saw an excellent opportunity in this desperate situation. They arranged shady business deals with "the Serb enemy," often during the night, at the main locations of exchange near the major frontlines.[12] Physical proximity to the frontlines was not accidental, since numerous fighters who would shoot at each other during the day would engage in illicit trade at night, to varying degrees. The war and military became a market, and "soldiers had the muscle to make the best deals" (Tsing 2005:37). Smuggling and black markets took over the economic dynamic, and while they did generate profits that could be declared illicit, they were also "essential for daily survival, providing a crucial supplement (albeit at highly inflated prices) to woefully inadequate international humanitarian aid" (Andreas 2004:33). Hence, at the epicenter of the war and its major frontlines, a new type of person emerged—the fusion between a solder and an illicit trader. The rise of these new elites provoked conflicting feelings among the larger population—a mixture of respect and bravery on the one hand, and frustration and detestation on the other. This open display of contradictory attributes, both "right" and "wrong," by the powerful people hints at the existence of the moral "gray zone"—the space at once ethical and corrupt (see Nordstrom 2004).

These trader/soldiers purchased flour, sugar, oil, soap, cigarettes, and other necessities from their business partners at low prices and resold the items in town at much higher cost, thus making an enormous profit literally overnight. All the money the starving population saved or received from relatives working abroad was spent on these basic foods, the prices of which were enormous, ranging up to 100 dollars for a bag (approximately 50 pounds) of flour. This "list" of items and prices was similar in all Bosnian cities under siege; for example, in Sarajevo a box of Marlboros could be bought for 20 German Marks and sold for 250 in the black market (Andreas 2008). The main traders were often small thieves and hooligans before the war, some of whom were good fighters during the conflict and who gained fortune quickly. Many have continued to this day to be among the richest and most influential politicians and businesspeople in postwar Bosnia-Herzegovina.

While the OHR constantly demands the end of rule by the war profiteers, ordinary Bosnians complain that the internationally generated anticorruption discourses are not successful. More critical citizens argue that the anticorruption talk is just a façade and that numerous international staff use external state-making in Bosnia-Herzegovina for their personal gain—international aid is not believed to be free of corruption (Transparency International 2009:1). While many international workers focused their energies on the official goals of peace-building and state-making, quite a few also engaged in illicit trade with the local residents, including trade of UN ID cards (Andreas 2008), thus calling into question the validity of seeing Bosnian corruption as a local phenomenon and adding transnational flavor and form to the new economies of morality. The initial rumors about international dimensions of "Bosnian corruption" were later supported by facts, showing that some internationals were indeed involved in illicit practices, including frequent visits to prostitution houses, trafficking in human beings, smuggling weapons, and accepting bribes (Vandenberg 2005). The presence of the UN troops on the ground thus did not lessen the corruption: "United Nations peacekeeping troops were making a fortune selling everything from cigarettes and alcohol to heroin and tanks in former Yugoslavia. Some estimated that upwards of half the economy was generated through these activities in the precarious times of war" (Nordstrom 2004:187). In 1999, the *New York Times* estimated that corruption and misuse of international aid was as high as US$1 billion (Transparency International 2009:9). This twofold role of the international workers generated a new category of a morally ambiguous person in the turbulent, peace-building context—the fusion between an international peacekeeper and a global smuggler, entirely congruent with the local soldier/trader.

In addition to these new categories of persons, the scope of the international humanitarian and military intervention created another stratum of the local population without much awareness of its larger social impact. First, the international presence required a large number of interpreters. Thousands of people, many young and fluent in English, got their first jobs with the foreign agencies, thus impacting the generational relations in the country. While interpreter salaries were much lower than the salaries of the foreign workers, these mostly young people still made at least two to four times as much money as the rest of the local population. For example, immediately after the war I got a job with Malteser Hilfsdienst (a German humanitarian aid organization), which paid its interpreters much less than larger organizations such as the UN or Red Cross. Still, my salary was higher than my parents' (both government employees) combined salary. In addition, these interpreters between internationals and locals were able to move in and out of country with much more freedom than the rest of the local population. This created multiple tensions between the confined population and those Bosnians and Herzegovinians employed by foreign organizations. The pressure was most intensely experienced in the domain of gender relations.

Most of the translators for foreign agencies were young women, which resulted in a swift gender restructuring in the disordered society, especially its urban areas. These women often served as immense inspiration for rumors circulating in public, mostly about their allegedly immoral behavior. At times, these women were characterized as "easy women" or even "whores" who slept with internationals, as these women worked long hours, often traveling with their almost exclusively male bosses for days, which made them frequently absent from home. These patterns of behavior were largely unfamiliar in prewar Bosnia-Herzegovina, and they signaled the rise of a new type of person in the Balkan social landscape: an educated, partly "Westernized," semi-independent, self-seeking young woman. In addition, the foreign presence required a great number of cooks, cleaning women, drivers, and other personnel who, regardless of their position, frequently made more than a teacher or doctor employed by the crumbling local government. This created chaotic and powerful economic and gender restructuring, even if temporarily. While many Bosnians felt grateful to the international organizations for creating these jobs, the same people remarked that the society in which *vozač zaradi više od doktora* (driver makes more than a doctor) cannot be good.

In addition to the soldier/traders, peacekeepers/dealers, and independent working women, the war produced a great number of internally displaced persons. In many ways, the displaced persons were the biggest casualties of war. I witnessed the arrival of thousands of these people who were forced out of their homes in the villages surrounding Bihać; after days of walking they reached Bihać and occupied the apartments left behind by local Serbs. The tension between the old inhabitants of the town and the village refugees[13] was sharp from the very beginning, and it increased over time. At first, people in Bihać were very welcoming and sympathetic to the misfortunate refugee population. Soon after their arrival, however, one could hear on the streets: "Serbs were better—at least we taught them good manners. Now we have to educate these guys from scratch."[14] The tension exploded into full-scale mistrust because of one alleged habit of the refugees—stealing bicycles. During the war, bicycles became the main mode of transportation for civilians (army personnel still used cars) due to the great shortage of fuel. But refugees, especially a group from the village of Glavica, almost immediately obtained the label "bike thieves" who could not be trusted. The initial rumors about their interest in stealing bikes created a reputation of morally dubious refugees, establishing a boundary between the old population and the newcomers that continues into the present day.

In order to understand the weight of the "bike thieves" label, one has to contextualize it—during socialist times people took pride in the belief that petty crime was almost nonexistent in Yugoslavia. This trust in the sincerity of one's community was widespread and people still remember it with nostalgia and longing. One cold night during the war, my friends and I gathered at Alen's apartment, since we were not allowed to leave the building due to the repeated shelling. We sat around, next to the improvised candlelight, laughing, complaining, and commenting on our lives under siege. The conversation carried us back to socialist times. After a few shots of cheap vodka, Adis, red in the face, commented: "What kind of times are these . . . during Tito's time you could leave your bag in the middle of the street and find it untouched the next day . . . we never even locked the doors of our home even when we went away for ten days." After a short moment of silence, another, by that time very drunk friend of ours, who was a refugee from the village near Bihać, got up from his chair, stood up on the table, yelling: "Dok je Tito bio živ, ti si mog'o u svakom grmu spavati, spavati, spavati/jebavati, jebavati, jebavati" (During Tito's time one could sleep and fuck in any bush [and no one would bother you]). Those times were over, everyone in the room agreed, while silently falling into the space of structural nostalgia. The war destroyed the socialist trust in *pošten narod* (genuine folk) and fabricated new economies of morality, social mistrust, and devious categories of persons—including the local and international elites at the centers of power, and marginalized and stigmatized citizens, such as the Glavica refugees/bike-thieves.

These actions performed by ordinary Bosnian people who sought goods and services by any means available "simply" to survive, contribute to the perception that "corruption has won over law and order" (D. J. Smith 2006). I heard numerous Bosnians complain about being compelled, attracted, and resigned to participate in corruption and at the same time feeling angry, frustrated, disappointed, and betrayed by their own actions. These conflicting new economies of morality amount to much cynicism and related detachment from the state among ordinary Bosnians, especially youth, who grow up in the context that engenders the production of new assemblages of persons and relationships. They have been absorbing these massive sociopolitical and economic transformations, while trying to envision and negotiate their future in the morally unstable, dubious, and disordered social world. Their world is full of opportunism, fast roads to money, and open display of power and connections, which became the main benchmark on the road to adulthood. This context generates two unique, corruption-related processes that symbolize the shift from socialist to neoliberal times: excessive bragging, even pride, in engaging in "corruption," and the emerging, geographically and temporally situated discourse of Bosnian (negative) exceptionalism.

"Because I Have a Hookup"

During the mid-2000s, the uncertainty about the rules and uses of corruption, nepotism, and informal networks was further complicated by increasingly open bragging about the use of connections. In other words, there was no discomfiture in using means other than knowledge and competition to achieve one's goals and hope for a better future; it was power, reach, and connections that counted and people openly said so. There was something about the manner in which this was being discussed that signaled a shift in the local political and social worlds and imaginations. The overt display of corruption takes verbal (e.g., bragging about one's connections) and nonverbal (e.g., conspicuous consumption) forms. This shift from relatively covert to more overt display of networks was visible not only in the behaviors of the corrupt elites who felt secure in their power, but also in all aspects of life in postwar Bosnia-Herzegovina, as the following excerpt from my field notes illustrates.

One morning as I was rushing to class using the now-familiar Mostar shortcuts that crosscut Mahala, I met one of the students from my class, a troublemaking young man who already had several police arrests for different misdoings, and who was among the least achieving in a class of excellent students. Still, I liked talking to him because he was straightforward and intelligent. He also had a great sense of humor, and he entertained the class. As we were walking past Mostar's ghostly ruins—leftovers from the recent war—I hesitantly asked what he planned to do in the future. He responded quickly and assertively: "I think I will study law." I could not resist asking: "How will you get into that department when you have bad grades?" He looked at me and without hesitation replied: "Jer ja imam štelu" (Because I have a hookup). Next November, I came back to Mostar to visit friends and found out that this student had indeed enrolled in the university and was studying law, side by side with students who studied hard throughout high school because they had no connections.

The new economies of morality that include public display and openness about illicit actions are related, in local discourse, to the vernacular connotations of state-making. The people's stories indicate that in general "things got worse" since the war ended and the socialist "system" vanished. When people would exhibit "immoral behavior" during the war, this was explained by abnormal conditions of living; corrupt behavior and informal networks became a contemporary skill that made one's survival more probable.

Overwhelmed by witnessing these cultural practices of unconcealed illicit activities, I approached Husein, an old acquaintance of mine, and asked for an explanation. He told me that most people, when talking about the injustices of everyday life, somewhat cynically say "Pa to ti je kapitalizam!!!" (Well, that is capitalism!!!), often followed by "Htjeli ste demokratiju, eto vam demokratije" (You wanted democracy, here you have it). These comments point at multiple ways in which Bosnians perceive, interpret, and live capitalism and democracy. Furthermore, discourses of corruption help define "the political," and they constitute anti-citizens who perceive themselves as acting against corruption and immorality, even if they are complicit in it. This explains how for the majority of Bosnians and Herzegovinians, democracy is described as just in principle and moderate capitalism is seen as a possibly proper way to organize the market economy in the global world; yet, in their unstable local world, the nexus between formal democracy and capitalism is described as altered and morally questionable.[15] Excessive and blatant, massive and petty corruption in Bosnia-Herzegovina is therefore not something linked to premodern, socialist, and traditional, but endemic to modernity, democracy, and capitalism, which provide new opportunities for the emergence of shadow economies and what people see as morally vague conduct. In this way, the discourses of corruption become means by which a complex, externally regulated, shallow state is symbolically constructed in public culture (Gupta 2006:223), including in the classrooms of the Mostar Gymnasium. The following vignette from the field captures one of those moments when an empty state and its corrupt leadership were discursively constructed and evaluated by a geography teacher.

In her lecture on Mostar landscape, the teacher introduced the rise of a new type of local elites and their dangerous, kitschy, and huge homes: "due to the type of soil on which the homes in the Strmina neighborhood [where many new elites construct their homes] in Mostar are built, if there is an earthquake or a big flood, all those houses with their big fake lions [one of the main symbols of kitsch and "bad" taste] are going to start sliding and they will push narod into the Neretva [River]." The teacher emphasized that the new elites who quickly and illicitly gained fortunes overnight were lacking in cultural capital,[16] and she labeled them as "uneducated and uncultured." Their "lack of culture" was visible in the absence of knowledge about the poor quality of Mostar's soil. These elites, who do not have deep roots in *gradska sredina* (urban environment) that generates cosmopolitan awareness and disposition, became the source of the overall cultural decline, dangerous for the social, moral, and even physical safety of (urban) Mostarians. The new elites "simply" *ne znaju kako imati* (do not know how to have) and they are *nezasiti* (insatiable). Their greediness is explained as a consequence of their fast and questionable accumulation of money during and after the war, their upbringing, and their habitus, described as raw, rural, and *prost* (vulgar). Furthermore, like Nino, who said that mixed families could not fit in the postwar spatial governmentality of the city and thus could easily end up in the middle, where lies only the river (see Chapter 5), the geography teacher also used the metaphor of a river to talk about the dangers awaiting "cultured," "normal," and urban Mostarians, who are being pushed into the river, thus disappearance, by the "flood" of unrefined new criminal elites, their fake lions, and hideous huge homes.

Puzzled by the rising scope, visibility, and audibility surrounding connections and corruption, I once again approached Husein. While we sat in front of the TV in his living room, watching an extremely popular and controversial CBS-inspired political show *60 Minuta* (60 Minutes), I shared with him my interest in the new articulations of corruption, especially among youth. He listened to me carefully, and then, after a moment of silence and in the spirit of structural nostalgia, he explained to me that connections were used during socialism as well, but to a much smaller extent and only to help someone with certain qualities, not to put someone unqualified in a position of power. Importantly, this was done secretly, due to social stigma and fear of the socialist state, as Husein recalls: "You could not say: 'I am the son of that person and that is why I got that job.' If you did, the police would come to your door. Today anyone could be a president, they do not even have to have a high school education, they only need to buy a Ph.D. That kind of injustice could not happen during Tito's time." Here Husein discloses yet another contextual and for many Western observers counterintuitive dimension of "Bosnian morality"—that it is more respectable (done "in style") to hide/discipline/limit illicit actions and behaviors, than to openly display them and boast about them.

When I hesitantly, during the commercial break on TV, mentioned to Husein that he recently used connections to help his niece pass an exam at the local university, he explained: "You do not understand. Things have changed. I have high moral standards. Everyone in this town knows that—you cannot buy Husein, I am transparent. You know my story—I lost several jobs because I refused to join SDA [the leading Bosniak nationalist party] and play their dirty game. I even, for a while, left the public life altogether." Husein paused for a second and then continued:

> You see, everything here is so unjust. For example, you know that professor Mirnad, don't you? He openly says to his students who do not know his subject too well that they will only pass into the next grade if they pay him a large amount [of money]. When I hear this and see how others get their diplomas, including some of the local elites, without ever showing up at the university at all, when I see how *tajkuni* [tycoons] buy degrees for their families, then I feel a *moral obligation* to help a student who tries hard but cannot pass because she does not have anyone to help her. She took that national history exam, how many times, maybe 13? And she keeps failing. How is that possible? I think that the only proper way to act in this situation is to use my connections to help her end this masquerade.

Husein's thoughts and actions demonstrate how, when confronted with multiple moral models, individuals combine their past experiences/ideologies and cruel optimisms (Berlant 2011) to confront their present uncertainties. In other contexts, this behavior could be seen as deviant or immoral. However, in times of external state-making, which Husein called "masquerade," and which allowed the local elites to engage in insatiable corruption, these actions are seen as being in-between, tolerable, or necessary, even moral, in order to scratch out a living and confront what is *truly* immoral—the new elites and the "elsewhere state" (Jašarević n.d.). At the same time, Husein utilizes complex moral interpretations and embodied frustrations to distance himself from the criminalized, morally empty state and from those in society who are "truly" immoral, mainly ethnonationalist politicians and *tajkuni*.

To learn more about the worlds of *tajkuni*, I decided to spend some time with Irena. She and I often shared the same desk at school and I appreciated her honesty and friendship. Irena reminded me of Paris Hilton, with her skinny figure and long blond hair. On that day, she was waiting for me, leaning against the glass door of the hip bar in west Mostar. She was dressed in a purple jacket and trendy orange tennis shoes. Irena "smelled" like money. Her eyes glowed when she saw me and her mouth opened in a big smile offering two rows of shiny braces to the sun. She pulled my hand and a second later I found myself following her to a centrally placed table, so that "we could be seen."

Irena was a daughter of a big *tajkun* in Mostar, the man who had a transportation company that was making vast profits at the time. Other students in class often called her *tajkunuša* or "*tajkun*-daddy's daughter," which made her smirk. As we were talking about her future in Zagreb, where she planned to continue her studies, we ordered Cedevita, a suspiciously orange vitamin drink, and shifted our conversation to money. I asked her how she could tell who had money. She pointed at some girls passing by and said: "See, the one to the right, she has it. . . . How I know, you ask? Well, the easiest way is based on what kind of clothes people wear. Like, here we have many copies of the original brand names . . . but when you see someone wearing an original Hugo Boss or D&G shirt, you know that that person has money." Several minutes later, Irena returned to the talk of fashion and *originali* (the original brands of clothes) and she said, proudly: "I only buy the originals! I will tell you how I do it. I buy clothes that were stolen. Yes, stolen. Who steals it? . . . Well, the Croats [from Croatia] do. They go to Italy and steal clothes there. Then our guys here buy them from them relatively cheaply. And they resell it here. So you can see an original price on a sweater of let's say 1,000 euros but we pay 200 euros! That is a good deal." Since I was very interested in the channels through which Irena obtains her *originali*, I asked where she goes to buy these stolen clothes. She explained: "We always buy from only one guy. Where? In private apartments . . . it all takes place in private apartments. We go to his place and pick and choose. Marko [Irena's boyfriend] always buys that way and I go with him." I could not resist but to ask Irena if she minds that the merchandise is stolen. Irena looked at me for a second, thought about my question, and said candidly and confidently "No, why would I?"

This example shows how corruption might be illegal, but it has, nonetheless, its own morality where illicit actions do not need to be perceived as immoral in a traditional sense. This shows that legality and morality are not synonymous, and that some illicit actions can be incorporated into the moral worlds of a certain subset of populations. That is how corruption can have its own, multifaceted morality. For example, in the eyes of elites, such as Irena, the shadow economy stretches the domains of moral behavior so that they include numerous illicit actions. Shadow economies (Nordstrom 2004) offer new possibilities for prosperity, and for hoping and achieving one's goals. In this instance, however, hope is dislocated from the socialist sphere of morality where one's future was imagined, planned, and hoped for based on one's intellectual capabilities, informal networks, and political loyalty. Post-Dayton Bosnia-Herzegovina, however, offered new spaces of hope and political and economic agency to open up within the emerging world of shadow economies, which stretch across official political, geographical, and moral boundaries. This world offered much optimism for people like Irena, armed with extensive connections and equipped with piles of money. At the same time, it excluded people like Husein and his niece, who were pushed to its margins, playing its "dirty" games to respond to and partially correct injustices done to them and those they cared about. Therefore, for Husein and his niece, postwar democratization and state-building felt less like a world of progress and opportunity, and more like hopelessness and impossibility, approximating existential crisis, and like the distorted and corrupt meaning of survival, where one "cheats" in order to endure.

Bosnian Negative Exceptionalism: Here and There, Now and Then

My friend Irena was not a good student, but she did not need to worry— her father had widespread connections in Croatia and she already knew she would be studying psychology in Zagreb. When I reminded her that she barely got a D in the psychology class, she waved her hand nonchalantly and said: "That does not matter *here*, I have connections."

Irena's notion of "here" is remarkable, since it points at the perceived exceptionalism of the Bosnian case. "Here" indexes a *geographical* (and temporal) space: the city and the state as social spaces where the rules of moral action are different from other places. These discursive "imaginative horizons" (Crapanzano 2004:4) give youth a hope of a better future elsewhere, while obstructing an articulation of "here and now," thus freezing youth's view and relationship to the reality that immediately confronts them. It is *here*, in postwar and postsocialist Bosnia-Herzegovina, that it does not matter if you do or do not have good grades—what matters is who you know and how much money you have. In other places, which are not *here*, it might be different. This dialectic of closeness and openness, and hereness and thereness, that imaginative horizons generate, keeps in suspension social agents and powerfully shapes their sensibilities toward the state. For example, those youth who cannot or do not want to engage in the *tajkun* style of life feel angry and hopeless, wishing to leave the country under any circumstance. The following example shows this clearly: once, during a sociology class when teachers and students engaged in a nonchalant discussion, Harun made his frustrations clear: "Because of these injustices which you see everywhere, from your teachers, from others around you . . . because of that one should leave Mostar. I know a guy, my parents know him, he has two or three college degrees and his children are hungry. Where else does that exist?" The student sitting behind Harun concludes: "Yes, teacher, we should leave; anyone who wants to stay is a fool. I say [turning to me], please write this down: 'Ivica would rather clean toilets in Belgium than be a director of a bank in Mostar.'"[17]

Harun's cynical comment, "*Where else* does that exist?" also indexes a geopolitical imagination/location and reveals the perceived contours and ills of Bosnian modernity where rules are bent to accommodate the behaviors that people engage in but cannot easily digest. While this situation is common to many places that face similar social and political turbulences, Bosnians complain that this "transitional" time from warlike behavior, explained insightfully by a local writer as *došlo vrijeme da pametni šute a budale vladaju* (the time has arrived when smart people are silenced while the fools rule), has continued for too long. Dino commented on the Bosnian exceptionalism that produces an agonizing social situation:

Look at many countries in the world! Look at Eastern Europe, for instance! They also had their Tigars, Ćelos, and Jutas [former Bosnian army soldiers who were among the leading war profiteers and mafia men in postwar Bosnia-Herzegovina] immediately after the fall of communism, but that period lasted for about 10 years, and then the intellectual elites regrouped, came together and took back the power. And things got better; the mafia guys are forgotten or at least they are less influential. But *here*, that transformation did not happen. No one came to replace the mafia men, the intellectuals are silent, and they either left, died, or got marginalized, while the same criminals still rule. People live in fear of them. And do you know what the real problem is? That if you go to any of the local Internet chat rooms, as I did it this morning, you see these guys such as Tigar [local mafia man] being talked about as idols of youth—they all want to become like them when they grow up.

This quote demonstrates, among other things, the belief in the exceptionalism of the Bosnian case, which manifests itself in the spatial indexical "here." As a number of scholars have pointed out, corruption has become one of the symbols of the transforming postsocialist world and its nonlinear transition to capitalism (see, e.g., Haller and Shore 2005). These new ethical forms, largely associated with consumption, such as clothes and educational credentials, hint at the folk models of capitalism. In addition, there is a prevailing sense among ordinary Bosnians that in the rest of the region, also marked by the outside world as "corrupt," these issues are dealt with more quickly, aggressively, and successfully, while Bosnia-Herzegovina continues to be plagued by corruption. People often say, dramatically: "Even Albania is ahead of us," showing how Bosnia is falling behind even Albania, which has been historically (and problematically) perceived by the majority of Yugoslavs as the darkest, most backward corner of Europe. In this way, space and time are intimately connected to create Bosnian negative exceptionalism.

These frustrations with Bosnian exceptionalism grow with time. Commenting on the aggressive behavior of three high school students in Tuzla who brutally attacked their fellow high schooler in front of multiple spectators armed with phones and cameras, Emir Imamović wrote:

Everywhere, in every society, there are incidents like the Tuzla one. We do not have an exclusive right on thieves, killers, vandalizers, and aggressive children. We, however . . . have a systematic production of scum, which started in the 90s of the last century, when the accentuated patriotism of individuals and groups became an excuse for their illicit behavior in the time between the battles. Teenage aggressors, let's repeat, are products of the broken system and as such these teenagers will grow up to be serious, big criminals.[18]

As a result of the perceived cancerous spreading of corruption, excessive projection of immoral behavior is experienced by ordinary people as a uniquely Bosnian quality, regardless of the widely documented spread of corruption globally (D. J. Smith 2006). The story of Bosnian particularity reveals that ordinary Bosnians believe that corruption is a pervasive problem of postwar political, economic, and social modernity. At the same time, the framing of this phenomenon as a particular feature of Bosnian life transforms the rest of the world into a place open to imagination and hope for better life and alternative modernity. This creates a sharp distinction between "here," seen as a morally corrupt Bosnian democratization where one has to withdraw from the state and its dirty politics in order to survive, and "there," imagined as a site where moral rules are more or less in place and where a person can choose not to engage in corrupt behavior and be a recognized, respected citizen. This stimulates the desire for youth to leave their country for a better place, and it creates a further gap between Bosnia-Herzegovina and "Europe," and between the youth and the state. As a consequence of this detachment, youth adopt an active stance of anti-citizenship—political "hibernation" in the contaminated present (see Hromadžić forthcoming)—which includes waiting for better times to arrive and a related aspiration to leave the state under any circumstance. This detachment is understood by numerous international staff and researchers as a sign of youth's apathy and lethargy. More recent ethnographic studies on nonparticipation as a site of agency, calculated choice, and political and moral preservation offer a much more complicated view of the situation, however. In these anthropological studies, youth's "social life of disappointment," including nonparticipation in "political life," is explained as a highly complicated and agentive process (see Fox 2004; Greenberg 2010, 2014; Kurtović n.d.). In other words, through indifference, apathy, humor, irony, and scorn, youth "eschewed participation in political establishment in favor of their own pragmatic needs" (Fox 2004:381).

Youth's active detachment from the state and their desire to leave Bosnia-Herzegovina permanently became especially apparent during the teachers' strike in February 2006.[19] The strike created a space in classrooms when teachers and several students who attended classes had more opportunities to speak about wider social problems. One of those heated discussions took place during a geography class when only eight (of thirty) students were present, so that the teacher decided not to start a new lesson. In the cold and mostly empty classroom, the students and the teacher energetically and informally chatted about education, corruption, the strike, youth and their future. Here is an excerpt from this conversation.

> Harun: Our society is made in a way that everyone tries to finish some school, to get a diploma, and not to gain any knowledge. The goal is just to get into university.
> Halid: This country should disappear from the face of the Earth!
> Teacher: It is not the country, it is the people! You will get out of here, [you will] go to university, you can change something. Students change the world, so why do not you take things into your own hands?
> Davor: Why do not you change the situation, professor?
> Teacher: We also agree that things need to change, that reform is needed. How many times did we go on strike? We do not get anything, but we start working again because of you. The problem is in the people. Here, I have a student who has straight As, his parents have no money, and he will probably stay in Mostar, probably will not be able to continue his education, and the one he shares his desk with has all Ds but he will go to Zagreb to the University because he is full of money.
> Daliborka: That is why we are all unmotivated and demoralized.
> Harun: We talked to the teacher Vedrana the other day about this—how can you start this school full of energy and leave feeling apathetic?
> Teacher: What can I say to a student who spends five hours every day studying at home, has all As and then someone who never studies, who just sits at home, comes here and passes into the next grade?
> Harun: Well, teacher, that is because there are new rules now, you know. It goes like this: "I can, I want, and I have connections!" "Takav smo mi narod" (That is the kind of narod we are).

This dialogue captures youth's approaches to their society, corruption, education, morality, and future. Students describe themselves as "demoralized and unmotivated," and they see no exit from the situation but to use their connections to achieve their goals, to withdraw from political life altogether in order to preserve their sense of (political) self for better times, or to hope they will eventually leave the country. The teacher agrees with the students, but she also challenges them to do something about the situation, because they are young and "should take things into their hands." Students are tired of being called on to change the situation and they call on the older generations "to clean up the mess they made," the attitude embedded in the student's response "why don't you change the situation, teacher?"

The teacher's continuous remarks about the problem being located in the Bosnian and Herzegovinian people and Harun's concluding remark, "that is the kind of people/nation we are," hint at the aforementioned notion of fundamentally honest and resilient narod being transformed into a morally "decaying" and "rotten" nation. This approach, which puts blame on narod and its mentality, suggests that there is something in the changing postwar culture emerging at the intersection between international practices, transnational forces, and local politics, that is twisted, immoral, stale, psychologically conditioned, and hard to change. This vision of an increasingly immoral narod leads to the idea that the excessive corruption is truly a Bosnian mark and Bosnian curse, which has become amplified, ironically, by processes of peace-building and democratization. This view makes many ordinary Bosnians assume their fellow citizens are prone to corruption and immorality, since it is in their "postwar culture." This creates an ironic situation where even those who most openly criticize corruption end up being prone to it; many students admit that they would use connections to get where they want to be if their connections were strong enough, since that is the only approach this state and its impoverished and disillusioned narod know and value. In this way, the youth who see themselves as the main critics of corruption become potential and skilled agents in it.

Finally, the transformation of the popular slogan "I want, I can, I will," into Harun's "I want, I can, and I have connections" is very telling. The first version, popular during Tito's regime, was used above all to motivate and describe Tito's socialist youth. It suggests individual agency, progress, and one's determination to achieve success by relying on one's own hard labor and willpower. The new, twisted version of this phrase, ironically uttered by Harun, suggests something different, however: the possessive verb "to have [connections]" shows ownership as well as displacement of individual agency to the web of connections, which are never under control of an individual agent.[20]

After observing transformations of socialist citizens into poor, unemployed people on the one side or into *tajkuni*, corrupt politicians, and criminals on the other, I realized that for a great majority of my informants, state-making and transition to capitalism were experienced as corrupt, impoverishing, and unjust. While the bulk of people had much appreciation for democracy as a principle, their experience of "here and now" midway democracy felt essentially stale, immovable, and immoral. These feelings strike tremendous cynicism among ordinary Bosnians about the future of the state that is both ethnically segregated and corrupt. The product of this social helix is, among other things, a stance of anti-citizenship among the youth who feel detached from any political public. Numerous youth in Bosnia-Herzegovina are thus actively and consciously resigning from involvement in the country's current workings, while planning and awaiting a better future, hopefully elsewhere. The following note, written (in Bosnian and Japanese languages) by an unknown youth participant on the interactive "map of crisis," prepared for the exhibit "Ništa više nije isto: Kultura krize i društvene promjene u Bosni i Hercegovini" ("Nothing is the same any more: the culture of crisis and social changes in Bosnia-Herzegovina") by Amir Husak, beautifully captures these sentiment. The note reads: "It is very sad that we live in a country in which the biggest success is to leave it."

Based on these insights, one might be tempted to suggest that recent "ethnic" violence at the end of the Cold War "unmade the world" (Scary 1985) of youth by creating political acquiescence and inertia, and by producing hierarchies of domination and submission based on corruption and uncertainty. Ordinary Bosnians feel that democratization fuels corruption, which then generates, together with political turbulences, anti-citizens and an empty nation. And yet, my data includes stories about enormous creativity and agency displayed by young people, who use both formal and informal networks and licit and illicit ways to navigate the novel configurations of disorder. As a result, I do not see the youth's withdrawal from the corrupt, internationally supervised and ethnonationally conceptualized state as a straightforward mark of apathy and lethargy. Instead, youth's resistance, individual rebellion, and participation (even if via corruption)

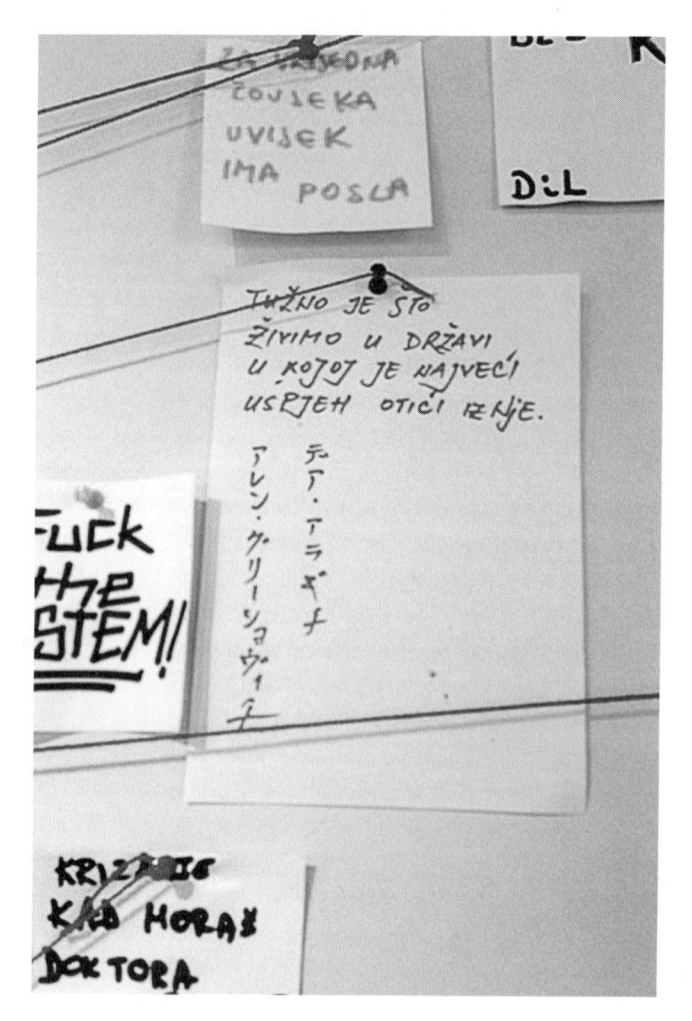

Figure 7. Bihać, August 2014. Photo by the author.

in the postwar state make them into complicated postwar political agents. Their ingenuity and political and economic awareness make me uncomfortable to label Bosnian youth, as is often the case, as a lost, sacrificed, and socially impotent group. Instead, I see them as active agents who try to maneuver, more or less successfully, their space and their role in the constantly shifting, morally confusing, and nationalism-prone context created by the recent war and ongoing international intervention.

Conclusion

Numerous international observers of Bosnia-Herzegovina still refer to the reconstruction of the new "Old" Bridge as one of the most important symbols of reconciliation in the country. For the majority of Mostarians, however, the bridge failed to fulfill the reconciliatory role envisioned by these discourses and projections. Rather, the Mostar Gymnasium has become a more representative symbol of the internationally directed programs of peace-building and state-making in Mostar and Bosnia-Herzegovina. Therefore, symbolically speaking, the Mostar Gymnasium *is* the new bridge—this school, its spatial governmentality, and its organic everyday life powerfully capture and reflect the spirit, the techniques, and the effects of the post-Cold War international humanitarian intervention.

In late spring 2012, I returned to Mostar. I was eager to visit the city and its people and to verify my ethnographic data. My goal was to capture and reflect on the changes that have taken place since the completion of my fieldwork in 2006. I knew from continuous email exchanges and phone conversations with people at the school and elsewhere that new progress toward integration had been made since I finished my fieldwork. For example, I was told that a joint Parents' Council had been established at the school in November 2008.[1] I learned that teachers and students have been communicating more across ethnic boundaries.[2] In addition, the computer science classes were integrated, so that for the first time since the beginning of the war in Mostar, Bosniak and Croat students jointly attend classes taught by a Serb teacher. Furthermore, the United World College opened its Mostar College in one wing of the Mostar Gymnasium, where chosen students from all three communities, the rest of former Eastern Europe, and the world jointly attend classes taught in English and work on, among other things, conflict resolution. Finally, the American Embassy installed the American Corner in the basement of the school, where students from

182   Conclusion

Figure 8. Mostar Gymnasium, reconstructed, June 2012. Photo by the author.

the two curricula mingle during breaks between classes and use the Corner's facilities, such as computers and books. Inspired by the news of these changes, for months before my scheduled return, I anticipated the visit—I wanted to witness, grasp, and make sense of these and other changes at the school and the town.

From the very start, the return was emotional and exhilarating. From a rain-spotted window of the Centrotrans bus that brought me from Sarajevo to Mostar, I looked at the heavy clouds and familiar surroundings. To add to the spectacular feeling of return, as I approached Mostar, the clouds separated and the Herzegovinian sun, unhesitant and self-assured, welcomed me into the city. I got off the bus as the sun was setting behind the rugged Mostar hills. Without much thinking, and unburdened by the heavy backpack, I strolled to the school; Stara Gimnazija stood there—in the middle of the revived Boulevard—proud, dominating the landscape, with its new, bright orange façade.

I came back at a very exciting time—many changes were unfolding in front of my eyes, and numerous events took place during the weeks of my return. While the experiences were many, they all condensed around one main notion articulated by the majority of my informants, which can be summarized in the following statement: "Yes, things are much better now, more relaxed, but people still have *podjelu u glavi* (division in their heads)." At first, I grappled to analytically capture that complexity; yes, things did get better, but divisions, albeit more fluid, are still there, resistant, embodied, dispositional, and (infra)structural. I struggled—I wanted to be able to show how much I appreciated the improvements that I witnessed and that people eagerly emphasized. At the same time, I wanted to take note of the still palpable and profound divisions and obstructions, and to depict everyday life in a perpetual state of spasm, where hope and lack of hope intermingle. I was able, once again, to witness the organic capacities of everyday life that continues to challenge the rigid ethnopolitical structures imposed on this life. And yet, as a consequence of still-divided, ethnicized lives, people got used to living in homogeneous territories and identities.

While the changes in cartography and geography of the school were plenty, my biggest surprise was the level of activity in the "empty" computer lab. During my time away from school, computer science classes had indeed been integrated and students attended classes together. Multiple factors, some coincidental and some calculated, made this "full integration" possible. Soon after the school was administratively unified, the Japanese government that financed the reconstruction of the lab realized that, given the divided curricula, the lab was going to stay empty of its intended beneficiaries. To avoid this situation, they decided to look for "cracks" in the ethnicization of curricula and to create an environment that would make integrated computer science classes possible. This required multiple interventions. For example, a questionnaire about the initiative, explaining the introduction of a very modern informatics curriculum that would accompany unification, was sent to all parents, who overwhelmingly supported the effort. The principal and vice-principal of the school, the city of Mostar, and the Cantonal Ministry of Education all had to approve the merger. Then the curricula had to be synchronized, since before unification, the computer science course was offered in the first (U.S. nine) grade in the Croatian curriculum and in the third (U.S. eleven) grade in the Federal curriculum. The Cantonal Ministry and Pedagogical Institutes agreed that the computer science course could be moved from the eleventh to the ninth grade in the Federal curriculum. Once this was accomplished, the classes had to be created. The school leadership decided that each ninth grade class in both curricula would be split in two, and half from each curriculum would be matched with half from the other. These students (half from each curriculum) would attend the lab portion of the course together. The theory portion of the course, however, was still to be taught separately, so that students could be instructed in their national languages.

Almost everyone I talked to about the computer class merger believed that this simultaneously divided and unified class is a good solution, "given the wider context." This wider context, still largely segregated, continues to make any open expression of solidarity and unification seem like a threat to the ideas of cultural heritage, plurality, and difference. This then triggers the fear of "identity loss" in the wider, ethnically conceived community, and creates an opportunity for ethnopoliticians to build on this fear, reinsert ethnic boundaries, and secure their position of power.[3] Therefore, this example of "full integration" of the school lab illuminates the constraints on "peace" under the regime of consociational democracy and ethnic nationalism, where any "progress" toward integration becomes a space for ethnic leaders to reinsert dominance, distrust, despair, and isolation within the language of cultural preservation, tolerance, autonomy, and respect.

In the midst of these changes and constraints, bathroom smoking continues to unfold behind the two sets of closed doors. One day, I found students standing by an open window, smoking and laughing. I explained to these "new youth" how we used to smoke in the bathroom six years ago, just to hang out with the "others." "Some of us did not even smoke," I concluded. The students started to laugh, and one girl said: "I danas je tako" ("It is like that today too"). Then she continued: "Too bad you did not come two hours ago; there were fifteen of us here, from both sides." As they were inhaling the last bits of smoke before they had to return to class, one young man looked at me, smiled, and said: "This is the only normal room in this school." Then they left the bathroom, and once again I was left in the smoky bathroom alone, surrounded by sad-looking cigarette butts on the floors. I felt the same curious sadness that I felt in a similar situation six years ago—like everything and nothing has changed. It is this ambivalence that I feel every time I think of "my" school—its story of simultaneous inclusion and exclusion, where the wider context and dominant ideologies of ethnic purity and nationalism favor and recognize exclusion as legitimate, while inclusion and interconnectedness continue to powerfully linger in the "cracks" between ethnicized territories and ethnically dominated political realities.

One thing that became clear to me during my return to Mostar in 2012 was how the floating, fragile, and organic everyday interactions at the school become hyper-invisible in the wider sociopolitical grid that the postwar state has become. In the structure that recognizes ethnic culture as its main and natural domain, and makes insertion of ethnic boundaries its primary sociopolitical and, important, economic task,[4] the fluid moments of commonality around the issues of shared fate, common suffering, and widespread political disenchantment and economic deprivation stay invisible because these voices, sentiments, and experiences have no place, no boundary, no language/name, no institutional space to claim or that would claim them. They cannot materialize into meaningful acts under the current system when the meaning itself has been hijacked by ethnopolitics. True, some people resist the ideologies and contours of ethnopolitics, but their resistance is immediately marginalized, estranged, eliminated, and suffocated by local elites' maneuverings and international diplomatic miscalculations, contributing to the profound sense of emptiness.

My return thus confirmed this book's main thesis that the consociational model of democracy, when coupled with continuous ethnonationalist politics, cultural fundamentalism, and related ethnicization of everyday life, generates an empty nation in Bosnia-Herzegovina. The empty nation is not some real entity or group, but a category of absence that captures the growing lack of social and political vision for Bosnia-Herzegovina, as it unfolded under Dayton, among its youth. The literal, mundane emptiness that youth encounter, experience, and inhabit is also giving rise to the ontological dimensions of emptiness, where absence can emerge as both paralyzing and productive of sociopolitical potentiality—one that is often located elsewhere, however, dwelling in different geography and/or futurity. These processes lead to the nation's being perpetually "emptied" of its youth citizens and to overall citizen "numbness." With its ordinary, hungry citizens being constantly denationalized, segregated, ethnicized, and stripped of citizen-identification, the Bosnian nation ends up holding too little—it exists primarily to harbor ethnically conceived and managed populations, while leaving the interconnected histories, economic solidarities, and hybrid lives socially marginalized and politically uncultivated. Hence, the Dayton-produced state in Bosnia-Herzegovina materializes as an "empty container," which, due to its ideology and (ir)rationality (Scott 1998), fails to recognize, provoke, and nurture panethnic identification and economic solidarity or to successfully "contain" citizens who belong to it territorially and historically. Consider, for example, a moving reader's response to the article published in *Slobodna Evropa* on November 21, 2013, marking the eighteenth anniversary of the signing of the Dayton Peace Agreement:

> Everything exists, but Bosnia. And I have to get used to that painful truth. I do not want to lie to myself anymore and to hope that I have something that was forcefully taken away from me, leaving me at the blowing winds [without shelter]. . . . One has to cure oneself from the false hope. And not regret. That which once existed was alive, providing me with warmth, courage . . . it is all gone now. And so be it! Probably it was not even good. If it were [good], it would be here, countries do not disappear from the face of Earth. And I cannot find Bosnia-Herzegovina. Not even to humanly say "goodbye" to her. And I used to love my Bosnia-Herzegovina.[5]

This comment illustrates how ordinary citizens, tired of "here and now politics," react to their fragmented, dysfunctional, and frustrated ethnopolis (Mujkić 2007). Assuming, as transnational actors and foreign observers often do, that the Bosnians-Herzegovinians now need to take things in their own hands, ignores the effects of war and postwar political ideologies and policies, simultaneously "local" and "international," which severely limit the possibility for "postethnic society" (Stojanović 2011:108) to emerge under the current arrangement in Bosnia-Herzegovina. Everywhere I went, people were saying that this situation only benefits the politicians in power who do not want to see any changes—their wealth grows with every additional day of living (post-)Dayton in Bosnia-Herzegovina. But most people are "normal," who want to live "normal" lives, have "normal" jobs, without explaining what the "new normal" might mean and what form it might take. When I would ask my interlocutors why people do not choose new leaders that could respond to these calls for "normalcy," one, a Banja Luka-born former refugee in her mid-forties, said:

> See, only people like you, our people abroad, show this kind of optimism, I dare to say naiveté. You believe that there is room for change. There is no optimism here . . . *why*? Well, first, it is all corrupt, contaminated from the top to the bottom [of society]. Who will make the necessary change then? No one [of the people in

power] wants to see people like you, normal educated Bosnians and Herzegovinians, return to lead the country. You scare them, and they will, if you confront them, say that you do not understand how it is here, that you left some time ago, that you are too intellectual, too Bosnian, or too utopian. That is how they manipulate people, through fear . . . *which fear, you ask*? The fear of the new war, of the "other" . . . the war hit us all so hard that today people are ready to tolerate everything: corruption, hunger, unemployment, tension . . . *samo da se ne puca* (for as long as there is no shooting).

This powerful mentality of *samo da se ne puca*, coupled with over two decades of divisive ethnopolitics that nurtures ethnic nationalism and homogenization of "culture," generates a vacuum of optimism and limits political activism. One last time, I shared my frustrations with Husein, who, listening to my description of the rigidity of changes in Mostar, concluded: "*Međunarodna zajednica je napravila grešku na startu, bez obzira što su dobro željeli*" ("the International Community made a mistake at the start [by seeing ethnopolitics and ethnopoliticians as the only partners for creating stability and peace in Bosnia-Herzegovina] regardless of their good intentions"). Then he paused, seeing my puzzled and possibly distressed facial expression. After only a few short moments of telling silence, he elaborated, however: "[But] *Narod je gladan* (people are hungry). People are voting for the nationalists because they feel that there is no other option, no alternative, and that nationalists will provide them with jobs. But wait and see, Azra, *narod će se dići* [people will rise]." Speechless, hopeful yet disillusioned, I nodded.

Epilogue: Empty Nation, Empty Bellies

It is mid-February 2014 and I am sitting in my office at Syracuse University. Husein's words, "but wait and see, Azra, *narod će se dići* (people will rise)," with which I concluded this book, are echoing in my mind while I am reading numerous reports, analyses, and predictions about the unfolding "Bosnian Spring." This movement of marginalized, disillusioned, angry, and hungry "ordinary" people—mainly unemployed workers and students—began on February 4 in Tuzla, once a prosperous Yugoslav industrial center located in the FBiH. The industrial potentials of this town were devastated during the war and destroyed by the shady processes of privatization and democratization. As a result, Tuzla today harbors among the highest numbers of unemployed people in the state.

On February 4 a significant crowd of "ordinary" people gathered in Tuzla to express their anger against *lopovi* (thieves, politicians) who, hiding behind the contours of Dayton and its ethnic nationalisms, grew rich—through self-interested policies—from peace-building and state-making. In this way, they directly contributed to the high levels of unemployment, delayed salaries for the employed people, and the related steep rise in poverty for the majority of ordinary workers and other citizens. While the event in Tuzla at first appeared to be yet another localized congregation of people suffocated by growing social inequality, elitism, and corruption, the protest quickly spread throughout the country. This included not only larger centers but, importantly, also smaller, primarily exindustrial towns facing severe poverty and highest unemployment levels, such as Bihać, Bosanska Krupa, Orašje, Živinice, Breza, Kalesija, and Maglaj.

During the first days of protests, and especially on February 7, while facing police brutality, protestors in Tuzla, Sarajevo, Mostar, and Bihać looted and burned government and, in some instances, private property.

Empty Nation, Empty Bellies 189

This rage is understandable—it is a symptom of and a reaction to decades of accumulated anti-citizen sentiments born out of frustration, negligence, feeling of betrayal, and overt snobbishness of local and international political elites. As the protests unfolded and the initial chaos and obliteration ceased, more and more ordinary people took to the streets and started to peacefully walk together under the banner of narod. This embodied political capacity of empty, growling bellies moving/protesting together in multiple town centers released new politics of visibility and possibility, culminating in the creation of citizen plenums. In these "open to all" citizen assemblies people come together and, in the spirit of direct democracy (without labeling it in this or any other political-science language), engage in discussions about their immediate political and economic concerns, their present and their future. In these meetings ordinary citizens produce lists of requests they then put in front of their cantonal decision-makers. This democratic exercise in the name of empty bellies has so far led to, among other things (such as eliminating the practice of paying "white bread," or salaries of politicians after they leave office), an overturn of four cantonal governments in FBiH and to people's growing commitment to continue to occupy the street until all their requests are addressed/fulfilled and a new government of people-chosen experts is elected.

This "new" and seemingly sudden politics/solidarity of empty bellies surprised many local and international politicians and observers, who kept on (fearfully) asking: "How is this possible? Where did this come from?" Fearing, for the first time in more than two decades, for their political lives and economic fortunes, local politicians (and the media houses that they control) attempted to mold these calls for political responsibility and socioeconomic transparency as acts of conspiracy (Who is really behind this? But *really* behind? People "here and now" could not do this (democratically organize) by themselves? Who is using narod?), or used ethnopolitical manipulation (by trying to absorb, control, and eliminate the rising anger born of hunger into an ethnically motivated issue, such as illuminating the fact that most of the protests happened in FBiH with limited activities in the Republika Srpska). Acting (once again) in synchrony with the local political elites, the "international community" in Bosnia-Herzegovina responded, via the mouth of high representative Valentin Inzko, by threatening to employ international troops if the protestors' violence continued. Protestors verbally lashed out against the high representative, indexing their impatience with the "international community's" perpetual misreading and miscalculation of the Bosnian people, actions, places, and histories.

The protestors replied to these framings, attacks, and threats by emphasizing, once again, that their solidarity rested on their shared predicament —one shaped by unemployment, excessive corruption, citizen-marginalization, and empty bellies. They openly told the media and politicians that they were not sheep to be manipulated by the fear of (the next) war anymore. Responding to the forceful attempts by local and regional politicians and mainstream media to reframe the "language" of economic solidarity into an issue of ethnonational conspiracy, protestors bespoke: "Gladni smo na tri jezika" ("We are hungry in three languages"). This linguistic act beautifully subverted the charges of ethnonationalism, while using and reinserting, yet trivializing, the "grammar" of ethnonational division.

While much of the European, regional, and local public discussions, diplomatic evaluations, and some academic analyses of this "unexpected" Bosnian awakening echoed disbelief that this kind of emerging mobilization could happen in contemporary Bosnia-Herzegovina, my ethnography of an empty nation (as well as some other ethnographically grounded and inspired scholarship) makes the timing and articulation of the current events not so surprising, but rather historically informed, contextually logical, and politically evocative (also see, among others, Jansen 2014; Kurtović 2014; M. Lovrenović 2014).[1] More specifically, in order to transform themselves from ethnicized anti-citizens into Bosnian citizens, *gladan i napaćen narod* (hungry folk, exhausted from suffering) *had to* claim the street. They could not act within the existing political (formally/procedurally) democratic system since this system does not recognize them as citizens but as ethnic collectivities. In order to act "just" as citizens, they had to be anti-citizens to the Dayton regime, and citizens of the streets/direct democracy where the future is presently being (re)written. This explains why the international and local elites do not know how to approach these hungry, emerging citizens, because they escape easy classifications and are instead using different "grammar," and thus a different citizen-script, unrecognized by the one-dimensional grammar of Dayton.

And yet, these citizen-struggles, I suggest (in contrast to some of my colleagues), cannot be understood as a total erasure or destruction of the ethnonationlist matrix—it is against this matrix that the protests materialized, to which structures they eventually refer, and with which script they stay entwined. The structures and grammar of Dayton are a necessary context from which to analyze the geographic unfolding of the protests—to understand and explain why they did not, for example, mobilize equally in time and space in the whole state. Rather, the protestors, while creating the political "outside" of the Dayton political machinery, still have to engage with Dayton and work against the boundaries/walls/divisions/people produced through Dayton's spatial governmentality. That is also why protestors "speak" of common hunger in "three languages," since this language of language difference/ethnicity is the only language that the local elites and the wider international community understand. More specifically, in order to resist the attempts of those in power to intentionally misread and reethnicize the politics of empty bellies, the protestors have to "perform ethnicity" and subvert it in its visibility, as the protestors in Jajce, a divided central Bosnian town, for example, did when they tied together Croatian, Serbian, and Bosnian-Herzegovinian flags. These strategies of political resistance shed light on the powerful relationship between the processes that created an empty nation and the ones that mobilized empty bellies, including the transformation of (anti-)citizens into citizens (or vice versa, depending on who is doing the interpretation). When put in the context of the twenty years during which the state has been perpetually emptied of its youth citizens, the current protests become logical in their formation timing, and vocalization.

As I write these last paragraphs, I am also watching a video from the latest protest in Mostar. I see a sign that reads: "Two prisons under one roof." The camera moves from the sign to the faces, young and old, in the crowd. People, as they slowly and symbolically walk in a circle in the middle of the Boulevard, shout: "Istok-Zapad-Sjever-Jug" (East-West-North-South). This speech act signals citizen solidarity across the city's suffocating spatial governmentality, while still acknowledging its existence. The camera slows down and zooms in on one face in the crowd and I recognize Jasenko. We first met Jasenko in Chapter 3, when he angrily talked about the racist connotations "hidden" in the language of mixing. I still remember his face as it looked through the cigarette smoke in the school's bathroom. He has changed since I last saw him; he is in his mid-twenties now, his facial hair attesting his maturity. He is 5,000 miles away, but I hear his voice and see his lips moving apart and coming together to shout: "Istok-Zapad-Sjever-Jug." In the background, as if supporting his back, the Mostar Gymnasium proudly stands.

Notes

Introduction

1. In this book I mostly use Bosnia-Herzegovina when referring to the state. Where stylistically more appropriate, however, I use the shorter construction, Bosnia.

2. BBC News Europe, "Mostar bridge opens with splash," 23 July 2004.

3. I use "ordinary people" with much caution in this work. As Veena Das (2007) has pointed out, "everyday" is where much deeply political work happens.

4. Numerous scholars have documented the importance of schools as primary sites in which images and ideas about national loyalties are disseminated and attachments to national states are formed (see, among others, Gellner 1983; Anderson 1991; Hobsbawm 1990; Althusser 1971; Levinson, Foley, and Holland 1996; Willis 1977).

5. The names of informants in the book are pseudonyms. The names of smaller towns and villages have been changed as well.

6. In order to carry out its mission, the OSCE relies on donations from its 57 member states, primarily in Europe, Central Asia, and North America; at times it receives support for specific projects from nonmember states, such as Japan.

7. There are three curricula used today in Bosnia-Herzegovina. The curriculum of Republika Srpska is used primarily in that Republic. The Federal curriculum was developed by the Bosnian Federal Ministry of Education; however, it is used almost exclusively by Bosniaks and was rejected by Croat leaders in Bosnia-Herzegovina, who, at the time of my research, have used the curriculum from Croatia, modified by the Institute of Education in West Mostar and the Ministry of Education of Hercegovačko-Neretvanski Kanton (Freedman et al. 2004:229).

8. Brotherhood and Unity was the policy of interethnic relations in Tito's Socialist Federal Republic of Yugoslavia. It was proposed that all Yugoslav ethnic groups should peacefully coexist and nurture the notion of cross-ethnic affiliation.

9. It is important and telling, however, that the decision-makers did not attempt to keep the flame on regardless of the gas shortages—certain institutions were spared from the shortages, but not this monument.

10. For a visual tour of twenty-five of these abandoned monuments, see http://www.cracktwo.com/2011/04/25-abandoned-soviet-monuments-that-look.html.

11. Ferhadija was a centrally located mosque and a cultural heritage site in the historically ethnically diverse city of Banja Luka, now the capital of the Republika Srpska. The mosque was destroyed, as part of ethnic cleansing, by the Serb militia in 1993, together with fifteen other mosques in the city. The mosque is currently being rebuilt.

12. The agreement's official name is the General Framework Agreement for Peace.

13. In the case of Bosnia-Herzegovina, the contours of consociational democracy are even more complex. The state has seven levels of governance, 13 constitutions, hundreds of ministers, and over 600 deputies (Bieber 2005:4). In addition, Bosnia-Herzegovina is best described as a "triple power-sharing system" (44), where power-sharing exists in entities and cantons, and to a much smaller degree, at the level of the state. The installation of this seemingly equal, but in reality unbalanced, political arrangement led an "asymmetrical" (Kasapović 2005:4), intolerably plural (Vlaisavljević 2005), inherently complex, unstable, and dysfunctional government (Bieber 2005:40).

14. The term Bosniak or Bosniac (Bošnjak) has its origins in the Middle Ages, when a slightly different but related term Bošnjanin was in use; it embraced all inhabitants of the medieval Bosnian kingdom, including Catholics, Orthodox, and Muslims in the territory of today's Bosnia-Herzegovina (Bringa 1995; Malcolm 1996). During the early years of Ottoman rule, the name was replaced with Bošnjak, with a territorial, not a national, connotation (nationhood did not exist as such in the Ottoman Empire). After the Austro-Hungarian Empire annexed Bosnia in 1878, the new administration tried to promote Bošnjak as a panethnic, national Bosnian identity. The efforts failed, mostly due to the rising nationalist movements in neighboring Serbia and Croatia, which mobilized and divided the ethnic communities in Bosnia along ethnonational lines. Bošnjak was revived in the 1990s; and at the congress of Bosnian Muslim intellectuals in 1993, it officially replaced Muslim in an ethnic sense. In everyday speech, however, Muslim and Bošnjak are often used synonymously.

15. For example, entities are in charge of "territory, population, citizenship, constitution, parliament, government, judiciary, administrative system, military, police, official languages, flag, coat of arms, anthem, and so on. The powers of the central state institutions are limited to foreign policy and trade, customs, monetary and migration policies, air-traffic control, the implementation of international obligations and regulations, [and] the regulation of transport between the entities" (Kasapović 2005:4).

16. The ten cantons in FBiH fall into three groups: five in which Bosniaks are the majority population, three Croatian-majority cantons, and two "mixed" cantons.

17. Over the last twenty years, however, there have been at times considerable efforts on the side of international state-makers to strengthen the state-level institutions and to limit the power given to entities and cantons in the Dayton Peace Agreement (Bieber 2005).

18. Here I expand on Sally Engle Merry's (2001) notion of spatial governmentality, which she, building on Foucault (1991), understands as (gendered) mechanisms of spatial segregation, discipline, and punishment found in postmodern cities.

19. Data gathering for this study was conducted in Mostar (primary site) and Bijelo Brdo (pseudonym, secondary site) between June 2004 and December 2006. Toward the end of my stay in Mostar, I realized that it would be useful if I could spend some time away from the publicity and fame of the Mostar Gymnasium to better understand processes of state-making in an area that received much less international and national attention. This is why I decided to spend the last three months of my fieldwork in Bijelo Brdo, an impoverished town populated by Bosniaks and Bosnian Serbs. In this account, I use the data from Bijelo Brdo only sporadically; I refer to it only where comparison is fruitful and where it allows for better grasping and explanation of the phenomena that are the main subject of this work. The majority of data, however, come from my participant-observation work at the Mostar Gymnasium, collected during numerous visits between 2004 and 2012, with the longest, nine-month stay taking place during the 2005–6 school year.

20. While there were some concerns that the violence would rise in the aftermath of the fierce fighting between Croats and Bosniaks elsewhere in the country, the tension never escalated into a full-scale conflict.

21. Herceg-Bosna was a quasi-state of Croats created during the war in the Croat-dominated regions of the country (Malcolm 1996:252).

22. For a similar reflection on Croatia, see Drakulić 1993.

23. These "top-down" restructuring and democratization efforts (Brown 2006:9) included a massive financial aid package: the initial, four-year recovery and reconstruction program for Bosnia-Herzegovina proposed by the international donor community (World Bank, the Western states, EU, UN, etc.) was US$5.1 billion (Coles 2007), dispersed among hundreds of local and international governmental agencies and NGOs. In addition, Smillie (2001) estimated that in 1996 there were between 156 and 240 NGOs in Bosnia-Herzegovina; in 1998, the UN Development Programme (UNDP) recorded 500–1,600 local and 185 international NGOs (Smillie 2001).

24. Responsibility for military security was initially given to the NATO-led Implementation Force (IFOR), replaced in 1996 by the NATO-led Stabilization Force (SFOR) and in 2004 by the European-led EUFOR Althea force.

25. PIC is composed of 55 states, six of which form the Contact Group (United States, UK, France, Germany, Italy, and Russia). Since February 2007, the Steering Board of the Peace Implementation Council has been aiming at closing the OHR institution in Bosnia-Herzegovina, hoping that the country would be able to take full responsibility for its own affairs. This transition has still to happen, even though the influence and visibility of the high representatives have been noticeably decreasing in recent years, http://www.ohr.int/ohr-info/gen-info/default.asp?content_id=38519, accessed March 18, 2011.

26. There have been seven high representatives: Carl Bildt, Carlos Westendorp, Wolfgang Petritsch, Paddy Ashdown, Christian Schwarz-Schilling, Miroslav Lajčák, and the current high representative, Valentin Inzko.

27. The organization was given a budget of 244.9 million Austrian shillings (US$24.4 million) (Coles 2007:51) to "organize and supervise elections, to further democratic values, monitor and promote human rights, and to implement arms control and security measures" (ICG 2001:2).

28. OHR Regional Office, Mostar, "Short History of the Office," May 14, 2003, http://www.ohr.int/ohr-offices/mostar/history/default.asp?content_id=5533.

Chapter 1. Right to Difference

1. Most people accept the beginning of the siege of Sarajevo, which started on April 6, 1992, as the start of the Bosnian war. Others, however, suggest that the beginning moment was the JNA attack, in November 1991, on the Croatian village Ravno in eastern Herzegovina.

2. Roma are a minority population in the former Yugoslavia, especially in Serbia and Bosnia-Herzegovina. They tend to inhabit poorer and marginal urban areas and are commonly derogatorily referred to as Cigani (Gypsies) by people of all ethnic groups in Bosnia-Herzegovina.

3. One shopping center has been completed since I left the field, but it is small and expensive. Therefore, Bosniaks in general still prefer to shop on the west side.

4. *Komšija*, or a neighbor, is one of the most prevalent vernacular ways to speak of social relations in Bosnia-Herzegovina, especially when it comes to social trust, affection, reciprocity, home visits, and exchange (Sorabji 1995:89; Bringa 1995). "Good neighbors," regardless of their ethnic/national/religious backgrounds, are crucial for one's cultural, social, and economic well-being and carry a significant moral dimension.

5. Not all Croat youth felt this way about "going east." For example, Davor was curious about the other side, so one day he crossed to the east side with a group of friends. On the way back from his first trip, as Davor was waiting for the green light to cross the boulevard, his parents drove by and saw him standing on the east side of the street: "They were shocked. They kept turning back and looking at me, their eyes wide open. When I got home, I said to them that one of my Croat friends from school moved back into his apartment on the east side so I went to visit with him after school. You know, my parents are really nationalistic. I could not care less."

6. This type of school is not unique to Bosnia-Herzegovina. Similar schools were developed independently in Scotland, where they are known as "shared schools" (Tony Gallagher, personal communication, Belfast, Northern Ireland, April 18, 2006). In addition, a new governmental direction in education policies in Northern Ireland argues in favor of seeing education as a continuum from segregation to integration, with several possibilities in between, including shared schools and federation principle schools (David Russell, personal communication, Belfast, Northern Ireland, April 26, 2006).

7. In January 2004, high representative Paddy Ashdown imposed a decree that abolished the six municipalities and replaced them with six electoral units.

8. Fra Dominik Mandić was a Croatian church historian who belonged to the Franciscan order.

9. Because of Croat leaders' resistance to integration, the U.S. offer was withdrawn.

10. This fear proved to be unfunded; the transition from a Croat to a Bosniak vice-principal was rather smooth.

11. The Croat side has, in addition to the reunited Stara Gimnazija, a New Gymnasium, which has become the most prestigious school on the Croat side since the beginning of the war. There is another, Second Gymnasium (language- and pedagogy-focused) on the Bosniak side, but my interlocutors reported that it lacked in quality and popularity.

12. According to the ICG 1996 report, the statistics for dead or missing in the aftermath of the war are 50.5 percent Bosniaks, 34.9 percent Serbs, 10.2 percent Croats, and 4.4 percent others (quoted in Bieber 2005:29).

13. In the first two years after the administrative unification of the school, the Croat curriculum struggled to attract students to enroll. One teacher said, "there was so much fear and resistance [by Croat parents] to send children to the school. We literally had to gather them from the streets and bring them into the classroom." This, however, changed once the first year of unified schooling ended with no incidents and the school continued to produce well-educated and internationally exposed students.

14. The janissaries were infantry units that formed the Ottoman troops and bodyguards. The janissary corps was originally staffed by Christian youths from the Balkan lands, including Serb and Croat boys in Bosnia-Herzegovina.

15. Many people on the streets of Mostar, however, argued that this collision between Croat leadership and Croat community was not a genuine one. The leaders, while saying that they agree with integration, argued that they cannot go against the wider community and neglect their resistance to incorporation. In that way they achieved two goals—they pleased the OSCE with their stance, while ensuring that integration did not take place since it lacked popular support.

16. In his writings, Taylor (1994) distinguishes between the "politics of dignity" and the "politics of difference." He defines the politics of dignity as a search for equality in what is "universal, the same, an identical basket of rights and immunities" (38). The "politics of difference," on the other hand, requires recognizing the unique identity of an individual or group, their distinctiveness from everyone else. The idea is that this distinctiveness has been consistently ignored, glossed over, and assimilated to a dominant or majority identity. Suppressing this difference or uniqueness is felt to be an instrument of political and social oppression.

17. The term "trapped minority" was first suggested by Dan Rabinowitz (2001).

18. The term "constituent people" is used to ensure that "minorities" or "national minorities" is not applied to the three primary groups, the Bosniaks, Croats, and Serbs (Perry 2002:2).

19. These figures are approximations—the first postwar census was taken in October 2013, with the final results to be released between one and one and a half years later. Meanwhile, anxious rumors and exaggerated figures flood the Bosnian public and private spaces.

20. Bosnia-Herzegovina and Croatia signed an official agreement about dual citizenship for Bosnian Croats in August 2005. The agreement legalized the common practice of allowing Bosnian Croats to acquire Croatian citizenship as well. The complexities of this arrangement might become even more visible now that Croatia has entered the European Union.

21. At times, this distinction fuels political desire for a secession of Herzegovina from Bosnia-Herzegovina (and possibly its inclusion in the Greater Croat state) or, in more moderate political circles, the aforementioned political demands for the creation of a third entity in Bosnia-Herzegovina for the Bosnian Croats. This was attempted during the war (1992–95), aiming for the creation of a Croat Herceg-Bosna parastate.

22. For an inspiring analysis of the workings of the triadic relationship among "nationalizing states," "national minorities," and their "external national homelands," see Brubaker 1996.

23. The proponents of Greater Croatia claim that all the territories that were part of Croatia (which was in union with Hungary) before the Ottoman invasion should be returned to full Croat control.

24. Dr. Falk Pingel, former head of the OSCE Department of Education.

25. For integrated schools in Northern Ireland see, among others, DENI 1988; Dunn 1986; Gallagher and Smith 2002; Gallagher, Smith, and Montgomery 2003; and McGlynn 2003. For studies that focus on bilingual education in Israel, see Feuerverger 2001 and Bekerman 2005.

26. Tony Gallagher, personal communication, Belfast, Northern Ireland, April 18, 2006.

27. During the war, the Bosnian Croat army forced most Bosniak families out of their homes, and the process of return has been slow and painful. The actual politics of desegregation is more complicated according to Karl, an OSCE staff member. On one occasion, he explained that the main obstacles to the integration of the gymnasium in Stolac were, in his opinion, created by Stranka Demokratske Akcije (Party of Democratic Action) or SDA, which is the main Muslim nationalist party, and not by the Croat leadership. SDA, he stressed, was also to be blamed for the recent separation of schools in the cities of Prozor-Rama and Čapljina.

28. Serbo-Croatian was taught as a second language in all schools where it was not the first language (Slovenia, Macedonia, Kosovo, and parts of Vojvodina). Military service was obligatory for all healthy men and it was twelve to eighteen months long. Men from the republics where Serbo-Croatian was not the first language learned this language during their military stay (they were almost exclusively based in republics other than their own).

29. They still tend to learn the Latin alphabet, however, due to its prevalence in the region and the "Western" world.

30. In *Pravopis bosanskog jezika* or *The Orthography of the Bosnian Language*, this author argues that Bosnian is the language spoken by 4.5 million people, meaning all people in Bosnia-Herzegovina and some other parts of the former Yugoslavia and its diaspora.

31. Serbs in Bosnia-Herzegovina speak a dialect of Serbo-Croatian that is closer to Croatian than to Serbian spoken in Serbia, but would never agree to call their language Croatian (see Longinović 2011:285).

32. For example, Young (2000:208) argues that if people want to live in a democracy, they have to inhabit the same public spaces, so that they can relate to each other's experiences and in that way, create a shared fate. For Barry (2002:79) in addition to shared fate there has to be a feeling of empathy for others, since "we cannot expect the outcomes of democratic politics to be just in a society that contains large numbers of people who feel no sense of empathy with their fellow citizens and do not have any identification with their lot." In other words, if people are to be in a community of fate, they have to share public spaces and institutions, such as schools and neighborhoods (Trappenburg 2003:307). Based on these insights, the aforementioned scholars would probably characterize the consociational democratization policies that reinforce war-generated segregation in the name of "peace" as undemocratic and unjust.

33. United World Colleges (UWC) exist in many parts of the world and "deliver a challenging and transformative educational experience to a diverse cross section of students, inspiring them to create a more peaceful and sustainable future." UWC Mostar, located on the second floor of the Mostar Gymnasium, is the first UWC with an explicit goal of helping to rebuild postwar society http://uwc.org/about_uwc/default.aspx, accessed February 4, 2014.

34. Personal communication with OSCE staff member, June 2010.

Chapter 2. Cartography of Peace-Building

1. The division between the two sides of the table was much less noticeable during the teachers' strike in February 2006. While the teachers still remained on separate sides, they all discussed, across the table, the news and plans for the strike (see Hromadžić under review).

2. Mostar's Serbs are the least visible group in the city today. There are too few Serb voters to elect even a single representative on their own; all elected officials of Serb nationality in the past were elected on tickets of other parties. Mostar thus "has Serb representatives, but not representatives of the Serbs" (ICG 2009:10).

3. Several students mentioned how they wished that they had lived during Tito's time, when people were, as one student said, "normal," and everyone talked to everyone else. On Tito and Yugonostalgia see, among others, Petrović 2010; Velikonja 2009; Volčič 2007.

4. Personal communication from Field Mission Chief for OSCE Mostar Unit, June 2010.

5. Some Croat administrators were convinced that the OSCE removed the wall photographs not to create equilibrium but to hide the "truth"—Jadranka, for example, said that the so-called Croat school had many non-Croats in its ranks before the reunification, including, at one time, a Bosniak principal.

6. "Arbeit Macht Frei" or "Work Liberates" is a German phrase well known because it was placed above entrances of Nazi concentration camps during World War II.

7. *Ustaša* literally means "insurgent"—"name taken by an extremist wing of the Croatian Party of Rights which, led by Ante Pavelić, accepted the patronage of fascist Italy in the interwar period; in 1941 the Ustaše were installed in power by the Nazis in the quisling 'Independent State of Croatia,' which included the whole Bosnia-Herzegovina, and in which they pursued genocidal policies against Serb, Jewish, Roma and other minorities" (I. Lovrenović 2001:232).

8. The official vice-principal, but all Bosniaks at the schools, both teachers and students, called him the principal.

9. Bosnian for Eid al-Fitr (festival at the end of Ramadan) and Eid al-Adha (festival of sacrifice).

Chapter 3. Bathroom Mixing

1. The bathrooms at the school were unisex during the duration of my fieldwork.

2. These writings illustrate the significance of access to public toilets in the construction of class, gender, and cast boundaries (Gupta 2006). For example, Arjun Appadurai argues that in India, distance from one's excrement can be seen as a marker of one's social class. Furthermore, he suggests that the "politics of shit" and "the transgressive display of fecal politics" are crucial material aspects of "deep democracy" (Appadurai 2002:38). Writing in the context of the urban United States, Emily Martin (1992) examines the society's and women's visions of female reproduction. Her study reveals the importance of public bathrooms for construction of gender differences and spaces of workers' resistance against authority. In addition, the role of bathrooms for generating resistance in the context of inner-city schools in New York City has been argued by John Devine (1996), who explains that in these schools the gaze of authority evaporates in the bathrooms, enabling students to engage in creative practices.

3. Mêlée in French includes the notions of fight and sexual mingling, as well as mixing, which are all lost in the English form "melee" (Nancy 2000:205n2).

4. The scarce and statistically oriented literature on mixed marriages in ex-Yugoslavia approaches mixed marriages as indicators of social acceptance and lack of discrimination (Gagnon 1994). These works link these statistical data to the calculations about probability of violence in mixed regions. Some researchers, for instance, Botev and Wagner (1993), argue that "the popular notion of a Yugoslav population characterized by increasing rates of interethnic marriage is highly erroneous." Similar,

others argued the actual number of mixed marriages was not enough to have a conflict-reducing effect (Smits 2010:15). Other scholars, such as Gagnon (1994), suggest that if we "break out rates for ethnically mixed regions within republics and provinces 2/3 of the maximum of potential marriages took place." Similarly to Gagnon, Donia and Fine argue that there was a 30 to 40 percent intermarriage rate for Bosnia's large cities prior to 1991(1994: 6).

5. As a reflexive verb, *miješati se* is best translated as "to mix oneself." In addition to the words *miješanje* and *miješati se*, my informants used many other versions of this word, such as *umiješati se* ("to mix (oneself) into something"), *pomiješati* ("to mix two or more components together") or *mješanac* (noun, "the mixed one, the one coming from two or more different parts"). Additionally, students and teachers at the reunified school often mentioned in passing that a certain student *voli da se miješa* (loves to mix).

6. Lovrenović continues: "To be Bosnian was to have a feeling for otherness, for the different part of the daily reality of one's most personal environment. It was this experience of different that made it possible to be Bosnian" (2001:209).

7. I am grateful to Larisa Kurtović for this comment.

8. An exception continues to be the city of Sarajevo, where 20 to 25 percent of marriages between 1996 and 2003 were mixed (Markowitz 2007:61).

9. *Balijkuša* is feminine for *balija*—a slang name used for Bosnian Muslims as an insult; *četnikuša* is feminine for *četnik*—"traditional Serb term for irregular fighters, adopted by forces of Draža Mihalović in WWII and subsequently by Serbian irregulars fighting in Croatia and Bosnia; also generally applied in Bosnia-Herzegovina after April 1992 to all Serb forces taking part in the aggression against their country" (I. Lovrenović 2001:229–30); for *ustaša* see Chapter 2n7.

10. This rivalry is the issue of constant tension between the two sides, especially since Zrinjski now uses Velež's old stadium on the west side, while Velež has to play on the small, rural stadium in a nearby village Vrapčići on the east side.

11. OIA is Omladinska Informativna Agencija Bosne i Hercegovine or Youth Information Agency of Bosnia-Herzegovina.

12. Srebrenica is an eastern Bosnian town in which a massacre of approximately 8,000 Bosniak men by the Serb forces took place in summer 1995 under the eye of the UN (among others, see Wagner 2008, and Halilovich 2013). Drežnica is a small town near Mostar in which torture and killing of the Croat civilians by the Bosnian-Herzegovinian army took place in 1993.

Chapter 4. Poetics of Nationhood

1. "The main objective of the Nansen Dialogue Center network is to contribute to reconciliation and peacebuilding through interethnic dialogue between strategic individuals and groups in the Balkans that have strong influence or decision making power in deeply divided communities," http://www.nansen-dialogue.net/content/view/13/4/, accessed June 16, 2011.

2. Working with the student and parent councils has become the focus of the OSCE since 2004. The idea of the "civic engagement" initiative was to bring in parents and students, who have been neglected in the OSCE programs prior to that time. So the OSCE refocused attention to Student Councils and Parent-Teacher Associations (author interview with education officer, OSCE Mostar, January 2006).

3. Here I understand peoplehood as the primary form of people or community, where "its proponents are generally understood to assert that its obligations legitimately trump many other demands made on its members in the name of other associations" (R. Smith 2003:20).

4. Following Brubaker (1996), I opt not to use nation but nationhood, where nationhood is understood as a "category of practice, institutionalized form, and contingent event" (7).

5. By a "Serb singer" Andrea actually means a turbo-folk singer. Turbo-folk is a mainstream musical genre, a subgenre of folk music that incorporates dance and pop elements. The genre originated in Serbia but is equally popular in Bosnia-Herzegovina, Croatia, Slovenia, and Macedonia.

6. I. Lovrenović (2001:210) writes: "It is a tragic illusion that ethnic ideologies and the fixing of boundaries are necessary for the realization of self, through the production of a pure culture and a return to roots . . . for it is a process that leads nowhere except to a ghetto mentality, to cultural stagnation and eventually death. The ghetto mentality reduces the fine Bosnian multiplicity of perspectives to the crude sway of three cultural paradigms. Each thinks it must turn to its own pure separate history, its own pure separate literature, and its own pure separate language."

7. Literally *fildžan* is a small cup for drinking Turkish coffee. In this context it means a small, round piece of land for Bosniaks.

8. *Baščaršija* is the old marketplace in Sarajevo.

9. *Sevdah* is a traditional Bosnian music form that originated during the Ottoman conquest of Bosnia-Herzegovina.

10. *Merhametli* (from Turkish) is a Bosnian word that means merciful, peaceful, hospitable, giving and forgiving.

11. Within Bosnia, people understand the difference between Serb, Croat, and Muslim narod. At the same time, they distinguish Bosnian members of these groups from their non-Bosnian conationals. As a result, Bosnian Croats are often referred to as Katolici (Catholics) and Serbs as Vlasi (Orthodox, can be used derogatorily) (see Sorabji 1995:89).

12. Under great pressure by the OSCE, the introduction of the common core curriculum was forced in geography classes, so the class I attended was covering Bosnia-Herzegovina regions, and no longer Croatia.

13. This has been somewhat changing with the introduction of "the common core" in all three curricula.

14. There are only two entities in Bosnia-Herzegovina, Federation of Bosnia-Herzegovina and Republika Srpska. It is worth revisiting Bosnian and Herzegovinian

political and geographical organization. Bosnia-Herzegovina is politically divided into two entities, the Federation of Bosnia-Herzegovina (predominantly Bosniak and Croat) and Republika Srpska (predominantly Serb), which are divided by an intrastate border. Both entities, however, stretch across two horizontal, geographically defined regions, Bosnia (north) and Herzegovina (south).

15. Sanja moved to Italy as soon as she finished high school in Mostar. She works for a car-selling business.

16. The official Bosnia-Herzegovina flag between 1992 and 1997 had a historical connection to the independent kingdom of Bosnia during the Middle Ages. It was white with the shield in the middle, which contained yellow lily flowers endemic to Bosnia (*lilium Bosniacum*) on a blue background. Bosnian Serbs and Bosnian Croats associated the flag with Bosniaks, and the country had to search for a new flag, which was created by the OHR and officially adopted February 4, 1998.

17. Coles addresses this phenomenon when she writes that "the position of the international was juxtaposed against that of the people being helped—the Bosnians. I use an international emic reference [Bosnians] to describe Bosnia-Herzegovina's residents and citizens. The designation has certain limitations in that it can be rightfully criticized as problematically assimilating Herzegovinians and excluding ethnic Serbs from national labeling" (2007:41).

18. The majority of western Herzegovinian inhabitants are Bosnian Croats.

19. *Fukara*—from Ottoman Turkish, and from Arabic (fuqarā'), meaning "poor man, pauper."

20. The media in Bosnia-Herzegovina were fragmented along ethnic lines during the war and they continue to be separated today. The OHR tried to promote the countrywide Bosnian-Herzegovinian Television, which still operates, but is less popular than the entity-based television stations. Within the FBiH, there is the Federal Television, which formally serves both Croat and Bosniak populations; most Croats, however, feel it is Bosniak-dominated, and they request their own TV channel, so far unsuccessfully. They continue to watch primarily the television of the Republic of Croatia.

21. The Hague is the official seat for the International Criminal Tribunal for the former Yugoslavia, where many alleged war criminals were prosecuted or are currently awaiting or undergoing trial.

22. The Croatian Republic of Herceg-Bosna was an officially unrecognized entity in Bosnia-Herzegovina that existed between 1991 and 1994, with west Mostar as its capital city.

23. Many people in Bosnia-Herzegovina did not know the Bosnian anthem at the time of research. After the leaders of the three ethnic groups could not agree on the words of the anthem, on February 10, 1998, as an inclusionist measure, a new anthem was adopted for Bosnia and Herzegovina, one without words. It was chosen by OHR "since the local communities could not agree on them. Another example of these undemocratic practices is the Bosnian flag. The leaders of the three ethnic groups

could not agree on the design of the flag, so the High Representative appointed a commission to design a 'neutral' flag. The commission chose a design with a gold triangle on a blue background with a row of white stars, where 'the triangle represents the three constituent peoples of Bosnia and Herzegovina, the gold color represents the sun, as a symbol of hope; the blue and the stars stand for Europe'" (*OHR Bulletin* 65, February 6, 1998). This and other state designs have more meaning to the OHR than to Bosnians themselves (Hayden 2002) Bosnian citizens' lack of emotional response to "their" flag was nicely captured by a reporter at the press conference when the flag was unveiled, who spontaneously uttered that the flag "looked like a cereal box" (170).

24. Independent State of Croatia was a puppet state of Axis powers during World War II.

25. *Nož, Žica, Srebrenica* is a Serb nationalist slogan glorifying the 1995 Srebrenica massacre of approximately 8,000 Muslim men and boys, the bloodiest in Europe since the end of World War II.

26. Before the war, Muslims composed about 15 percent of the municipality's population, and the majority in the city's urban core. Today, in the aftermath of "ethnic cleansing," Bosniaks are estimated to be 4 percent of the total.

27. Radovan Karadžić was a Bosnian Serb leader before and during the Bosnian war. As of July 30th 2008 he has been at the International Criminal Tribunal for the former Yugoslavia, charged with acts of crime against humanity and genocide, among others.

28. I am grateful to Svetlana Đurić for sharing this anecdote with me.

29. Here "ours" stands for local, domestic, regional, and former Yugoslav political elites, and "foreign" denotes the international peace-makers and democracy-builders that have been shaping Bosnian political, social, and military realities since at least the end of the war in 1995.

30. Of course, when I asked people about specific politicians, they distinguished among individuals and political parties—they emphasized that there were some good and honest politicians. However, skepticism about *politika* remained—people said that with time, everyone would become *zaražen* (contaminated) by "dirty politics."

31. This attitude is problematic for several reasons—like (ethno)nationalism, it romanticizes, compartmentalizes, reduces, and essentializes its object, in this case, the common "Bosnian mentality."

32. The complicated and powerful gendering and degendering of politics in postwar Bosnia-Herzegovina is beyond the scope of this chapter. See, however, Helms (2007, 2013) for an insightful discussion of these processes.

33. Stolac is a small town in southwest Bosnia and Herzegovina, not far from Mostar.

Chapter 5. Invisible Citizens

1. I use quotation marks to hint at the complexity of citizen-invisibility—these people are officially citizens of Bosnia-Herzegovina, but they are excluded from the

ideology of ethnic citizenship. I omit quotation marks in the remaining part of the chapter, however, to avoid a cumbersome read.

2. For an interesting and historically driven analysis on how mixed marriages were either neglected (during the times of relative stability) or made hypervisible and problematic (during the times of social upheavals), see Fedja Burić's Ph.D. dissertation, "Becoming Mixed: The Mixed Marriages of Bosnia-Herzegovina and the Creation of Ethnic Difference."

3. I am grateful to Larisa Jašarević for this comment.

4. Fedja Burić, personal communication, May 8, 2011.

5. The population had not been counted in Republika Srpska, however (see Markowitz 2007).

6. While some accounts suggest that in prewar Mostar up to 10 percent of all marriages were mixed (see Matejčić 2009), my calculation of this percentage, using the population survey from 1991 available at the Federal Office of Statistics in Sarajevo, gives a smaller number. Based on this data, the total number of families in Mostar in 1991 was 34,131, among which 2,829 or 8.29 percent were ethnically mixed households. The statistic also shows that in 2004 there were 651 or 4.8 percent mixed marriages in FBiH, with huge disparity between different cities. For example, Markowitz (2007:61) found that in Sarajevo, 20 to 25 percent of marriages between 1996 and 2003 were mixed, while in Mostar, these numbers are much lower: in 2000, the total number of registered marriages was 176. None of them were "mixed" marriages, and of 527 registered marriages in 2004, only 6 or 1.14 percent were mixed (see Matejčić 2009).

7. The story of Goran's forced crossing of the Boulevard in the middle of the war is both chilling and unbelievable. I leave the details of this event out to protect Goran's identity.

8. A fellow anthropologist, Larisa Kurtović, told me about an informant of hers who called her friend, a "product of a mixed marriage," *mješanče*, combining the words for *miješanje* (mixing) and *mladunče* (baby animal). While the term was meant to index intimacy, endearment, and affection, it also has a deeper connotation of immaturity and animal-like qualities.

9. Veena Das understands practical kinship as strategies of families to absorb politically isolated and socially labeled individuals (such as women and children abducted by "ethnic others" during the partition of India). The notion of practical kinship was first introduced by Pierre Bourdieu (1977).

10. Caritas is a Catholic agency for aid and development.

11. Abrašević is a cultural center on the east side that attracts alternative youth from both sides. The center offers Mostar youth a space where they can engage in creative projects, especially those that focus on alternative art, music, diversity-promotion, tolerance, and critical thinking (see http://www.okcabrasevic.org/o-abra%C5%A1evi%C4%87u)

12. The center is also sometimes described by older generations as a place where troubled kids experiment with drugs.

13. I am grateful to an anonymous reviewer for this comment.

Chapter 6. Anti-Citizens

1. This detachment is complicated and can be seen as a youth's engagement and critique of the state, and not as a "simple" withdrawal (see Greenberg 2011; Kurtović n.d.).

2. Personal communication with Paddy Ashdown, Sarajevo, July 2002.

3. http://www.reci.ba/usr/106/scr/mojglas.php?voxpopuli_id=463, accessed July 31, 2008.

4. "Captured state" refers to the process by which political elites use legal frameworks to serve their own interests (Blagovčanin 2014).

5. The academic and nonacademic literature on corruption in Bosnia-Herzegovina is vast. See, among others World Bank (2005), Transparency International (Marie Chêne) (2009), UNODC study (2011) *Corruption in Corruption in the Western Balkans: Bribery as Experienced by the Population*, http://www.unodc.org/documents/data-and-analysis/statistics/corruption/Western _balkans_corruption_report_2011_web.pdf.

6. According to UNODC (2011), 20.1 percent of citizens sixteen to sixty-four admitted they have been exposed to a bribery experience (3).

7. By definition, corruption is a "violation of norms and standards of conduct" (Gupta 2006:225). The formal definition is an abuse of public office for private gain (World Bank 1997). In this chapter I do not engage with the vast literature on corruption since it mostly focuses on finding "the set of universal, invariable norms that would help decide if certain actions are to be classified as 'corrupt'" (Gupta 2006:235n44) and thus does not have much to contribute to my analysis of the everyday functioning of an empty nation and materialization of anti-citizenship. As many anthropologists have noted, this narrow notion of corruption assumes a clean cut between public and private. This dichotomy runs counter to anthropological knowledge, which reveals that the public-private partition is often random and intrinsically vague (Haller and Shore 2005; D. J. Smith 2006). Anthropologists interested in morality describe the ways "moral actions are produced, how different models of moral reasoning emerge in their response, and how people creatively interact with these moral codes and behaviors" (Heintz and Rasanayagam 2005:2). As a result, when anthropologists study corruption, they include a much wider range of social behaviors, such as government bribery, rigged elections, medical quackery, cheating in school, and in the case of Nigeria, for example, deceiving a lover. Similarly, when Bosnians talk about corruption, they do not mean only the abuse of the state office for private gain, but they index a whole range of social behavior in which various forms of morally questionable actions are used to achieve power, affluence, esteem, and other more commonplace ambitions (D. J. Smith 2006).

8. Anthropologists interested in the former Eastern Europe have extensively researched the phenomenon of informal networks and their implications for the people they study (Bringa 1995; Sampson 2002; Solioz 2003). For example, much has been written on patron-client relationships in communism, as well as about the cult of *komšiluk* and kin-solidarity. During socialism, informal networks were experienced as necessary to gain access to a variety of public goods, such as obtaining a job, paying a gas bill, entering a university, or avoiding long lines at a doctor's office (Solioz 2003; D. J. Smith 2006). In addition, "corrupt" actions assisting family and friends were often undertaken out of a sense of social obligation that "trumps the notion of the duty to the state" (D. J. Smith 2006:222). This reveals that informal relations unique to socialism appear as paradoxical, since they "inhibit the proper functioning of the institutions while enabling people to survive suppression by foreign powers, dictatorial regimes, and innumerable conflicts" (Sampson 2002:4). In this way, informal networks could be seen as not contrary to stable bureaucratic structures; rather they can be interpreted as complementary and needed arrangements for maintaining stability (Haller and Shore 2005). Furthermore, one of the main characteristics of informal networks is their supposed invisibility. The "hidden" networks are sometimes truly concealed, but at other times they are candidly displayed, where the informal economy of small favors and services are "open secrets" (12).

9. The majority of bribes are paid in cash (80 percent of the time), and mostly in the health sector, including cash paid to doctors and nurses (UNODC 2011:4). Even though this is seen as a petty form of corruption, the sums are not trivial, the average bribe paid being 220 KM (approximately U.S.$140) (4).

10. According to the UNODC (2011) report, men pay more bribes than women. While men usually pay cash, women are more inclined to pay in kind—in the shape of food or drink, for example (3–4).

11. The incapacity (or unwillingness) of the UN to protect "protected" regions came to full light with the fall of Srebrenica enclave in summer 1995.

12. Collaboration between parties took place for commercial purposes all the time. Military resources were sold from Serbs to the Bosnian army, as in June 1992 when the leader of the Bosnian Serbs, Radovan Karadžić, gave written authorization for a shipment of weapons and communication equipment to be delivered to Jusuf "Juka" Prazina, an organized crime leader and coordinator of the transfer of people across the border in exchange for money (Andreas 2008: 65).

13. Officially, these people were not refugees but internally displaced. In the vernacular discourse, however, everyone referred to them as refugees.

14. This statement also reflects the historical settlement pattern of the three ethnic groups in Bosnia-Herzegovina before the war. According to the 1991 census, only Muslims lived in the same proportion in rural and urban areas, while Croats and Serbs made up a larger share of the rural population (Bieber 2005:14).

15. It is true that we can find the same blatant use of connections in many other countries, including the United States. Connections are at the heart of the value and

the idea of "networking" in the United States, since they are seen as essential to success. In the United States, however, blatant statements about use of connections are often reserved as a threat more than they are actually used (I am grateful to Gerald Creed for this comment). Furthermore, in their study of corporate scandals and organized crime in the West, Schneider and Schneider "raise the question whether organizational crime, extortion and illegal trafficking are not full-fledged elements of the workings of capitalism, as such" (Jane Schneider and and Peter Schneider, "Sack of Two Cities: Organized Crime and Political Corruption in Youngstown and Palermo" quoted in Haller and Shore 2005:5).

16. Cultural capital includes forms of knowledge, skills, and education that a person has that give them a status in society. It is embodied in the individual; it is both an inherited (through culture and socialization into family) and an acquired form of self (Bourdieu 1986).

17. Harun and Ivica left Mostar after high school to attend universities in Austria and Croatia respectively.

18. http://radiosarajevo.ba/novost/130815/djeca-s-kolodvora-zlo-#, accessed February 24, 2014.

19. Teachers' strikes became a regular phenomenon in postwar Bosnia-Herzegovina, mostly for economic reasons such as being unpaid or because salaries were low compared to those of other government employees. This time, the main reason for the strike was the request of the teachers' unions of primary and secondary schools to receive the same base salary as those employed in the city and cantonal administrations (see Hromadžić under review).

20. I am grateful to Jessica Greenberg for this insight.

Conclusion

1. OSCE Education Officer, e-mail to author, February 22, 2009.
2. Principal of the Gymnasium, e-mail to author, February 20, 2008.
3. In order to demonstrate the tensions that emerge from proposing (re)unification while taking ethnicity as an a priori foundation for educating youth in Bosnia-Herzegovina, I will shortly explain an exchange that took place at the end of one of the joined computer classes and was told to me by a teacher at the school. Two girls from the Federal curriculum were discussing the work of one of the most famous Bosnian authors of all time, Meša Selimović. Two other girls, from the Croat curriculum, sitting in the row behind them, interrupted their discussion: "Who is that Meša you are talking about?" Shocked by the question that demonstrated lack of knowledge about this famous author, Irma, the student in the Federal curriculum, said: "I cannot believe that you did not study his works in elementary school!" After a few long moments of silence, the bell rang announcing the end of class. As they were leaving the room, the two girls from the Federal curriculum heard the other two students converse: "Do you know that Meša?" one asked. The other one answered, quickly and dismissively: "Ma ne znam ti ja nikoga sa one strane" (I do not know anyone from

the other side). This tragicomic encounter captures two different and opposing impulses at play: on the one side, by unifying computer science instruction, youth are brought into close physical proximity. And yet the structures of ethnic division and exclusion are so deep and penetrating in the rest of the school and the society at large that by sixteen students are formed as members of two exclusive groups. This perpetual distancing, accomplished by the war and cemented by the implementation of the postwar political vision that separates citizens into politicized ethnicities, becomes especially visible in situations of proximity, including this encounter in the computer lab.

4. The relationship between ethnopolitics and economic gain has been captured in the report by Transparency International, where its author writes: "The war left a political vacuum in the country, leading to the emergence of a corrupt political elite that uses ethnic divisions to disguise its corruption-seeking agenda" (Transparency International 2009:2).

5. http://www.slobodnaevropa.org/content/nerzuk-curak-dejtonskog-sporazuma-ne-bi-bilo-da-nema-bih/25175379.html, accessed February 27, 2014.

Epilogue: Empty Nation, Empty Bellies

1. For example, many forget that numerous citizens in Bosnia-Herzegovina occupied the streets in summer 2013 to protest the fact that newborns were not being issued ID numbers, due to the political elite's manipulations (see M. Lovrenović 2014).

Bibliography

Agha, Asif. 2001. "Register." In Alessandro Duranti, ed., *Key Terms in Language and Culture*. 212–15. Oxford: Blackwell.

Althusser, Louis. 1971. *Lenin and Philosophy, and Other Essays*. New York: Monthly Review Press.

Anderson, Benedict. 1991. *Imagined Communities*. London: Verso.

Andreas, Peter. 2008. *Blue Helmets and Black Markets: The Business of Survival in the Siege of Sarajevo*. Ithaca, N.Y.: Cornell University Press.

Appadurai, Arjun. 1996. *Modernity at Large: Cultural Dimensions of Globalization*. Minneapolis: University of Minnesota Press.

———. 2002. "Deep Democracy: Urban Governmentality and the Horizon of Politics." *Public Culture* 14, 1: 21–47.

Arnautović, Suad. 1996. *Izbori u Bosni i Hercegovini '90*. Sarajevo: Promokult.

Arsenijević, Damir. 2007. *Protiv Oportunističke Kritike*. European Institute for Progressive Cultural Policies, November. http://eipcp.net/transversal/0208/arsenijevic/bhs.

Bardoš, Gordon. 2010. *Bosnian Lessons*, July 16. http://www.nationalinterest.org/commentary/bosnian-lessons-3674.

Barnett, Michael, and Martha Finnemore. 1999. "The Politics, Power and Pathologies of International Organizations." *International Organization* 53, 4: 699–732.

Barry, Brian. 1990. "Social Criticism and Political Philosophy." *Philosophy & Public Affairs* 19: 360–73.

———. 2002. *Culture and Equality: An Egalitarian Critique of Multiculturalism*. Cambridge, Mass.: Harvard University Press.

Barth, Fredrik. 1969. *Ethnic Groups and Boundaries. The Social Organization of Culture Difference*. Boston: Little, Brown.

Bauman, Zygmunt. 2000. *Liquid Modernity*. London: Polity.

———. 2003. *Liquid Love: On the Frailty of Human Bonds*. London: Polity.

BBC News. 2004. "Mostar Bridge Opens with Splash." Friday, 23 July.

Berlant, Lauren. 2011. *Cruel Optimism*. Durham, N.C.: Duke University Press.

Bhabha, Homi K. 2004. *The Location of Culture*. London: Routledge.

Bekerman, Zvi. 2005. "Complex Contexts and Ideologies: Bilingual Education in Conflict-Ridden Areas." *Journal of Language Identity and Education* 4, 1: 1–20.

Bieber, Florian. 1999. "Consociationalism: Prerequisite or Hurdle for Democratisation in Bosnia?" *South-East Europe Review* 2, 3: 79–94.

———. 2005. *Post-War Bosnia: Ethnic Structure, Inequality and Governance of the Public Sector*. London: Palgrave.

Blagovčanin, Srađan. 2012. "Bosnia and Herzegovina: Captured State." In Džihić Vedran and Daniel Hamilton, eds., *Unfinished Business: The Western Balkans and the International Community*. Washington, D.C.: Center for Transatlantic Relations, Johns Hopkins University.

———. 2014. *Kratka istorija korupcije u BiH*. http://balkans.aljazeera.net/vijesti/kratka-historija-korupcije-u-bih, accessed February 28, 2014.

Bojkov, Victor. 2003. "Democracy in Bosnia and Herzegovina: Post-1995 Political System and Its Functioning." *Southeast European Politics* 4, 1: 41–67.

Bose, Sumantra. 2002. *Bosnia After Dayton: Nationalist Partition and International Intervention*. New York: Oxford University Press.

Botev, Nikolai, and Richard Wagner. 1993. "Seeing Past the Barricades: Ethnic Intermarriage in Yugoslavia During the Last Three Decades." In *War Among the Yugoslavs*, Special issue, *Anthropology of East Europe Review* 11, 1–2: 27–34.

Bougarel, Xavier. 1996. "Bosnia and Herzegovina: State and Communitarianism." In *Yugoslavia and After: A Study in Fragmentation, Despair and Rebirth*, eds. Dyker, D.A. and Vejvoda, I. 87–113.

Bougarel, Xavier, Elissa Helms, and Ger Duijzings, eds. 2007. *The New Bosnian Mosaic: Identities, Memories and Moral Claims in a Post-War Society*. Aldershot: Ashgate.

Bourdieu, Pierre. 1977. *Outline of a Theory of Practice*. Cambridge: Cambridge University Press.

———. 1986. "The Forms of Capital." In John Richardson, ed. *Handbook of Theory and Research for the Sociology of Education*. 241–58. New York: Greenwood.

———. 1990. *Other Words: Essays Towards a Reflexive Sociology*. Stanford, Calif.: Stanford University Press.

Bringa, Tone. 1993. "Nationality Categories, National Identification and Identity Formation in 'Multinational' Bosnia." In David A. Kideckel and Joel Halpern, eds., *The Yugoslav Conflict*, Special issue, *Anthropology of East Europe Review* 11: 9–76.

———. 1995. *Being Muslim the Bosnian Way: Identity and Community in a Central Bosnian Village*. Princeton, N.J.: Princeton University Press.

———. 2003. "The Peaceful Death of Tito and the Violent End of Yugoslavia." In John Borneman, ed., *The Death of the Father: An Anthropology of the End of Political Authority*. 63–103. New York: Berghahn.

Brown, Keith, ed. 2006. *Transacting Transition: The Micropolitics of Democracy Assistance in the Former Yugoslavia*. Bloomfield, Conn.: Kumarian Press.

Brubaker, Rogers. 1992. *Citizenship and Nationhood in France and Germany*. Cambridge, Mass.: Harvard University Press.

———. 1994. "Rethinking Nationhood." *Contention* 4, 1: 3–14.

———. 1996. *Nationalism Reframed: Nationhood and the National Question in the New Europe*. Cambridge: Cambridge University Press.

Bugarski, Ranko. 1995. *Jezik od mira do rata [Language from Peace to War]*. Belgrade: Biblioteka XX vek.

Burg, Steven, and Paul Shoup. 1999. *The War in Bosnia-Herzegovina: Ethnic Conflict and International Intervention*. Armonk, N.Y.: M.E. Sharpe.

Burić, Fedja. 2011. "Becoming Mixed: The Mixed Marriages of Bosnia-Herzegovina and the Creation of Ethnic Difference." Ph.D. dissertation, University of Illinois.

Campbell, David. 1998. *National Deconstruction: Violence, Identity, and Justice in Bosnia*. Minneapolis: University of Minnesota Press.

———. 1999. "Apartheid Cartography: The Political Anthropology and Spatial Effects of International Diplomacy in Bosnia." *Political Geography* 18: 395–435.

Chandler, David. 1999. *Bosnia: Faking Democracy After Dayton*. London: Pluto.

———, ed. 2006. *Peace Without Politics? Ten Years of State-Building in Bosnia*. New York: Routledge.

Chatterjee, Partha. 1998. "Community in the East." *Economic and Political Weekly* 33, 6: 277–82.

Cohen, Robert, and Mihailo Marković. 1975. *The Rise and Fall of Socialist Humanism: A History of the Praxis Group*. Nottingham: Spokesman Books.

Coles, Kimberly. 2002. "Ambivalent Builders: Europeanization, the Production of Difference, and Internationals in Bosnia." *PoLAR* 25, 1: 1–18.

———. 2007. *Democratic Designs: International Intervention and Electoral Practices in Post-War Bosnia-Herzegovina*. Ann Arbor: University of Michigan Press.

Cox, Marcus, and Gerald Knaus. 2003. "After the Bonn Powers: Open Letter to Lord Ashdown." European Stability Initiative. July 16.

Crampton, Jeremy. 1996. "Bordering on Bosnia." *GeoJournal* 39: 353–61.

Crapanzano, Vincent. 2004. *Imaginative Horizons: An Essay in Literary-Philosophical Anthropology*. Chicago: University of Chicago Press.

Croegaert, A. 2011. "Who Has Time for Ćejf? Postsocialist Migration and Slow Coffee in Neoliberal Chicago." *American Anthropologist* 133, 3: 463–77.

Ćurak, Nerzuk. 2002. *Geopolitika kao sudbina: Slučaj Bosna. Postmodernistički ogled o perifernoj zemlji*. Sarajevo: Fakultet političkih nauka.

———. 2004. *Dejtonski Nacionalizam: Ogledi o Političkom*. Sarajevo: Buybook.

Čorkalo, Dinka et al. 2004. "Neighbors Again? Intercommunity Relations After Ethnic Cleansing." In Eric Stover and Harvey M. Weinstein, eds., *My Neighbor, My Enemy: Justice and Community in the Aftermath of Mass Atrocity*. Cambridge: Cambridge University Press.

D'Alessio, Vanni, and Eric Gobetti. 2006. "Monuments and Memory Competitions in Post-War Mostar: Between Ideology, Identity and Politics." Paper presented at ASN Conference "Globalization, Nationalism and Ethnic Conflicts in the Balkans and Its Regional Context," Belgrade, September 2006.

Dahlman, Carl, and Gearoid Ó Tuathail. 2005. "Broken Bosnia: The Localized Geopolitics of Displacement and Return in Two Bosnian Places." *Annals of the Association of American Geographers* 95, 3: 644–62.

Das, Veena. 1995. "National Honor and Practical Kinship: Unwanted Women and Children." In Faye D. Ginsburg and Rayna Rapp, eds., *Conceiving the New World Order: The Global Politics of Reproduction*. 212–33. Berkeley: University of California Press.

———. 2007. *Life and Words: Violence and the Descent into the Ordinary*. Berkeley: University of California Press.

De Certeau, Michel. 1984. *The Practice of Everyday Life*. Trans. Steve Rendall. Berkeley: University of California Press.

DENI (Department of Education, Northern Ireland). 1988. *Education Reform in Northern Ireland: The Way Forward*. Belfast: DENI.

Devine, John.1996. *Maximum Security: The Culture of Violence in Inner-City Schools*. Chicago: University of Chicago Press.

Donia, Robert, and John Fine. 1994. *Bosnia and Hercegovina: A Tradition Betrayed*. New York: Columbia University Press.

Douglas, Mary. 1966. *Purity and Danger: An Analysis of the Concepts of Pollution and Taboo*. London: Routledge.

Drakulić, Slavenka. 1993. *The Balkan Express: Fragment from the Other Side of War*. New York: HarperPerennial.

Duffield, Mark. 2001. *Global Governance and the New Wars: The Merging of Development and Security*. New York: Zed.

Dunn, Seamus. 1986. "The Role of Education in the Northern Ireland Conflict." *Oxford Review of Education* 12, 3: 233–42.

Farrell, Séamus. 2001. "An Investigation into the Experimental School Strategy in the Promotion of School Improvement and of Social Cohesion Through Education, in Bosnia and Herzegovina." Master's thesis, University of Ulster.

Ferguson, James. 1994. *The Anti-Politics Machine: Development, Depoliticization, and Bureaucratic Power in Lesotho*. Minneapolis: University of Minnesota Press.

Ferguson, James, and Akhil Gupta. 2002. "Spatializing States: Toward an Ethnography of Neoliberal Governmentality." *American Ethnologist* 29, 4: 981–1002.

Fernandez, James. 1986. *Persuasions and Performances: The Play of Tropes in Culture*. Bloomington: Indiana University Press.

Feuerverger, Grace. 2001. *Oasis of Dreams: Teaching and Learning Peace in a Jewish-Palestinian Village in Israel*. New York: Routledge.

Foucault, Michel. 1991. "Governmentality." In Graham Burchell, Colin Gordon, and Peter Miller, eds., *The Foucault Effect: Studies in Governmentality*. 87–104. Chicago: University of Chicago Press.

Fox, Jon E. 2004. "Missing the Mark: Nationalist Politics and Student Apathy." *East European Politics and Societies* 18, 3: 363–91.

Freedman, Sarah et al. 2004. "Public Education and Social Reconstruction in Bosnia and Herzegovina and Croatia." In Eric Stover and Harvey M. Weinstein, eds., *My Neighbor, My Enemy: Justice and Community in the Aftermath of Mass Atrocity*. Cambridge: Cambridge University Press.

Friedman, Sarah. 2008. "Intimacy of State Power: Marriage, Liberation, and Socialist Subjects in Southeastern China," *American Ethnologist* 32, 2: 312–27.

Gagnon, V. P., Jr. 1994. "Reaction to the Special Issue of AEER: War Among the Yugoslavs." *Anthropology of East Europe Review* 12, 1: 50–51.

———. 2004. *The Myth of Ethnic War: Serbia and Croatia in the 1990s*. Ithaca, N.Y.: Cornell University Press.

———. n.d. "Liberal Multiculturalism and Post-Dayton Bosnia: Solution or Problem?" Manuscript.

Gallagher, Tony, and Alan Smith. 2002. "Attitudes to Academic Selection, Integrated Education and Diversity Within the Curriculum." In Ann Gray, Katrina Lloyd, Paula Devine, Gillian Robinson, and Deirdre Heenan, eds., *Social Attitudes in Northern Ireland: The Eighth Report*. London: Pluto.

Gallagher, Tony, Alan Smith, and Alison Montgomery. 2003. *Integrated Education in Northern Ireland: Participation, Profile and Performance*. Coleraine: UNESCO Centre, University of Ulster.

Gellner, Ernest. 1983. *Nations and Nationalism*. New Perspectives on the Past. Ithaca, N.Y.: Cornell University Press.

Gilbert, Andrew. 2008. "Foreign Authority and the Politics of Impartiality in Postwar Bosnia-Herzegovina." Ph.D. Dissertation, University of Chicago.

Gordy, Eric. 1999. *The Culture of Power in Serbia: Nationalism and the Destruction of Alternatives*. University Park: Pennsylvania State University Press.

Greenberg, Jessica. 2010. "'There's Nothing Anyone Can Do About It': Participation, Apathy and 'Successful' Democratic Transition in Postsocialist Serbia." *Slavic Review* 69, 1: 41–64.

———. 2011. "On the Road to Normal: Negotiating Agency and State Sovereignty in Postsocialist Serbia." *American Anthropologist* 113, 1: 88–100.

———. 2014. *After the Revolution: Youth, Democracy and the Politics of Disappointment in Serbia*. Palo Alto: Stanford University Press

Gupta, Akhil. 1995. "Blurred Boundaries: The Discourse of Corruption, the Culture of Politics, and the Imagined State." *American Ethnologist* 22, 2: 375–402.

———. 2006. "Blurred Boundaries: The Discourse of Corruption, the Culture of Politics, and the Imagined State." In Aradhana Sharma and Akhil Gupta, eds., *The Anthropology of the State: A Reader*. Carlton, Australia: Blackwell.

Hajdarpašić, Edin. 2008. "Museums, Multiculturalism, and the Remaking of Postwar Sarajevo." In Robin Ostow, ed., *(Re)Visualizing National History: Museums and National Identities in Europe in the New Millennium*. 109–39. Toronto: University of Toronto Press.

Halilovich, Hariz. 2013. *Places of Pain: Forced Displacement, Popular Memory and Trans-Local Identities in Bosnian War-Torn Communities*. New York: Berghahn Books.

Halilović, Senahid. 1996. *Pravopis bosanskoga jezika* [*The Orthography of the Bosnian Language*]. Sarajevo: Preporod.

Haller, Dieter, and Cris Shore, eds. 2005. *Corruption: Anthropological Perspectives*. London: Pluto.

Hammel, Eugene. 1997. "Ethnicity and Politics: Yugoslav Lessons for Home." *Anthropology Today* 13, 3: 5–9.

Hammel, Eugene, Carl Mason, and Mirjana Stevanović. 2007. "Pitanja nastala analizom etničke strukture stanovništva u SFR Jugoslaviji." *Stanovništvo* 45, 2: 7–24.

Harley, John Brian. 1990. "Cartography, Ethics and Social Theory." *Cartographica* 27: 1–23.

Hayden, Robert M. 1992. "Constitutional Nationalism in the Formerly Yugoslav Republics." *Slavic Review* 51, 4: 654–73.

———. 1996. "Imagined Communities and Real Victims: Self-Determination and Ethnic Cleansing in Yugoslavia." *American Ethnologist* 23, 4: 783–801.

———. 2005. "Democracy Without a Demos? The Bosnian Constitutional Experiment and the Intentional Construction of Nonfunctioning States." *East European Politics and Societies* 19, 2: 226–59.

———. 2002. "Intolerant Sovereignties and 'Multi-Multi' Protectorates: Competition over religious Sites and (in)tolerance in the Balkans." In C. M. Hann, ed., *Postsocialism: Ideals, Ideologies and Practices in Eurasia*. London: Routledge.

———.2007. "Moral Vision and Impaired Insight: The Imagining of Other Peoples' Communities in Bosnia." *Current Anthropology* 48, 1: 118–19.

Henig David. 2012. "Knocking on My Neighbor's Door: On Metamorphoses of Sociality in Rural Bosnia" *Critique of Anthropology* 32, 1:3–19.

Heintz, Monica, and Johan Rasanayagam. 2005. "An Anthropology of Morality." In *Max Planck Institute Report 2004–2005*. 51–60. Halle/Saale: Max Planck Institute for Social Anthropology.

Helms, Elissa. 2003. "Women as Agents of Ethnic Reconciliation? Women's NGO's and International Intervention in Post-War Bosnia-Herzegovina." *Women's Studies International Forum* 26, 1: 15–33.

———. 2007. "Politics Is a Whore: Women, Morality and Victimhood in Post-War Bosnia-Herzegovina." In *The New Bosnian Mosaic*. Xavier Bougarel, Elissa Helms and Ger Duijzings eds., Aldershot: Ashgate.

———. 2010. "The Gender of Coffee: Women, Refugee Return, and Reconciliation Initiatives After the Bosnian War." *Focaal: Journal of Global and Historical Anthropology* 57: 17–32.

———. 2013. *Innocence and Victimhood: Gender, Nation, and Women's Activism in Postwar Bosnia-Herzegovina*. Madison: University of Wisconsin Press.

Hemon, Aleksandar. 2005. "Nataša u Inostranstvu [Nataša Abroad]." *DANI* 416:1. from http://www.bhdani.com/default.asp?kat = kol&broj_id = 416&tekst_rb = 22, accesed February 28, 2009.

———. 2012. "National Subjects." *Guernica: A Magazine of Art and Politics*, January 15.

Herzfeld, Michael. 2005. *Cultural Intimacy: Social Poetics in the Nation-State*. 2nd ed. New York: Routledge.

Hobsbawm, Eric. 1990. *Nations and Nationalism Since 1780: Programme, Myth, Reality*. Cambridge: Cambridge University Press.

Horowitz, Donald L. 1985. *Ethnic Groups in Conflict*. Berkeley: University of California Press.

Horvat, Branko. 1982. *The Political Economy of Socialism: A Marxist Socialist Theory*. New York: Sharpe.

Hromadžić, Azra. Forthcoming. "'Only When the Spider Web Becomes Too Heavy': Youth, Unemployment and the Social Life of Waiting in Postwar and Postsocialist Bosnia-Herzegovina." In *Youth Unemployment: Policies, Measures and Challenges*, Special issue, *Journal of Social Policy* 11.

———. (under review). "Intimate Citizens: Teacher's Strike and Politics of Interethnic Solidarity in Postwar Mostar, Bosnia-Herzegovina." *Perspectives on European Politics and Society* 16(3), Special Issue *Europeanizing the Spaces for Lived Citizenship in the Post-Yugoslav States*.

Hunt, Swanee. 2011. *Worlds Apart: Bosnian Lessons for Global Security*. Durham, N.C.: Duke University Press.

Husanović, Jasmina. 2006. "Politika svjedočenja nasuprot stanja poricanja:ogledi o repolitizirajućim praksama u polju kulture i umjetnosti u BiH" ["The Politics of Witnessing Verses the State of Denial: Reflections on the Repoliticizing Practices in the Field of Culture and Art in BiH"]. In Husanović, Jasmina and Damir Arsenijević, eds. *Na tragu novih politika: Kultura i obrazovanje u Bosni i Hercegovini* [On the Path to New Politics: Culture and Education in Bosnia and Herzegovina]. Tuzla: Centar Grad.

Imamović, Emir. 2014. "Djeca s kolodvora zlo" ["Children from the Terminal of Evil"]. http://radiosarajevo.ba/novost/130815/djeca-s-kolodvora-zlo-#, accessed February 24, 2014.

International Crisis Group (ICG). 2001. "Bosnia: Reshaping the International Machinery." Report 121, November 29.

———. 2009. "Bosnia: A Test of Political Maturity in Mostar." Europe Briefing 54, July 27.

———. 2012. "Bosnia's Gordian Knot: Constitutional Reform." Europe Briefing 68, July 12.

———. 2013. "Bosnia's Dangerous Tango: Islam and Nationalism," February 26.

James, Erica. 2010. *Democratic Insecurities: Violence, Trauma and Intervention in Haiti*. Berkeley: University of California Press.

Jansen, Stef. 2005. "National Numbers in Context: Maps and Stats in Representations of the Post-Yugoslav Wars." *Identities: Global Studies in Culture and Power* 12, 1: 45–68.

———. 2007. "The Privatisation of Home and Hope: Return, Reforms and the Foreign Intervention in Bosnia-Herzegovina." *Dialectical Anthropology* 30, 3–4: 177–99.

———. 2014. "Can the Revolt in Bosnia and Herzegovina Send a Message to the Wider World?" *Balkan Insight*, February 13.

Jašarević, Larisa. 2011. "Lucid Dreaming: Revisiting Medical Pluralism in Postsocialist Bosnia." *Anthropology of East Europe Review* 29, 1: 109–26.

———. n.d. *Intimate Debt: Health and Wealth on the Bosnian Market*. Bloomington: Indiana University Press, forthcoming.

Kaplan, Robert. 1993. *Balkan Ghosts: A Journey Through History*. New York: St. Martin's.

Kardelj, Edvard. [1957] 1960. *Razvoj slovenačkog nacionalnog pitanja*. Belgrade: Kultura.

Kasapović, Mirjana. 2005. "Bosnia and Herzegovina: Consociational or Liberal Democracy?" *Politička Misao* 42, 5: 3–30.

Khan, Aisha. 2004. *Callaloo Nation: Metaphors of Race and Religious Identity Among South Asians in Trinidad*. Durham, N.C.: Duke University Press.

Kolind, Torsten. 2007. "In Search of 'Decent People': Resistance to the Ethnicization of Everyday Life Among the Muslims of Stolac." In Xavier Bougarel, Elissa Helms, and Ger Duijzings, eds., *The New Bosnian Mosaic: Identities, Memories and Moral Claims in a Post-War Society*. Aldershot: Ashgate.

Kordić, Snježana. 2010. *Jezik i nacionalizam*. Zagreb: Durieux.

Kristeva, Julia. 1982. *Powers of Horror: An Essay on Abjection*. New York: Columbia University Press.

Kurtović, Larisa. 2011. "What Is a Nationalist? Some Thoughts on the Question from Bosnia-Herzegovina." *Anthropology of Eastern Europe Review* 29, 2: 242–53.

———. 2014. "The Spectre of a Lost Future." *Mediacentar Online*.

———. n.d."Limits of In/Action: Everyday Politics of Dis/Engagement in Postwar Bosnia-Herzegovina." Unpublished paper.

Kymlicka, Will. 1995. *Multicultural Citizenship: A Liberal Theory of Minority Rights*. Oxford: Clarendon.

Latour, Bruno. 2000. "When Things Strike Back: A Possible Contribution of Science Studies." *British Journal of Sociology* 5, 1: 107–23.

Lefebvre, Henri. 1991. *The Production of Space*. 2nd ed. Oxford: Blackwell.

Lévi-Strauss, Claude. 1969. *The Elementary Structures of Kinship*. London: Eyre and Spottiswoode.

Levinson, Bradley, Douglas Foley, and Dorothy Holland, eds. 1996. *The Cultural Production of the Educated Person: Critical Ethnographies of Schooling and Local Practice*. Albany: State University of New York Press.

Lijphart, Arend. 1977. *Democracy in Plural Societies: A Comparative Exploration.* New Haven, Conn.: Yale University Press.
Lockwood, William G. 1975. *European Muslims: Economy and Ethnicity in Western Bosnia.* New York: Academic Press.
Longinović, Tomislav. 2011. "Serbo-Croatian: Translating the Non-Identical Twins." In Dimitis Asimakoulas, ed., *Translation and Opposition,* 283–95. Bristol: Multilingual Matters.
Lovrenović, Ivan. 2001. *Bosnia: A Cultural History.* London: Saqi.
Lovrenović, Maja. 2014. "Mogućnost novog događaja." *Mediacentar Online,* February 20.
Maček, Ivana. 2009. *Sarajevo Under Siege: Anthropology in Wartime.* Philadelphia: University of Pennsylvania Press.
Magaš, Branka. 2003. "On Bosnianness." *Nations and Nationalisms* 9, 1: 19–23.
Magner, Thomas. 1996. "New Languages in the Balkans?" *Geolinguistics* 22: 117–29.
Malcolm, Noel. 1996. *Bosnia: A Short History.* New York: New York University Press.
Markowitz, Fran. 2007. "Census and Sensibilities in Sarajevo." *Comparative Studies in Society and History* 49, 1: 40–73.
———. 2010. *Sarajevo: A Bosnian Kaleidoscope.* Champaign: University of Illinois Press.
Martin, Emily. 1992. *The Woman in the Body: A Cultural Analysis of Reproduction.* Boston: Beacon Press.
Massey, Doreen. 1994. *Space, Place and Gender.* Oxford: Polity Press.
Matejčić, Barbara. 2009. "U našem braku vide braststvo i jedinstvo pa nemamo mira." *Jutarnji List,* June 11. http://www.jutarnji.hr/ne-daju-nam-mira-jer-u-nasem-braku-vide-brastvo-i-jedinstvo-/337392, accessed 4 January 2011.
Mbembe, Achille. 1992. "The Banality of Power and the Aesthetics of Vulgarity in the Postcolony." *Public Culture* 4, 2: 1–30.
McCann, Eugene. 1999. "Race, Protest, and Public Space: Contextualizing Lefebvre in the U.S." *Antipode* 31, 2: 163–184.
McGlynn, Claire. 2003. "Integrated Education in Northern Ireland in the Context of Critical Multiculturalism." *Irish Educational Studies* 22, 3:11–27.
Merry, Sally Engle. 2001. "Spatial Governmentality and the New Urban Social Order: Controlling Gender Violence Through Law." *American Anthropologist* 103, 1:16–30.
Mertus, Julie. 2004. *Bait and Switch: Human Rights and U.S. Foreign Policy.* New York: Routledge.
Miklavcic, Alessandra. 2008. "Slogans and Graffiti: Postmemory Among Youth in the Italo-Slovenian Borderland." *American Ethnologist* 35, 3: 440–53.
Mosse, David. 2005. *Cultivating Development: An Ethnography of Aid Policy and Practice.* New York: Pluto Press.
Mosse, David, and David Lewis, eds. 2005. *The Aid Effect: Giving and Governing in International Development.* London: Pluto.

Mujkić, Asim. 2007. "We, the Citizens of Ethnopolis." *Constellations* 14, 1: 112–28.
———. 2008. "Ideološki problemi konsocijacijske demokratije u Bosni i Hercegovini." *Status: Magazin za Političku Kulturu i Društvena Pitanja* 13: 122–32.
Nancy, Jean-Luc. 2000. *Being Singular Plural.* Palo Alto, Calif.: Stanford University Press.
Neofotistos, Vasiliki. 2010. "Cultural Intimacy and Subversive Disorder: The Politics of Romance in the Republic of Macedonia." *Anthropological Quarterly* 83, 2: 279–315.
———. 2012. *The Risk of War: Everyday Sociality in the Republic of Macedonia.* Philadelphia: University of Pennsylvania Press.
Norbu, Dawa. 1999. "The Serbian Hegemony, Ethnic Heterogeneity and Yugoslav Make-Up." *Economic and Political Weekly* 34, 14: 833–38.
Nordstrom, Carolyn. 2004. *Shadows of War: Violence, Power and International Profiteering in the Twenty-First Century.* Berkeley: University of California Press.
OHR (Office of High Representative). 1995. The General Framework Agreement for Peace in Bosnia and Herzegovina, Article X.
———. 2012. Introduction. February 16.
OIA (Omladinska Informativna Agencija [Youth Information Agency]). 2005. "Independent Evaluation of National Youth Policy in Bosnia and Herzegovina." http://www.un.org/esa/socdev/unyin/documents/wpaysubmissions/bosnia.pdf, accessed August 6, 2006.
OSCE (Office for Security and Cooperation in Europe). 2003. "Statistical Report on the Implementation of the Interim Agreement on Accommodation of the Specific Needs and Rights of Returnee Children." Sarajevo.
———. 2005. "Gymnasium Mostar, Mostar's 'Other Landmark': Reconstruction and Revitalization Efforts." Unpublished Report, Mostar.
Palmberger, Monika. 2013. "Practices of Border Crossing in Post-War Bosnia and Herzegovina: The Case of Mostar." *Identities: Global Studies in Culture and Power* 20, 5: 544–60.
Palmer, Kendall. 2005. "Power-Sharing Extended: Policing and Education Reforms in Bosnia-Herzegovina and Northern Ireland." Ph.D. Dissertation, University of North Carolina.
Pandolfi, Mariella. 2010. "From Paradox to Paradigm: The Permanent State of Emergency in the Balkans." In Didier Fassin and Mariella Pandolfi, eds., *Contemporary States of Emergency: The Politics of Military and Humanitarian Interventions.* 153–72. New York: Zone.
Perry, Valerie. 2002. *Constitutional Reform and the "Spirit" of Bosnia and Herzegovina.* European Centre for Minority Issues Brief 7. Flensburg: Center for Minority Issues.
Petersen, Roger. 2011. *Western Intervention in the Balkans: The Strategic Use of Emotion in Conflict.* London: Cambridge University Press.

Petrović, Tanja. 2010. "Nostalgia for the JNA? Remembering the Army in the Former Yugoslavia." In Maria Todorova and Zsuzsa Gille, eds., *Post-Communist Nostalgia*. New York: Berghahn.

Pickering, Paula. 2009. *Peacebuilding in the Balkans: The View from the Ground Floor*. Ithaca, N.Y.: Cornell University Press.

Povinelli, Elizabeth. 2002. *The Cunning of Recognition: Indigenous Alterities and the Making of Australian Multiculturalism*. Durham, N.C.: Duke University Press.

Rabinowitz, Dan. 2001. "The Palestinian Citizens of Israel, the Concept of Trapped Minority and the Discourse of Transnationalism in Anthropology." *Ethnic and Racial Studies* 24, 1:64–85.

Radovanović, Milorad, ed. 1989. *Yugoslav General Linguistics*. Amsterdam: Benjamins.

Ramet, Sabrina. 1992. *Balkan Babel: Politics, Culture, and Religion in Yugoslavia*. Boulder, Colo.: Westview Press.

———. 2006. *The Three Yugoslavias: State-Building and Legitimation, 1918–2005*. Bloomington and Indianapolis: Indiana University Press.

Rieff, David. 1995. "The Lessons of Bosnia." *World Policy Journal* 12, 1: 76–88.

Sampson, Steven. 1996. "The Social Life of Projects: Importing Civil Society to Albania." In Chris Hann and Elizabeth Dunn, eds., *Civil Society: Rethinking Western Models*. 120–38. London: Routledge.

———. 2002. "Weak States, Uncivil Societies and Thousands of NGOs Western Democracy Export as Benevolent Colonialism in the Balkans." In S. Rečić (Ed.) *Cultural Boundaries of the Balkans*. Lund University Press. http://www.anthrobase.org/Txt/S/Sampson_S_01.htm, accessed August 13, 2008.

Sarajlić, Eldar. 2011. "The Convenient Consociation: Bosnia and Herzegovina, Ethnopolitics and the EU." In Francis Cheneval and Sylvie Ramel, eds., *From Peace to Shared Political Identities: Exploring Pathways in Contemporary Bosnia-Herzegovina*. Special issue, *Transitions* 51, 1–2: 61–80.

Scarry, Elaine. 1985. *The Body in Pain. The Making and Unmaking of the World*. Oxford: Oxford University Press.

Schechner, Richard. 1985. *Between Theater and Anthropology*. Philadelphia: University of Pennsylvania Press.

Scott, James. 1990. *Domination and the Arts of Resistance: Hidden Transcripts*. New Haven, Conn.: Yale University Press.

———. 1998. *Seeing like a State: How Certain Schemes to Improve the Human Condition Have Failed*. New Haven, Conn.: Yale University Press.

Sells, Michael. 1996. *The Bridge Betrayed: Religion and Genocide in Bosnia and Herzegovina*. Berkeley: University of California Press.

Sharma, Aradhana, and Akhil Gupta, eds. 2006. *The Anthropology of the State: A Reader*. Malden, Mass.: Blackwell.

Smillie, Ian, ed. 2001. *Patronage or Partnership: Local Capacity Building in Humanitarian Crisis*. Bloomfield, Conn.: Kumarian.

Smith, Daniel Jordan. 2006. *A Culture of Corruption: Everyday Deception and Popular Discontent in Nigeria.* Princeton, N.J.: Princeton University Press.

Smith, Rogers. 2003. *Stories of Peoplehood: The Politics and Morals of Political Membership.* Cambridge: Cambridge University Press.

Smits, Jeroen. 2010. "Ethnic Intermarriage and Social Cohesion. What Can We Learn from Yugoslavia?" *Social Indicators Research* 96, 3: 417–432.

Solioz, Christophe. 2003. "The Complexity of [In]formal Networks in Bosnia and Herzegovina." *Muabet: Local Dimensions of Democracy Building in Southeast Europe.* http://www.watsoninstitute.org/muabet/docs/christophe_solioz.doc, accessed September 9, 2008.

Sorabji, Cornelia. 1995. "A Very Modern War: Terror and Territory in Bosnia- Hercegovina." In Robert A. Hinde and Helen Watson, eds., *War: A Cruel Necessity?: The Bases of Institutionalized Violence.* 80–98. London: I.B. Tauris.

Stefansson, Anders. 2010. "Coffee After Cleansing? Co-Existence, Co-Operation, and Communication in Post-Conflict Bosnia and Herzegovina." *Focaal: Journal of Global and Historical Anthropology* 57: 62–76.

Stojanović, Nenad. 2011. "Limits of Consociationalism and Possible Alternatives: Centripetal Effects of Direct Democracy in a Multiethnic Society." In Francis Cheneval and Sylvie Ramel, eds., *From Peace to Shared Political Identities: Exploring Pathways in Contemporary Bosnia-Herzegovina.* Special issue, *Transitions* 51, 1–2: 99–114.

Stolcke, Verena. 1995. "Talking Culture: New Boundaries, New Rhetorics of Exclusion in Europe." *Current Anthropology* 36, 1: 1–24.

Stubbs, Paul. 2002. "Globalisation, Memory and Welfare Regimes in Transition: Towards an Anthropology of Transnational Policy Transfers." *International Journal of Social Welfare* 11, 4: 321–30.

Škiljan, Dubravko. 1988. *Jezična politika.* Zagreb: Naprijed.

Štiks, Igor. 2006. "Nationality and Citizenship in the Former Yugoslavia: From Disintegration to European Integration." *Southeast European and Black Sea Studies* 6, 4: 483–500.

———. 2010. "A Laboratory of Citizenship: Shifting Conceptions of Citizenship in Yugoslavia and Its Successor States." *CITSEE Working Paper Series* 2: 1–28.

Taylor, Charles. 1994. "Multiculturalism: Examining the Politics of Recognition." In Amy Gutman, ed. *Multiculturalism: Examining the Politics of Difference*, 25–73. Princeton, N.J.: Princeton University Press.

Taylor, Diana. 1997. *Disappearing Acts: Spectacles of Gender and Nationalism in Argentina's "Dirty War."* Durham, N.C.: Duke University Press.

Taylor, Lawrence. 2001. "'Paddy's Pig': Irony and Self-Irony in Irish Culture." In James W. Fernandez and Mary Taylor Huber, eds., *Irony in Action: Anthropology, Practice and the Moral Imagination.* 172–87. Chicago: University of Chicago Press.

Torsti, Pilvi. 2003. *Divergent Stories, Convergent Attitudes: Study on the Presence of History, History Textbooks, and the Thinking of Youth in Postwar Bosnia and Herzegovina.* Helsinki: Kustannus Oy Taifuuni.

Transparency International (Marie Chêne). 2009. "Corruption and Anti-Corruption in Bosnia and Herzegovina." http://www.u4.no/publications/corruption-and-anti-corruption-in-bosnia-and-herzegovina-bih, accessed March 15, 2013.
Trappenburg, Margo. 2003. "Against Segregation: Ethnic Mixing in Liberal States." *Journal of Political Philosophy* 11: 295–319.
Tsing, Anna. 2005. *Friction: An Ethnography of Global Connection.* Princeton, N.J.: Princeton University Press.
UNDP (United Nations Development Programme). 2000. *Human Development Report on Youth.* Sarajevo: UNDP.
———. 2003. Youth in *Bosnia and Herzegovina: Are You Part of the Problem or Part of the Solution?* Sarajevo: UNDP.
UNODC (UN Office on Drugs and Crime): 2011. *Corruption in Bosnia and Herzegovina: Bribery as Experienced by the Population.* http://www.unodc.org/documents/data-and-analysis/statistics/corruption/Bosnia_corruption_report_web.pdf, accessed 15 March.
Vandenberg, Martina. 2005. "Peacekeeping, Alphabet Soup, and Violence Against Women in the Balkans." In Dyan Mazurana, Angela Raven-Roberts, and Jane Parpart, eds., *Gender, Conflict, and Peacekeeping.* 150–67. Lanham, Md.: Rowman and Littlefield.
Van den Berghe, Pierre. 2002. "Multicultural Democracy: Can It Work?" *Nations and Nationalism* 8: 433–49.
Vaša prava Bosne i Hercegovine (Your rights Bosnia and Herzegovina). 2012. http://www.vasaprava.org/?p=1345, accessed June 21, 2012.
Velikonja, Mitja. 2003. *Religious Separation and Political Intolerance in Bosnia-Herzegovina.* College Station: Texas A&M University Press.
———. 2009. "Lost in Transition: Nostalgia for Socialism in Post-Socialist Countries." *East European Politics & Societies* 23: 535–51.
Verdery, Katherine. 1994. "Ethnicity, Nationalism, and State-Making. Ethnic Groups and Boundaries: Past and Future." In Hans Vermeulen and Cora Govers, eds., *The Anthropology of Ethnicity: Beyond Ethnic Groups and Boundaries.* 33–58. Amsterdam: Het Spinhuis.
Vetters, Larissa. 2007. "The Power of Administrative Categories: Emerging Notions of Citizenship in the Divided City of Mostar." *Ethnopolitics* 6, 2: 187–209.
Vlaisavljević, Ugo. 2005. "Demokratska konsocijacija i nepodnošljivi pluralizam." *Status: Magazin za političku kulturu i društvena pitanja* 6: 112–22.
Volčič, Zala.2007. "Yugo-nostalgia: Cultural Memory and Media in the former Yugoslavia." *Critical Studies of Media Communication,* 24, 1: 21–38.
———. 2011. *Serbian Spaces of Identity: Narratives of Belonging by the Last "Yugo" Generation.* New York: Hampton Press.
Wagner, Sarah. 2008. *To Know Where He Lies: DNA Technology and the Search for Srebrenica's Missing.* Berkeley: University of California Press.

Weinstein, Harvey, Sarah Freedman, and Holly Hughson. 2007. "School Voices: Challenges Facing Education Systems After Identity-Based Conflicts." *Education, Citizenship and Social Justice* 2, 1: 41–71.

Willis, Paul. 1977. *Learning to Labor: How Working Class Kids Get Working Class Jobs.* Lexington, Mass.: Lexington Books.

Wimmen, Heiko. 2004. "Territory, Nation, and the Power of Language: Implications of Education Reform in the Herzegovinian Town of Mostar." *GSC Quarterly* 11: 1–21.

Woodward, Susan. 1995. *The Balkan Tragedy: Chaos and Dissolution After the Cold War.* Washington, D.C.: Brookings Institution.

World Bank. 1997. *World Development Report: The State in a Changing World.* Washington, D.C.: World Bank.

———. 2005. *Bosnia and Herzegovina: Diagnostic Surveys of Corruption*, January 1. www1.worldbank.org/publicsector/anticorrupt/Bosnianticorruption.pdf, accessed March 7, 2014.

Young, Iris. 1990. *Justice and the Politics of Difference.* Princeton, N.J.: Princeton University Press

———. 2000. *Inclusion and Democracy.* Oxford: Oxford University Press.

Index

Abrašević cultural center (Mostar), 147, 148–49, 206nn11–12
Aluminij d.d. (company), 30
Andrić, Ivo, 115–16
Appadurai, Arjun, 37, 128, 200n2
Ashdown, Paddy, 157, 195n26, 196n7
Austro-Hungarian Empire, 194n14

balija/balijkuša, 96–98, 201n9
Banja Luka (capital of Republika Srpska), 8, 126, 127, 194n11, 204n26
Barry, Brian, 199n32
Barth, Fredrik, 88
bathroom mixing at Mostar Gymnasium, 86–102, 184; experimentation with ethnoreligious identity, 94–95, 102; friendships (superficial/true), 100–101; and lack of interethnic shared public social spaces, 92–93, 101; and memories of wartime violence, 95–98, 101, 102; scholarship on public bathrooms and identity construction, 87, 200n2; and tensions of postwar spatial governmentality/consociational democracy, 87–88, 90, 92–96, 99, 101–2; during 2012 school year, 184; wall graffiti, 98–99
Bihać (wartime): author's experiences and war-interrupted schooling, 2–3, 14; internal refugees and bicycle theft, 166–67; as UN "safe haven," 163–64; war profiteering and corruption, 163–66
Bijelo Brdo (pseudonym), 113, 116–18, 126–28, 195n19
bike thieves, 166–67
Bildt, Carl, 195n26
border-crossers, 73–74, 83, 85

Bosanac (territorial identity-marking term), 111–12
Bosnia-Herzegovina (prewar): citizen-morality and moral foundations, 163–68; interethnic social mixing, 88–93; mixed marriages/mixed families, 91, 143, 148–49, 205n6; Mostar, 3–4, 147–48, 205n6. *See also* Yugoslavia, communist
Bosnia-Herzegovina (wartime), 29–30; Bihać, 2–3, 14–15, 163–67; corruption and war-profiteering, 163–67, 207n12; destruction of Old Bridge, 30; Drežnica massacre (1993), 201n12; effect on social mixing, 11, 91–92; "ethnic cleansing," 8, 113; ethnic *narod* and experiences of victimhood, 117–18; international military and humanitarian intervention, 18–19, 195n23; Mostar, 29–30, 76, 131; official flag, 122, 203n16; Srebenica massacre, 201n12, 204n25; statistics on war dead and missing, 197n12; UN "safe havens," 163–64, 207n11; vision of ethnic groups (*etničke grupe*), 111; war stories, 131; and Washington Peace Agreement (March 1994), 30
Bosnia-Herzegovina (postwar), 9–11, 29–32; Adriatic coastal towns, 105; Bosnian exceptionalism, 173–80; citizen protests (summer 2013), 209n1; emptiness, 5–9; everyday life in Mostar, 30–32; flag, 122, 203n16, 204n23; media and television, 124, 203n20; national anthem, 125, 204n23; possibilities for postethnic society, 186–87; teachers' strikes, 177, 199n1, 208n19; tensions and memories from wartime past, 95–98; three constituent

Bosnia-Herzegovina (*continued*)
peoples, 38–39, 197n18; two political entities, 10, 194n15, 203n14. *See also* corruption in postwar Bosnia-Herzegovina; Federation of Bosnia-Herzegovina; international peace-building and state-making projects in postwar Bosnia-Herzegovina; mixing and public sociality in postwar Bosnia-Herzegovina; Mostar (city); Republika Srpska
Bosniak-Croat Federation, 30
Bosniaks (Bosnian Muslims): Bosniak national consciousness, 36; conflation of Bosnia-Herzegovina and Bosniak identity, 115–17; ethnic narod and Bosniak youth, 114–19, 202n11; families living on Mostar's west side, 31; fear of "identity loss," 36–37, 45; Islamization and growing influence of Islam, 15, 39; language and linguistic nationalism, 48–49, 50, 54–55, 199n30; leaders' support for prointegrationist policies, 34–35, 37–38, 45; and Mostar Gymnasium integration, 34–38, 45, 80–81; and Mostar's divided city, 30–32, 33–34; multiculturalism idioms and notion of *ravnopravnost* (pannationalism), 118; population statistics, 38–39, 198n19; and SDA party, 33, 171, 198n27; temporary schools on Mostar's east side (Mahala), 33–35, 37, 80, 81–82; term Bosniak/Bosniac (Bošnjak), 15, 17–18, 194n14; true homeland (*domovina*) as Bosnia-Herzegovina, 116–17, 122; war dead and missing, 197n12; war experiences of victimhood, 36, 117–18
Bosnian Croats: anti-integrationist stance at Mostar Gymnasium, 35–41, 44–46, 49, 50–58, 59, 79–80, 197n15; Croat curriculum, 51, 54–55, 120–21, 124–25, 183–84, 193n7, 208n3; Croat language and linguistic ethnonationalism, 45–46, 48–55; and Croat media/television, 124, 203n20; Croat nationalism, 14–15, 37–41, 44–46, 48–55, 116–17, 123–25; dual citizenship, 39–40, 53, 106–7, 119–23, 125, 198n20; ethnic narod, 49, 53, 119–25, 202n11; and HDZ party, 33, 59; and Herzegovinian regional identity, 40, 123–24, 203n18; and Mostar's divided city, 14–15, 30–32, 34, 196n5; narod in former Yugoslav state, 111–12; passports, 106–7, 119–20, 121–22; population statistics, 38–39, 198n19; self-perception as disadvantaged minority, 37–41, 69, 125; students' knowledge of Croatia and Bosnia-Herzegovina, 120–21, 124–25, 208n3; transborder notion of *domovina* (Croatia), 40–41, 53–54, 116–17, 123–25; youth detachment from Bosnia-Herzegovina, 40, 120, 124
Bosnian Federal Ministry of Education, 193n7
Bosnian Serbs: and Bosnian narod in former Yugoslav state, 111–12; Bosnian passports and Republika Srpska stamps, 106–7, 125–26; and curricula of Republika Srpska, 127–28, 193n7; ethnic narod, 125–30, 202n11; identification with Republika Srpska as their true state, 116–17, 125–29; living in FBiH, 128; Mostar, 67, 199n2; population statistics, 38–39, 198n19; Serbian language and linguistic nationalism, 48–49, 199n31
Bosnian Spring (spring 2014), 188–91
Bourdieu, Pierre, 205n9
bribery, 160–62, 206n6, 207nn9–10; "doctor money," 162, 207n9; and gender, 162, 207n10. *See also* corruption in postwar Bosnia-Herzegovina
Bringa, Tone, 91
Brubaker, Rogers, 108, 202n4

Campbell, David, 37
Cantonal Ministry of Education, 34, 183, 193n7
Čapljina, school integration in, 42–43, 198n27
"captured states," 158, 206n4
CARE International (NGO), 19
četnik/četnikuša, 96, 201n9
Chandler, David, 12
Chatterjee, Partha, 85, 109
Cigani (Gypsies). *See* Roma
citizen-morality: and anti-citizenship, 156–57, 159, 169, 179, 206n7; war effects on prewar moral foundations, 163–68; youth detachment and preservation of, 156–58, 168, 173–80, 206n1. *See also* corruption in postwar Bosnia-Herzegovina
Clinton, Bill, 12

Index   227

coffee shops and "having a coffee," 90–91, 99–100
Coles, Kimberly, 17, 21, 22, 44, 70, 158, 195n23, 196n27, 203n17
communist Yugoslavia. *See* Yugoslavia, communist
consociational power-sharing model of democracy, 10–13, 39, 61–62, 84–85, 194n13; critics and resisters of, 72; Croat suspicions of, 39; and empty nation of Bosnia-Herzegovina, 61, 185–86; and institutionalization of ethnonational differences, 10, 17–18; and linguistic nationalism, 55–56, 58, 199n32; and OSCE school integration projects, 43, 46, 61, 84; and shrinking shared spaces for interethnic interaction, 51–52, 92–93, 101, 114, 144, 148, 199n32; tensions at heart of, 11–13, 61–62; and "two-schools-under-one-roof" plan, 43. *See also* spatial governmentality
corruption in postwar Bosnia-Herzegovina, 156–80, 209n4; anthropologists' notions of, 206n7, 207n8; and anticorruption efforts, 164–65; "bike thieves" and internal refugees, 166–67; Bosnian exceptionalism, 173–80; and Bosnian Spring protests, 190–91; bribery, 160–62, 206n6, 207nn9–10; citizen-morality and anti-citizenship, 156–57, 159, 169, 179, 206n7; defining corruption, 206n7; and emerging shadow economies, 173; "international community" and transnational corruption, 159–60, 161, 163–66; international state-making programs and democratic transition, 158–60, 161–66, 169–70, 173, 179; misuse of international aid, 165; new economies of morality, 158–60, 161–62, 167–68, 169, 172–73; and nostalgia for communist Yugoslavia, 158, 159–60, 161, 162–63, 167, 169, 170–71; ordinary people's everyday encounters with, 156, 158–63, 167–80; pride/bragging about one's connections, 160–61, 168–73, 177–79, 208n15; and "rotten" narod, 162, 163, 178; state and corruption viewed as synonymous, 157–58, 176; and *tajkuni* (tycoons), 171–73, 179; transformation of Tito's slogan ("I want, I can, and I have connections"), 177–79; and transition to neoliberal capitalism, 158–60, 169–70,

175; war profiteering and trader/soldiers, 163–66, 207n12; war effects on prewar moral foundations, 163–68; and youth detachment, 156–58, 168, 173–80, 206n1; and youths' desires to leave country, 174, 176–77
Croat curriculum, 193n7, 208n3; computer science instruction, 183–84; language and linguistic nationalism, 51, 54–55; and students' knowledge of Croatia/lack of knowledge of Bosnia-Herzegovina, 120–21, 124–25, 208n3. *See also* Mostar Gymnasium (divided curricula)
Croat Democratic Union. *See* Hrvatska Demokratska Zajednica (HDZ)
Croat language and linguistic nationalism, 45–46, 48–55
Croat Municipality South West, 34
Croatia, Greater, 40, 198nn21, 23
Croatia, Republic of: Bosnian Croat students' knowledge of, 120–21, 124–25; Bosnian Croats' dual citizenship, 39–40, 53, 106–7, 119–23, 125, 198n20; Bosnian Croat identification with true homeland, 40–41, 53–54, 116–17, 123–25; and European Union, 40, 198n20; universities in, 53–54
"Croatia, Independent State of," 200n7, 201n9, 204n24
Croatian Defense Council. *See* Hrvatsko Vijeće Obrane
Croatian Party of Rights, 200n7, 201n9
Croatian Republic of Herceg-Bosna, 15, 29–30, 124, 195n21, 198n21, 203n22
Croatian Spring (1970s), 141
cultural capital, 170, 208n16
cultural fundamentalism, ideologies of, 10–11

Das, Veena, 193n3, 205n9
Dayton Peace Agreement and Dayton state, 10–11, 19, 46, 61, 70, 85, 190–91; and Croat anti-integration stance, 39, 46; division of Bosnia-Herzegovina into two entities, 10–11, 194nn15, 17; eighteenth anniversary (2013), 186; establishment of Republika Srpska, 129; ethnonationalism, 10–11, 190–91; and linguistic separation of Serbo-Croatian, 48; OSCE role in implementation, 19, 70, 196n27. *See also* consociational power-sharing model of democracy

Devine, John, 200n2
Dizdar, Mak, 115
Dodik, Miroslav, 126
domovina (homeland), 40–41, 53–54, 116–17, 122–29; Bosniak notion of, 116–17, 122; Bosnian Croat transborder notion of, 40–41, 53–54, 116–17, 123–25; Bosnian Serb identification with Republika Srpska, 116–17, 125–29; Herzegovina, 40, 123–24
Donia, Robert, 200–201n4
Drakulić, Slavenka, 16
Drežnica massacre (1993), 201n12

economies: emerging shadow economies, 173; ethnopolitics and economic gain, 185, 209n4; new economies of morality, 158–60, 161–62, 167–68, 169, 172–73; transition to neoliberal capitalism, 158–60, 169–70, 175; war-profiteering, 163–67, 207n12. *See also* corruption in postwar Bosnia-Herzegovina
ethnonationalism and ethnopolitics, 13–18, 38; and Bosnian Spring, 190–91; and cultural fundamentalism, 10–11; and Dayton's spatial governmentality, 10–11, 190–91; and economic gain, 185, 209n4; effect on Bosnian culture of interconnectedness and social mixing, 91–92; and "politics of difference," 36, 38, 45–46, 197n16; resistance to, 17–18, 144–45, 152–54, 185; and use of terms "Bosniaks," "Croats," and "Serbs," 17–18. *See also* ethnoreligious identity; linguistic nationalism
ethnoreligious identity: Bosniak Islamization, 15, 39; Bosnian youths' limited knowledge of other religious practices, 130; holidays and Mostar Gymnasium school year organization, 67–68, 82–83; increasing importance in lives of Bosnia-Herzegovina citizens, 15, 130; Ramadan wall exhibit at Mostar Gymnasium, 75–76; school bathroom mixing and experimentation with, 94–95, 102; transformation into ethnonational politics, 16
EUAM. *See* European Union Administration of Mostar
EUFOR. *See* European-led EUFOR Althea force

European Union, 19, 40, 198n20
European Union Administration of Mostar (EUAM), 20
European-led EUFOR Althea force, 195n24
exceptionalism, Bosnian, 173–80; comparing Bosnia to rest of Eastern Europe/world, 175–76; and corruption, 173–80; and spatial indexical "here," 174–75, 176; transformation of Tito's slogan into "I want, I can, and I have connections," 177–79

FBiH. *See* Federation of Bosnia-Herzegovina
Federal curriculum. *See* Mostar Gymnasium (divided curricula)
Federation of Bosnia-Herzegovina (FBiH): Bosniak leadership support for prointegrationist policies, 35; Bosnian Serb youth in, 128; and Bosnian Spring (2014), 188–91; media and television, 203n20; as one of two political entities in state, 10, 194n15, 203n14; populations, 10, 35, 38–39, 142, 198n19; ten autonomous cantons, 10, 194n16
Ferhat Paša (Ferhadija) mosque (Banja Luka), 8, 194n11
Fine, John, 200–201n4
Foucault, Michel, 194n18
Freedman, Sarah, 37

Gagnon, V. P., Jr., 111, 200–201n4
Gaj, Ljudevit, 46
Gehrecke, Ljiljana, 149
General Framework for Peace. *See* Dayton Peace Agreement and Dayton state
Gilbert, Andrew, 17
Gupta, Akhil, 159, 206n7

Halilović, Senahid, 48, 199n30
hateful language/hate speech and youth slang, 80–81, 96–99, 200n6
HDZ. *See* Hrvatska Demokratska Zajednica (Croat Democratic Union)
Hemon, Aleksandar, "Nataša u Inostranstvu," 127
Herceg-Bosna, Croatian Republic of, 15, 29–30, 124, 195n21, 198n21, 203n22
Herzegovina: Croats' notions of regional and territorial belonging, 40, 123–24, 203n18; secession discussions, 198n21

Hrvatska Demokratska Zajednica (HDZ) (Croat Democratic Union), 33, 59
Hrvatsko Vijeće Obrane (Croatian Defense Council), 131
Hunt, Swanee, 12
Husak, Amir, 179
Husanović, Jasmina, 127

ICG. *See* International Crisis Group
IDPs. *See* internally displaced persons
Imamović, Emir, 175–76
"Independent State of Croatia," 200n7, 201n9, 204n24
informal networks and socialism, 161, 207n8
Institute of Education in West Mostar, 79, 193n7
integration, 33–41; Bosniak fear of "identity loss," 36–37, 45; Bosniak leadership favoring, 34–35, 37–38, 45; Bosniaks' doubts about, 36–37, 80–81; Bosnian Croat community anti-integrationist stance, 35–41, 44–46, 49, 50–58, 59, 79–80, 197n15; ethnonationalism and "politics of difference," 36, 38, 45–46, 197n16; local notion of integration and phrase *biti zajedno* ("to be together"), 41–42; meaning of integrated schools, 41–46; and Mostar Gymnasium, 33–46, 50–62; OSCE shift from "integration" to "administrative unification," 59–61; OSCE unclear messages and discourses, 41, 43–44, 59. *See also* mixing and public sociality in postwar Bosnia-Herzegovina; Mostar Gymnasium (integration and reunification process)
internally displaced persons (IDPs), 166–67, 207n13
"international community" in Bosnia-Herzegovina, 18–23; ambassadors and embassies, 19; as complex entity, 19; cosmopolitan rhetoric and recognition of mixed marriages, 149; employment of young women as interpreters/translators, 165–66; EUAM in Mostar, 20; headquarters and regional offices, 19–20; local and international governmental organizations and NGOs, 19, 195n23; military and humanitarian intervention and reconstruction, 18–23, 195n23; Mostar special status, 20; principal actors coordinating transition and recovery, 19, 195nn24–25; response to Bosnian Spring, 189–90; and sociology of transnational governmentality (including Spanish monument in Mostar), 76–78; and transnational corruption, 159–60, 161, 163–66. *See also* international peace-building and state-making projects in postwar Bosnia-Herzegovina
International Criminal Tribunal for former Yugoslavia at Hague, 124, 203n21, 204n27
International Crisis Group (ICG), 19, 197n12
international peace-building and state-making projects in postwar Bosnia-Herzegovina, 10–13, 84; anticorruption efforts, 164–65; and Bosnian youth situation, 157; consociational model of democracy, 10–13, 39, 61, 84–85, 194n13; Dayton Agreement and Dayton state, 10–11, 19, 46, 70, 85, 190–91; disjuncture between nation and state, 12; education mandate and school integration projects, 3, 20, 32–36, 41–46, 52, 58–64, 68–70, 84, 193n4; and myth of ancient Balkan animosities, 12; and myth of Bosnian multiculturalism, 12, 70, 118; and state corruption in democratic transition, 158–60, 161–66, 169–70, 173, 179; tensions at heart of, 7, 11–13, 22–23, 61–62, 85. *See also* Organization for Security and Cooperation in Europe; spatial governmentality
Inzko, Valentin, 189–90, 195n26
Islamization, 15, 39
Israel, integrated schools in, 41
Istorija (history textbook used in Republika Srpska), 128

Jansen, Stef, 13, 20, 142, 190
Japanese donors and Mostar Gymnasium computer lab, 6–7, 183
JNA. *See* Yugoslav People's Army
Jugoslovenska Narodna Armija. *See* Yugoslav People's Army

Karadžić, Radovan, 127, 204n27, 207n12
Karadžić, Vuk Stefanović, 46–47
Kasapović, Mirjana, 11, 194n15
Khan, Aisha, 140

Kieffer, Claude, 43
komšija (neighbors), 31, 91, 196n4
komšiluk, cult of, 90–91, 207n8
Kordić, Snježana, 49
Koschnick, Hans, 20
Kurtović, Larisa, 14, 132, 176, 190, 201n7, 205n8, 206n1

Lajčák, Miroslav, 195n26
language purism, 45–46, 48–50, 53–55. *See also* linguistic nationalism and institutionalized language differences
Lévi-Strauss, Claude, 88
linguistic nationalism and institutionalized language differences, 45–58; alphabets (Cyrillic/Latin), 47, 48, 199n29; as barrier to development of common curricula, 50–51; Bosniak (Bosnian) language, 48–49, 50, 54–55, 199n30; Bosnian Serbs and Serbian language, 48–49, 199n31; and consociational model of democracy, 55–56, 58, 199n32; Croat language and Bosnian Croat nationalism, 45–46, 48–55; effects on everyday cross-ethnic interactions, 50–58; *ekavski* speech, 49; and language purism/purity, 45–46, 48–50, 53–55; *mješanac* (mixed language), 50; and narod (Croatian), 49, 53; performances of linguistic difference, 55–58; pursuit of language/national preservation at expense of "true" democracy, 51, 199n32; Serbo-Croatian language and variants/registers, 46–47, 48, 51, 55, 57–58, 198n28; and shrinking spaces for interethnic interaction, 51–52, 199n32; teachers' adaptations to classroom environments, 54–55; three official languages, 48, 55–58, 134
Longinovic, Tomislav, 46, 57, 199n31
Lovrenović, Ivan, 92, 202n6; on "Bosnian experience" and "feeling for otherness," 91, 113–14, 201n6

Macedonian language, 46
Malteser Hilfsdienst (humanitarian aid organization), 165–66
Mandić, Fra Dominik, 34, 197n8
Markowitz, Fran, 7–8, 205n6
Martin, Emily, 200n2

Medeno Polje (pseudonym) western Herzegovina town, 106
media/television in Bosnia-Herzegovina, 124, 203n20
mêlée, 88, 200n3
Merry, Sally Engle, 11, 194n18
miješanje (mešanje), 89, 90, 201n5
mixed marriages: and bureaucratic invisibility of mixed ("invisible") citizens, 140, 145–46, 205n1; children of, 145, 146–49, 205n8; communist Yugoslav regime and, 141–43, 146; international community cosmopolitan rhetoric and recognition of, 149; Mostar attitudes, 91, 92, 143–55; Mostar Gymnasium students'/teachers' views on, 86, 95, 150–55; and narod, 141–43; prewar Bosnia-Herzegovina, 91, 143, 148–49, 205n6; Sarajevo, 201n8; treatment in Balkans scholarship, 89–90, 200n4. *See also* mixing and public sociality in postwar Bosnia-Herzegovina
mixing and public sociality in postwar Bosnia-Herzegovina, 11, 88–90, 91–92, 139–55; Abrašević cultural center (Mostar), 147, 148–49, 206nn11–12; avoidance of, 151–52; bathroom mixing, 86–102, 184; bureaucratic invisibility of mixed ("invisible") citizens, 140, 145–46, 205n1; category of Others (*Ostali*), 142–43, 146; and (anti-)citizens, 143; elimination of shared public social spaces, 51–52, 92–93, 101, 114, 144, 148, 199n32; and international community cosmopolitan rhetoric, 149; and limitations of ethnonationalist ideologies of spatial governmentality and consociational model of democracy, 139–46, 149, 151, 154; mixed families' exclusion in no-man's-lands, 140–41, 142–43; Mostar citizen attitudes toward mixed marriages/families, 91, 92, 143–55; Mostar Gymnasium students'/teachers' views on dating and, 86, 95, 150–55; and narod, 141–43; and practical kinship, 145–46, 205n9; resistance/rebellion against segregation, 144–45, 152–54; spatial metaphor of river, 144, 170; vernacular discourse and notions of, 88–90, 140–41
mixing and public sociality in prewar Bosnia-Herzegovina, 88–93; coffee visits,

Index   231

90–91, 99–100; and mêlée, 88, 200n3; mixed marriages/mixed families, 91, 143, 148–49, 205n6; neighbors (*komšija*), 31, 196n4; rural/urban, 90–91; scholarship on, 88, 89–90, 140, 207n8; smoking, 88, 90–91; term *miješanje* (*mešanje*), 89, 90, 201n5, 205n8

mješanac (mixed language), 50, 201n5

Mostar (city): Abrašević cultural center, 147, 148–49, 206nn11–12; Bosniak families living on west side, 31; Bosniak-Croat violence and distrust, 14–15, 29–30; Bosnian Serbs of, 199n2; Bosnian Spring protests, 191; divided city and Bosniak-east side and Croat-west side, 1, 14–15, 30–32, 33–34, 196n5; divided city and empty central boulevard, 1, 3–4, 8, 196n5; and "international community," 20; JNA attack on, 29–30; Mahala neighborhood and temporary Bosniak schools, 34, 37, 80, 81–82; new "Old" Bridge (reconstruction and reopening), 1–2, 4–5, 31, 181; Old City and prewar notions of mixing, 147–48; postwar everyday life, 30–32; prewar, 3–4, 147–48; return to (2012), 181–87; shopping, 30–31, 196n3; Spanish Square, 76–78; spatialization of problem of cultural difference, 32; two main ethnonationalist political parties, 33; war in, 29–30, 76, 131

Mostar College (United World College), 181

Mostar Gymnasium (Stara Gimnazija): American Corner, 181–82; *Dan škole* ("Day of School") celebration, 65–66; ethnographic fieldwork and participant-observation at, 195n19; as historical institution and national monument, 3–4; location at center of Mostar, 3–4; Moorish revival style building, 3; photographs (summer 2005/2012), 4, 182; postwar Croatization, 34, 36, 75, 200n5

Mostar Gymnasium (divided curricula), 6–7, 36–37, 45, 50–51, 54–55, 64–74, 81–82, 193n7, 208n3; alternating classroom sequences, 64–65, 73; class books, 67; computer science classes, 6–7, 183–84, 208–9n3; Croat curriculum, 34, 51, 54–55, 120–21, 124–25, 183–84, 193n7, 197n13, 208n3; and Croat linguistic nationalism, 51, 54–55; and Croat student lack of knowledge of Bosnia-Herzegovina, 120–21, 124–25, 208n3; ethnic symmetries/spatial governmentality and fragmentation of school space by, 54–55, 64–74, 81–82, 208n3; language issues, 50–51, 54–55; OSCE introduction of a common core curriculum, 203n12; school year organization and ethnoreligious holidays, 67–68, 82–83; teacher employment by, 67, 81

Mostar Gymnasium (integration and "international community"), 20–23, 32–33, 41–46, 49, 58–61, 181; donors, 34, 76, 197n9; and empty computer lab, 6–7, 23, 183–84, 208–9n3; local reception of international actors as *stranci* (foreigners), 20–22; local representatives in negotiations, 33; negotiations and conflicting agendas of multiple actors, 2, 32–33, 62, 80; OSCE, 6–7, 20, 32–36, 41–46, 52, 58–64, 68–70, 84; school as icon/symbol of internationally directed peace-building and state-making, 4–5, 43, 181. *See also* Mostar Gymnasium (integration and reunification process)

Mostar Gymnasium (integration and reunification process), 20–23, 32–62, 63–85, 181–87; administrative and legal reunification (February 2004), 33, 62, 197n13; alternating classroom sequences, 64–65, 73; bathroom mixing, 86–102, 184; Bosniak temporary schools on Mostar east side (Mahala), 33–35, 37, 80, 81–82; Bosniak doubts about integration project, 36–37, 80–81; and cartography of ethnic difference, 63–85; class books, 67; concerns about past acts of school-related ethnic violence, 78–79; Croat community anti-integrationist stance/fears of reunification, 35–41, 44–46, 49, 50–58, 59, 79–80, 197n15; empty computer lab, 6–7, 23, 183–84, 208–9n3; ethnic symmetries and fragmentation of school space by curriculum, 63–74, 83–85; failures of "two-schools-under-one-roof" plan, 42–43, 70; first year of reunification, 78–83, 197n13; mandatory joint activities and joint extracurricular activities, 6–7, 71; OSCE goals in bringing Strana students to Mostar, 52; OSCE organization of school space and reliance on

Mostar Gymnasium (*continued*)
ethnic ideologies, 63–64, 68–71, 84; OSCE original vision of integration, 44–45, 59; OSCE shift in discourse from "integration" to "administrative unification," 59–61; OSCE unclear discourses of integration, 41, 43–44, 59; OSCE vision of future cross-ethnic interactions, 68–70;␣prointegration Bosniak leaders, 34–35, 37–38, 45; prointegration teachers, 70–72; relationships between Croat and Bosniak teachers and students, 78–83, 134–35; school decorations/wall exhibits and symbols of ethnic identification, 75–76, 200n5; school management, 67, 79; school year organization and ethnoreligious holidays, 67–68, 82–83; a student's creation of no-man's-land, 73–74, 84–85; teachers' room and segregated table-seating, 64–66, 199n1; tensions by wartime memories of violence, 95–98, 101, 102; 2012 school year, 65–66, 181–87

Nancy, Jean-Luc, 88
Nansen Dialogue Center, 105, 202n1
napolica, 145–46, 205n8
narod (nationhood, peoplehood), 105–38; complex and multidimensional scope of meanings, 109–12, 130–33; in former Yugoslav state, 109–12, 141–43; and language, 49, 53; and limitations of ethnonationalist ideologies, 113, 142–43; notion of *običan svijet* (ordinary world, people), 112; notions of exoticism and ethnic "others," 107–8; notions of nationhood, 107, 108, 202n3; notions of peoplehood, 107, 202n3; as "people" in everyday vernacular, 112; and postwar mixed marriages, 141–43; "rotten" narod and corruption of postwar state, 162, 163, 178. *See also* narod, ethnic; narod, transethnic
narod, ethnic, 112–30, 202n11; Bosniak youth, 114–19; Bosnian Croat youth, 119–25; Bosnian Croat transborder notion of *domovina* (homeland), 40–41, 53–54, 116–17, 123–25; Bosnian Serb youth, 125–30; Croat notions of Herzegovinian regional identity, 40, 123–24, 203n18; and homelands (*domovinas*), 40–41, 53–54, 116–17, 122–29; *podjela u glavi* (division in heads), 66, 113, 153, 183; and youth detachment from state, 40, 120, 124, 128, 129
narod, transethnic, 129–38; as an "avoidance" strategy to talking about politics, 134–35; and children, 137; as counter-discourse, 132–33, 136; enactment of, 133–38; strategic use to separate oneself from *politika* (as dissent and discursive mechanism), 112, 131–3, 204nn29–30; stressing one Bosnian *zajednički mentalitet* (common mentality), 133–34, 204n31; student experiences of, 129–30; and student interest in different religions, 130
narod in former Yugoslav state, 109–12, 141–43; Bosnian narod, 111–12; and "ethnic groups" (*etničke grupe*), 110–11; nations (*narodi*) and distinction from *narodnosti* (nationalities/people), 110, 118; and scholarly literature of former Yugoslavia, 109–10; territorial identity-marking term Bosanak, 111–12; Yugoslav Serbs, Yugoslav Croats, Yugoslav Muslims, 111
Narodno-oslobodilačka borba (People's Liberation Movement), 110
NATO. *See* North Atlantic Treaty Organization
neighbors (*komšija*), 31, 91, 196n4
Neofotistos, Vasiliki, 38
neoliberal capitalism, 158–60, 169–70, 175
Neum (coastal town), 105; teacher seminars, 97–98; workshop of student representatives (2005), 57, 105–8, 120–21, 125–26, 129–30
"no-man's-lands," 92; at Mostar Gymnasium, 73–74, 84–85; Mostar's empty boulevard and divided city, 3–4; postwar mixed families' exclusion in, 140–41, 142–43
"normal": and narod, 137; "new normal," 186–87; and spatial governmentality, 144–45, 161; Tito's, 199n3
North Atlantic Treaty Organization (NATO): Mostar force, 76–77; NATO-led Implementation Force (IFOR), 195n24; NATO-led Stabilization Force (SFOR), 195n24
Northern Ireland: ethnographic fieldwork in North Belfast, 94–95; integrated schools in, 41, 196n6

Office of the High Representative (OHR), 19; decision-making power, 19; and PIC, 19, 195n25; promotion of Bosnian-Herzegovinian Television, 203n20; selection of Bosnia-Herzegovina national anthem, 204n23; selection of new flag, 203n16, 204n23; seven high representatives, 195n26; and war profiteering, 164–65

OHR. *See* Office of the High Representative

OIA. *See* Omladinska Informativna Agencija Bosne i Hercegovine

Omladinska Informativna Agencija Bosne i Hercegovine (OIA) (Youth Information Agency), 201n11; study of Bosnian youth attitudes (2005), 99–100, 157

Organization for Security and Cooperation in Europe (OSCE), 19; civic engagement initiative, 202n2; Dayton implementation, 19, 70, 196n27; discourses of integration, 41, 43–44, 59; donors, 6–7, 20, 32, 34, 76, 183, 193n6, 197n9; education mandate and integration of Mostar Gymnasium, 6–7, 20, 32–36, 41–46, 52, 58–64, 68–70, 84, 99; introduction of common core curriculum, 203n12; original vision of integration at Mostar Gymnasium, 44–45, 59; as principal international actor coordinating Bosnian transition and recovery, 19, 20; programs and workshops with student and parent councils, 57, 105, 202n2; shift from "integration" discourse to "administrative unification," 59–61; so-called "two-schools-under-one-roof" plan, 42–43, 70; vision of future cross-ethnic interactions at Mostar Gymnasium, 68–70

OSCE. *See* Organization for Security and Cooperation in Europe

Ottoman Empire, 194n14, 197n14, 198n23; janissaries, 197n14

passports: Bosnian Croats with Bosnia-Herzegovinian, 121–22; Bosnian Croats with Croatian, 106–7, 119–20, 121–22; Bosnian Serbs' Bosnian passports and Republika Srpska stamps, 106–7, 125–26

Pavelić, Ante, 200n7, 201n9

Peace Implementation Council (PIC), 19, 195n25; Contact Group, 195n25; Steering Board, 195n25

Pedagogical Institute (Mostar), 135, 137, 183

People's Liberation Movement. *See* Narodno-oslobodilačka borba

Perez Casado, Ricard, 20

Petritsch, Wolfgang, 195n26

PIC. *See* Peace Implementation Council

podjela u glavi (division in heads), 66, 113, 153, 183

"politics of difference," 36, 38, 45–46, 197n16

politika: Bosnian youth as complicated postwar political agents, 179–80; strategic use of transethnic narod to separate oneself from, 112, 131–38, 204nn29–30; transethnic narod as "avoidance" strategy to talking about, 134–35

Povijest (Croat history book), 125

practical kinship, 145–46, 205n9

Prazina, Jusuf "Juka," 207n12

Prozor-Rama, school integration in, 42–43, 198n27

ravnopravnost (Bosniak pannationalism), 118

Red Cross (NGO), 19

religion. *See* ethnoreligious identity

Republika Srpska (RS): Banja Luka, 8, 126, 127, 194n11, 204n26; Bosnian Croat youth with little knowledge of, 121, 123; curriculum of, 127–28, 193n7; and Dayton Peace Agreement, 129; ethnic narod and Bosnian Serb identification with, 116–17, 125–29; as one of two political entities of Bosnia-Herzegovina, 10, 125–26, 194n15, 203n14; and wartime Yugoslav People's Army, 29; youth with Bosnian passports and Republika Srpska stamps, 106–7, 125–26

Roma, 30, 108, 110–11, 196n2

RS. *See* Republika Srpska

Sarajevo: eternal flame monument, 7–8, 193n9; international organizations in, 19–20; JNA attack, 29, 196n1; Markowitz ethnography, 7–8; mixed marriages, 201n8; Muslim character and population, 119, 127; myth of urban core as prewar multicultural heaven, 12; postwar emptiness, 8; siege of, 196n1

Save the Children (NGO), 19

Schechner, Richard, 57
Schneider, Jane, 208n15
Schneider, Peter, 208n15
Schwarz-Schilling, Christian, 195n26
Scotland, "shared schools" in, 196n6
SDA. *See* Stranka Demokratske Akcije (Bosniak nationalist party)
Selimović, Meša, 55, 114–15, 208–9n3
Serbia (Greater Serbia): narod, 126–27, 128–29; *Nož, Žica, Srebrenica* (nationalist slogan), 126, 204n25; Serbian language, 48–49, 199n31
Serbian language: Cyrillic alphabet, 48; *ekavski* speech, 49; and linguistic nationalism, 48–49, 199n31
Serbo-Croatian language, 46–47, 48, 51, 55, 57–58, 198n28; alphabets (Cyrillic/Latin), 47, 48, 199n29; Dayton Agreement and separation into three languages, 48
shadow economies, 173
Široki Brijeg (western Herzegovina town), 30
60 Minuta (television program), 170–71
Slobodna Evropa, 186
Slovenian language, 46
Smillie, Ian, 195n23
Smith, Rogers, 202n3
soccer fans and rivalries, 98–99, 126, 201n10
social mixing. *See* mixing and public sociality in postwar Bosnia-Herzegovina; mixing and public sociality in prewar Bosnia-Herzegovina
Socialist Federal Republic of Yugoslavia. *See* Yugoslavia, communist
socialist humanism, 4–5
Sorabji, Cornelia, 110, 112
Spanish Square (Mostar), 76–78
spatial governmentality, 13, 73–74; and bathroom mixing at Mostar Gymnasium, 87–88, 90, 92–96, 99, 101–2; consociational model of democracy enshrining into law, 13; defining, 11, 194n18; and narod, 113, 142–43; and "normal," 144–45, 161. *See also* consociational power-sharing model of democracy; international peace-building and state-making projects in postwar Bosnia-Herzegovina
Srebrenica massacre (1995), 201n12, 204n25
Stara Gimnazija. *See* Mostar Gymnasium
Stolac (town), 42–43, 137, 198n27, 205n33
Strana (pseudonym) central Bosnia-Herzegovina town, 52–53

Stranka Demokratske Akcije (SDA) (Bosniak nationalist party), 33, 171, 198n27
structural nostalgia, 142–43, 160, 167, 170–71

Taylor, Charles, 38, 197n16
Taylor, Diana, 57
Tito, Josip Broz: Brotherhood and Unity ideology, 8, 70, 110, 142, 193n8; language policies, 47; Mostar students' romanticized nostalgia for, 70, 199n3; slogan ("I want, I can, I will"), 177–79; slogan "I want, I can, I will," 178–79; Yugoslavism and narod, 110, 141–43
Torsti, Pilvi, 117, 118, 125, 128
Transparency International, 209n4
turbo-folk music, 202n5
Turkey, 119, 126
Tuzla, 175–76, 188–91
"two-schools-under-one-roof," 42–43, 70

UN Development Programme (UNDP): and NGOs in Bosnia-Herzegovina, 195n23; survey of Bosnian youth attitudes (2003), 99–100, 157
UN Mission in Bosnia and Herzegovina (UNMBiH), 19
UNDP. *See* UN Development Programme
Union of Student Councils in Herzegovina, 105, 202n2
United Nations: "safe havens," 163–64, 207n11; wartime corruption and war profiteering, 165. *See also* UN Development Programme
U.S. Agency for International Development (USAID), 19
United World Colleges (UWC), 59, 181, 199n33
UNMBiH. *See* UN Mission in Bosnia and Herzegovina
USAID. *See* U.S. Agency for International Development
Ustaša, 80–81, 96–99, 200n7, 201n9

war profiteering and trader/soldiers, 163–66, 207n12
Washington Peace Agreement (March 1994), 30
Western European Police, 20
Westendorp, Carlos, 195n26

"whores" (young women working as interpreters/translators for international community), 165–66
Wimmen, Heiko, 38
World War II, 7–8, 18, 110, 200nn6–7, 201n9, 204n24

Young, Iris, 51, 199n32
youth detachment from state: anthropological studies of nonparticipation in political life, 176; Bosnian Croats, 40, 120, 124; Bosnian Serbs living in FBiH, 128; desires to leave country, 174, 176–77; and ethnic narod, 40, 120, 124, 128, 129; exercise of anti-citizenship to preserve citizen-morality, 156–58, 168, 173–80, 206n1; public discourse about youth situation, 157; and youth as complicated postwar political agents, 179–80

Youth Information Agency. *See* Omladinska Informativna Agencija Bosne i Hercegovine (Youth Information Agency of Bosnia-Herzegovina)
Yugoslav People's Army (Jugoslovenska Narodna Armija) (JNA), 29–30, 131, 196n1
Yugoslavia, communist: Brotherhood and Unity ideology, 8, 70, 110, 142, 193n8; informal networks, 161, 207n8; mixed marriages, 141–43; Mostar students' romanticized nostalgia for, 70, 199n3; narod as state doctrine, 109–12, 141–43; official languages and language policies, 46, 47; postwar nostalgia/memories of communist corruption, 158, 159–60, 161, 162–63, 167, 169, 170–71; scholars of, 109–10; Tito regime, 47, 70, 110, 141–43, 199n3. *See also* Bosnia-Herzegovina (prewar)

Acknowledgments

Since the beginning of my training in anthropology, I have been intrigued by the seemingly solitary nature of the anthropological (field) work and my own experience of collaboration and team effort. This book would have never materialized if I did not enjoy the continuous and selfless support of numerous individuals, foundations, organizations and groups.

A very special "thank you" goes to the people of Mostar and Bijelo Brdo (pseudonym), and especially to the students, teachers, and management at the Mostar Gymnasium and Bijelo Brdo High School. These individuals readily opened their schools, their homes, and their hearts to me, and I remain humble in front of their kindheartedness. Throughout my research, I was overwhelmed by their benevolence and their persistence to tell and explain to me "their story." Every sentence written in this account is an expression of my admiration of their commitment to, their hopes for, and their belief in a better future.

I also would like to thank Kathy Hall at the University of Pennsylvania, for believing in me from the very beginning of our work together. Without her guidance, patience, and her ability to deliver constructive criticism in a graceful, friendly manner, this work would not be possible. Ritty Lukose, Adriana Petryna, Brian Spooner, Greg Urban, and Liliane Weissberg also provided continual guidance and encouragement throughout this project.

My colleagues at Syracuse University provided a generous intellectual, moral, and logistical support inspiring me to work hard on completing this project. Thank you all. In addition, exchanges with a number of colleagues and experts on the Balkans provided my intellectual home, where I have been and continue to be challenged as a scholar and a person. Special thanks go to Kimberly Coles, Ana Dević, Andrew Gilbert, Eric Gordy, Jessica Greenberg, Elissa Helms, Larisa Kurtović, Stef Jansen, Larisa Jašarević, Danijela Majstorović, Tomislav Longinović, Monika Palmberger, Paul Stubbs, Larissa Vetters, and Sarah Wagner.

There are many friends and colleagues who helped me along the way, by providing their support, advice, and editing skills to the "English as a second language" friend. These people are numerous, but several individuals particularly deserve to be mentioned. I am especially grateful to Kimberly Coles, Helen Cunningham, Liz Greenspan, Genevra Murray, Heather M. Riddle, and Stephanie Spehar for proofreading and/or commenting on different components of this work. I am particularly indebted to Erin Mooney, my loyal friend and "big sister," who edited the entire manuscript in record time.

The research and writing of this project have been supported by a number of grants and fellowships received from the Social Science Research Council Book Fellowship (a special "thank you" goes to Joel Score); the Social Science Research Council International Dissertation Field Research Fellowship; the United States Institute of Peace, the American Council of Learned Societies; the American Association of the University Women; the Spencer Foundation; Penfield; the Josephine De Karman Fellowship; the Appleby-Mosher Fund from Maxwell School, Syracuse University; the Program for the Advancement of Research on Conflict and Celebration at Maxwell School, Syracuse University; the National Council for Eurasian and East European Research Short-term Travel Grant; and the New Europe College Regional Fellowship. In addition, the Department of Anthropology at the University of Wisconsin at Oshkosh provided me with a space and logistical support during several years of writing; I am especially grateful to Pete Brown for sharing his second office with me.

The book publishing process can be extremely challenging and frustrating at times. Peter Agree and Toby Kelly at the University of Pennsylvania Press made this whole journey smooth and enjoyable—I am honored to publish my book with your Press and in this particular series. I am also deeply indebted to the reviewer who provided excellent—critical yet encouraging—comments on different versions of the manuscript.

Finally, I am enormously thankful to the three families whose love and support enabled me to work hard, respect people around me, and never give up. My Bosnian family, especially my parents Hasan and Rasema Hromadžić, and my brother Hajrudin Hromadžić, provide my safety net wherever I am. They did the hardest thing a family can do—they sent their daughter and sister to a foreign land to search for a better life. I am extremely beholden by their unselfishness, and their ability to always be there for me, even if there are thousands of miles between us.

I was extremely lucky to have landed, on my arrival the U.S., into the hands and hearts of Helen Cunningham and Ted Newbold. They are my American parents whose care and genuine love of a "complete stranger" persistently motivate me to become a better person and to never forget what is important in life. Finally, during this journey, I was tremendously fortunate to start my own family. Aaron, Una, and Levi's existence made this intricate book publishing journey meaningful. I am very much grateful to them for tolerating an ambitious wife and a mom who needed her own time.